Green Crime

Also by Dr Julia Shaw

The Memory Illusion
Making Evil
Bi

Green Crime

Julia Shaw

CANONGATE

First published in Great Britain in 2025
by Canongate Books Ltd, 14 High Street, Edinburgh EH1 1TE

canongate.co.uk

1

Copyright © Dr Julia Shaw, 2025

The right of Dr Julia Shaw to be identified as the
author of this work has been asserted by her in accordance
with the Copyright, Designs and Patents Act 1988

No part of this book may be used or reproduced in any manner for the purpose
of training artificial intelligence technologies or systems. This work is reserved
from text and data mining (Article 4(3) Directive (EU) 2019/790)

British Library Cataloguing-in-Publication Data
A catalogue record for this book is available on
request from the British Library

ISBN 978 1 80530 115 8
Export ISBN: 978 1 83726 066 9

Typeset in Plantin Light by
Palimpsest Book Production Ltd, Falkirk, Stirlingshire

Printed and bound by CPI Group (UK) Ltd, Croydon CR0 4YY

The manufacturer's authorised representative in the EU for product safety is
Authorised Rep Compliance Ltd, 71 Lower Baggot Street, Dublin D02 P593
Ireland (arccompliance.com)

To Annette. My island in the storm.

CONTENTS

Introduction   1

1. The Con Men
   Emissions fraud in the US and how perpetrators
   rationalise environmental crimes   7

2. The Murderers
   Deaths in the Amazon and the question of whether
   nature needs its own rights   56

3. The Traffickers
   Poaching syndicates from China and the complex
   relationship between humans and animals   105

4. The Outlaws
   Illegal fishing in Antarctica and how we behave
   when no one is watching   154

5. The Thieves
   Zama Zama miners in South Africa and how
   narratives about environmental criminals
   become distorted   200

6. The Negligent
   The oil spill in the Gulf of Mexico and why
   it's so hard to change our minds   249

Conclusion: Capable Guardians   293

Acknowledgements	299
Notes	303
Index	332

Dear future generations: Please accept our apologies. We were rolling drunk on petroleum.

Kurt Vonnegut

INTRODUCTION

NEVER HAVE I felt more hopeful about Earth's future than after diving into some of the world's worst environmental crimes. It has been a bizarre, and unexpected, twist of perspective.

For years I was furious about the climate crisis. It felt like we were standing at the precipice of a black hole, about to be pulled in by sheer gravity. All of us knowingly feeding into our impending destruction. Then, one day, it dawned on me that killing the planet isn't simply an inevitable tragedy. It's the result of deliberate choices and environmental crimes. And crime is something that I know a lot about.

My work as a criminal psychologist involves trying to understand why people do bad things. I write about some of the darkest human behaviours. And, I am an expert witness in cases involving horrific allegations of violence, which includes sifting through graphic footage and files. Now I am taking that same approach to understanding the people destroying the planet, by examining the evidence, analysing their motivations, and figuring out how to stop them.

I have also come to realise that one of the reasons I used

to feel so hopeless about the climate crisis was because I only ever heard about the perpetrators. Rarely did I learn about the people fighting on our side, protecting the Earth. That needs to change.

In this book, I am going to introduce you to the environmental defenders, investigative journalists and scientists who make green crimes visible and refuse to be silenced. The undercover agents, international police, industry regulators and environmental lawyers who track down perpetrators and hold them accountable. And the researchers at the United Nations and universities around the world who help us to make sense of it all.

Unfortunately, we tend to fear that which we do not understand. The antidote to this fear is bringing light into the darkness of the unknown. In order to do this, I have spoken to experts on some of the biggest threats to our future: air pollution, deforestation, wildlife loss, overfishing, toxic waste, and the evolving concerns with the oil and gas industry. Fostering and refining scientific literacy on these issues can help everyone to join the conversation on these existential issues.

This book also covers the recent monumental changes to how people think about the Earth, and the new push for the criminalisation of acts that harm nature. Legal concepts like ecocide are now being used to place the rights of nature in the same category as fundamental human rights.[1] And, in some places, breaking environmental regulations is no longer something that just results in a fine. Now, it can land people in prison. This is important. Calling it a crime, and penalising it as such, psychologically places environmental offences alongside other acts that society has deemed horrific or intolerable. Can you imagine a world where we think of green criminals the same way we think of murderers? This would be a radical shift. It would mean we have finally understood what is really at stake.

That said, most acts of environmental destruction are currently not criminalised. We can, and should, debate whether individual acts should be punished by law. But this book focuses on laws that are already in place, and cases brought before the courts where people have been convicted.

'Green crime' is a phrase that is synonymous with environmental crime, and it is used by researchers in the social sciences. Lawyers prefer the term 'environmental crime', and I think the best technical definition of this was formulated, after much deliberation, by the European Parliament in 2024. They crafted the Environmental Crime Directive which states that environmental crime is unlawful conduct, done with intent or serious negligence. It involves releasing materials or substances, energy or ionising radiation. It can be an act, or a failure to act. And, it must cause either serious injury or death to a person, or substantial damage to the quality of air, soil, water, animals, plants or an entire ecosystem.[2]

In this book I'm going to break it down by looking at six fascinating and horrifying cases that allow us to dig deep into green crime and address the big question: *why* are people willing to destroy the Earth?

To help answer this, I will profile the perpetrators and reconstruct the thinking that drove them to commit these crimes. I will apply psychological concepts like unethical prosocial behaviour, disconfirmation bias, temporal discounting, corruptibility, and the paradox of feedback. I will also use the new language of green psychology to explain things that many of us are feeling, like eco-anger and eco-grief, and look at the importance of biospheric values and psychological ownership, which can turn our wild spaces into a natural resource to be protected rather than one we are willing to burn down. By weaving together history and social science, we can reconstruct how we got here and why we do, or don't, choose to protect the planet.

I am someone who likes to see patterns in the world around me. Otherwise, my brain feels adrift on the turbulent sea of information, especially when it comes to topics as big as those covered in this book. I prefer to carefully organise ideas, facts and questions by their feeling and shape. To turn the chaos into something useful.

In the years I spent writing this book, I found a pattern of psychological factors driving green crime which I call the 'six pillars': ease, impunity, greed, rationalisation, conformity and desperation. In each chapter I will return to these six pillars, though I am not going to tediously point out every facet of every crime that fits the model. Instead, I hope that as you read, they provide a foundation to help you to organise your newfound knowledge.

The first pillar is **ease**. Human behaviour tends to follow the path of least resistance. When lies, pollution or environmental destruction are faster or seem more convenient than choosing a sustainable option, people will often make a choice that causes harm.

The second pillar is **impunity**. By this I mean the psychological effect of believing – or knowing – that you can get away with crimes. Whether on the high seas, deep in the

Amazon or even in corporate boardrooms, there are people who act the way they do because they think no one can see them or stop them.

The third pillar is **greed**. It involves deciding to sacrifice the common good for personal enrichment. When the boss of an organised crime group kills animals almost to extinction so he can live in a big house, for example; or when a CEO cuts corners for personal gain, resulting in huge environmental costs.

The fourth pillar is **rationalisation**. This is when people tell themselves stories to make their actions seem less harmful than they really are. For example, a poaching boss arguing that his work is actually good because he is creating jobs, or an engineer thinking that their dirty technology won't make any difference in the grand scheme of global pollution.

The fifth pillar is **conformity**. Peer pressure, both real and perceived, plays a big role in creating the social foundations of green crime. For example, a company's employees might knowingly engage in greenwashing because they see people in other companies doing it too. Similarly, people from towns where illegal fishing is common can see dangerous levels of overfishing as just another job, rather than as the crime that it really is.

The sixth pillar is **desperation**. In many parts of the world, green crime wouldn't exist without extreme poverty. But that's only one form of desperation; it can happen whenever people feel trapped or are scrambling to get out of a situation that is causing them a huge amount of stress.

By systematically applying the six pillars model, it becomes easier to see that the minds of environmental criminals are not as complicated, or as different from our own, as they might first appear.

As we head into the furtive world of green crime, these offences of global proportions will be revealed layer by layer.

We will find, and unmask, Earth's killers.

1

THE CON MEN

THEY KNEW THE con couldn't last.

For years they had stood in meetings, spinning a story they all knew didn't add up. But with questions being asked and the damning evidence finally coming to light, the facade was crumbling. It was only a matter of time until the world knew what they'd been doing.

That's why, in August 2015, the Volkswagen employee found himself standing at a crossroads. Should he keep lying, or come clean? As the most senior regulatory executive at Volkswagen North America, the employee had decided to attend one of the big technical conferences in California. He'd known that regulator Alberto Ayala would be there too. They weren't friends exactly, but years of working side by side had instilled in them more than just a sense of mutual respect. They liked each other.

People tend to imagine a battlefield between companies and regulators, but the reality is often quieter and more collaborative. And yet the employee had been lying straight to Ayala's face.

He had been a coward.

Now he had to choose which side of history he wanted to be on.

After the last conference dinner, the employee scanned the bustling crowd. It was a sea of geeks, each blending into the next. A frustrating game of find-the-regulator. Then, finally, he spotted Ayala as he was walking out of the dining hall.

The employee took a breath that didn't seem to reach his lungs. A beer in each hand, smile twitching on his lips, he approached Ayala. They exchanged pleasantries, hollow and rehearsed, and both started to move away from the crowd. The chatter of the conference faded, replaced by the heavy weight of what needed to be said.

That was when the truth about almost a decade of fraud began to tumble out of the employee.

At first, Ayala's face stoically masked his disbelief. He had expected something like this, but nothing could have prepared him for the moment of impact. The betrayal hit hard, like a slap. Then came the fury. Words exploded from him, his anger raw and unrestrained. They'd wasted years on these lies. All those public resources, gone. The company had taken him, his team, and much of the world for fools.

The murmur of the crowd was barely audible now, as the two men kept walking, still sipping their beers. Remorse was met with anger. Fear with a sense of betrayal. But neither man quite understood the enormity of what had just been unleashed.

This chapter systematically deconstructs the psychological factors that make people decide to lie about their companies' environmental harm. It tells the story of one of the biggest corporate fraud cases in history, and the global response.

For a decade, the international press has chronicled the prosecutions and lawsuits surrounding the international diesel emissions scandal that became known as Dieselgate. The investigations bounced back and forth between the US and Germany, and then extended to countries all over the world. But, still, very few people know the whole story.

To guide me through the details of what really happened, I spoke to the man who was directly responsible for exposing Volkswagen's lies, Alberto Ayala. For years he had to stay silent as he worked with detectives to uncover the extent of the company's crimes. 'I haven't been able to talk fully about this until now,' he explained to me. My reconstruction of that pivotal moment when the Volkswagen employee fessed up and made the whole conspiracy collapse is based on his account.

Ayala's work as an air quality regulator isn't the paper-pushing job you might expect. 'We are the resistance,' as he put it. Ayala and his colleagues, and those doing similar jobs around the world, are key to protecting the air we breathe from the companies and politicians who are all too willing to suffocate us.

The Dieselgate case is infuriating and mind-bending in equal measure. It involves the psychology of eco-anger, malevolent companies who make us complicit in their crimes, and architects of choice who build a world riddled with greenwashing booby traps. It also raises important questions about who is able to spot corporate environmental fraud, and what we actually want to do with the perpetrators of green crimes when we catch them.

This is a case where people covered up lies with more lies . . . and then decided to lie some more. Why did so many Volkswagen employees agree to join in, even risking imprisonment for the sake of the company?

To answer that question, we need to head back to the very beginning. It all began with the invention of 'clean diesel'.

HOW CUTE

'When people talked about efficiency and low carbon emissions, the first thing that came to mind was the diesel car,' Alberto Ayala told me. 'And that's how we got to paying attention. We started simply by being curious about these "clean diesel" emissions.'

Ayala is an environmental protection regulator. Back in 2011, he was working at the California Air Resources Board, or CARB, which is the state agency in charge of ensuring clean air and climate action. Part of Ayala's job at CARB was 'to understand every carmaker in the world'. He was the most senior person at the agency who had day-to-day interactions with all the major carmakers, including Volkswagen.

By the time I spoke with him, Ayala had left CARB and was the executive director of the Sacramento Metropolitan Air Quality Management District. He was also writing a book on the Volkswagen case, *Three Forks in the Road: Dieselgate – The Volkswagen Cheating Scandal*. Dieselgate was his most famous case, his biggest success, and it had taken quite a lot out of him. But Ayala also told me he wants to use his experiences to make sure people understand the crucial role that regulators play in the fight for the necessities of life. Now, and in the future.

'Everybody likes to turn a water faucet and expect clean water,' he explained. 'When they go outside they expect clean air. They expect to buy food that is not going to kill them. A cell phone that is not going to explode. I mean, how do you think these things happen? When you think about the conveniences of modern life, regulations are simply the guardrails.'

We don't notice things when they work well, frictionlessly allowing us to live our lives. It's only when things break that we perceive them. And rather than appreciating the work of the people behind the scenes, we often just feel a sense of entitlement to safe utilities and products. That's the tragedy of the army of regulators who keep society moving smoothly. They are taken for granted most of the time, and then blamed when things go wrong. 'You don't see all the day-to-day testing that we do,' said Ayala. 'When nothing happens, there's no news article about it because everything is fine.'

Granted, following regulations can be annoying. They almost always force companies to do more tests than they would otherwise want to do, and limit what they can make or sell. Then there's the paperwork, which everybody hates. Sometimes regulations should be streamlined or simplified, but getting rid of them entirely is always a bad idea. According to Ayala, 'Without regulations you have absolutely no way of knowing whether what you're getting as a consumer is good or bad. It's just as simple as that.' And 'that would be a pretty scary world'.

There are two opposing misconceptions that irritate Ayala. The first is that regulators are just getting in the way of the businesses they regulate. To him, the people working for the carmakers and the regulators are on the same team. 'We spend a lot of time in the lab testing and pulling apart technology, talking to them' – by 'them' he means the engineers working at the carmakers – 'talking to other experts in the industry to try to understand how we should craft regulations that preserve all the attributes of the wonderful vehicles that we have on the road today and yet minimise the impact on the environment.'

The second, and opposite, misconception is that regulators are in bed with the regulated industry. The fact that Ayala is friendly with people from some of the companies he regulates is simply a by-product of spending so much time together, and 'a regulator is never going to be as good as the actual automaker at understanding the cars they sell'. Collaboration, and a certain degree of respect, is essential to this work.

Until Volkswagen launched their 'clean diesels' in the US in 2007, which were marketed as being far more environmentally friendly than any other diesel on the market, Ayala hadn't really thought much about diesel passenger cars at all. 'Diesel cars were never really important to us [in the US market] because we never really had any of them. For every diesel car we had, we probably had a thousand gasoline cars. So when we started to hear about how the Germans are bringing cars to the US, we looked at the clean diesel technology that Volkswagen was selling. And thought, how cute. But we never really gave it much attention.' With limited resources, regulators had to prioritise the biggest sources of environmental harm, which meant petrol engines came first.

But as the proportion of clean diesel cars in the market grew, so did the regulators' interest in them. When in 2012 California adopted new stringent greenhouse-gas emissions standards, Ayala and his colleagues at CARB wanted to understand how these cars were excelling in environmental tests. They headed over to Volkswagen, expecting a friendly response. But when Ayala started asking Volkswagen's representatives to explain how it all worked, things got weird.

'They would try to come back to us with some response. Some explanation. But they just started making less and less sense.' Still, for three whole years, the regulators' emissions team gave Volkswagen the benefit of the doubt.

Eventually, they began to suspect the cars' green credentials were not what they seemed. 'We just went through the list, the process of elimination,' said Ayala. 'And we realised that the only possible explanation that remained was that they were cheating.'

The question now was how they were cheating, and who exactly was behind it. It would take another year for Ayala and his colleagues to figure it out. Only after that would they get to the bottom of the 'defeat device'.

But before we get into that, and the psychology of all the people who went along with Volkswagen's lies, I want to give a brief summary of the history of air pollution. Global awareness of what air pollution means for human and environmental health only truly began in the mid-twentieth century, and companies have spent decades being dragged – kicking and screaming – into the modern clean-air era. While the US and the UK were among the first large nations to introduce national laws to regulate air pollution, it took a series of disasters to initiate the process of large-scale change.

Like the 'disaster at Donora'.[1]

AIR AWAKENING

For the town of Donora, Pennsylvania, and the nearby communities, the smoke from the local steel and zinc plants was just a part of life. Pollution was seen as a sign of prosperity, of a thriving local economy, not a problem.[2] So, when heavy smog rolled in on 27 October 1948, the people in the small town assumed it was just business as usual. They found that the smog had been caused by a mix of fumes from the nearby factories, which then got trapped in the area by unusual weather called an inversion blanket.[3] That's when cool air is trapped close to the ground by a layer of warm air.

Despite the poor air quality, many tried to keep up their day-to-day activities. At the Halloween-themed parade, children dressed up and wandered down smoggy Main Street. The local American football team even played their usual Friday night game, despite being unable to see the ball.

But within days, things turned dire. People began falling ill, gasping for air, and doctors' phones were ringing off the hook. Emergency crews mobilised, but navigating the smog was a challenge. Ambulances crawled through the dense fog, guided by someone walking ahead with a torch. Firefighters went door-to-door carrying oxygen tanks. Roads out of town were impassable, trapping residents in the toxic cloud.

By 30 October, seventeen people had died, most of them in their sixties.[4] When after five breathless days the smog finally lifted, the death toll had risen to twenty, and over 5,000 people – half the town's population – were left with moderate to severe illness. It was a public health crisis.

A year later, twenty-five researchers were sent to investigate what happened. They called the day the heavy smog began 'S-day', and the illness was labelled 'smog sickness'.[5] Symptoms ranged from sore eyes and coughing to severe oxygen deprivation that turned skin blue or caused unconsciousness. At the time, the research was praised for being 'the most exhaustive ever made on a problem in air pollution', and there were calls for 'an attack on this new frontier of atmospheric pollution'.[6]

According to researcher Clarence Mills, who conducted an independent investigation into the disaster after the original research team had left, the Donora disaster was 'America's first mass killing from industrial air pollution'. He pointed out that in addition to human lives being lost, there had also been a 'terrible devastation' of the wider environment, including the death of nearly all plant life within about a mile radius of one of the factories. And, Mills realised that, rather than the immediate risk of death, it was the long-term damage from breathing polluted air that would be the biggest problem for society. He finished his report in 1950 with a clear message: 'Let us hope that the Donora disaster will awaken people everywhere to the dangers they face from pollution of the air they must breathe to live.'[7]

But the people did not awaken. At least, not right away. And just two years later, across the Atlantic, another deadly smog event forced a similar reckoning in the United Kingdom.

In December 1952, London was hit with the Great Smog, a catastrophic pollution event that lasted five days and was again caused by toxic emissions being blanketed by unusual weather. The smog from the coal plants created a thick fog, like pea soup, which stank of rotten eggs. Visibility dropped to just a few metres, paralysing the city. Thousands of people died, and hundreds of thousands suffered long-term health impacts.

The Great Smog remains one of the most significant environmental disasters in British history.[8] It led to the UK's Clean

Air Act 1956, a groundbreaking piece of legislation that forced both industries and households to switch to cleaner technologies in towns and cities. As in every Act of Parliament, it started with the most quintessentially British opening, 'Be it enacted by the Queen's most Excellent Majesty', and it included as its first provision that 'dark smoke shall not be emitted from a chimney of any building, and if, on any day, dark smoke is so emitted, the occupier of the building shall be guilty of an offence'. It also established that people were not allowed to put in new furnaces unless they were 'so far as practicable capable of being operated continuously without emitting smoke when burning fuel'.[9]

Smoke was now the enemy.

Local councils were tasked with designating 'smoke control areas' where only smokeless fuel was allowed to be burned. Factories also needed to minimise pollution. Inspectors enforced compliance, issuing fines to violators. And to support the continued phase-out of smog-creating smoke, scientific research was carried out at the Warren Spring Laboratory in Stevenage.[10] One of the main research areas of the lab was the 'occurrence of oxides of nitrogen', or NOx, which would become important in the Dieselgate scandal decades later.

Criminalising air pollution was a huge shift, but change didn't happen as fast as was hoped. In 1962, a decade after the first Great Smog, a deadly smog once again suffocated London. It hit in December and lasted for five days. Once again, people died.[11] It also led to a revision of the Clean Air Act, because clearly the original legislation wasn't working well enough.[12]

Earlier that year, the publication of *Silent Spring* by Rachel

Carson had challenged the idea that all technology signals progress. Carson's book exposed the devastating effects of the pesticide DDT on wildlife, showing that innovation could also lead to harm, and became a cornerstone of the growing global environmental movement. The catastrophic smog events in the US and UK, combined with this new environmental movement and iterative local laws regarding pollution, led to the US adopting its own national Clean Air Act in 1963.

Over the next two decades, much of the world followed suit.

Predictably, industry immediately began to push back against these strategies for pollution control.[13] A particular point of contention was the perceived incompatibility of economic growth and environmental protection. One small-town American mayor was cited as saying 'if you want this town to grow, it has got to stink'.[14] For some, pollution was seen as an inevitable and justified cost of progress. Companies and politicians continued to actively resist the new environmental standards, as many still do today. But the public was beginning to see the benefits of cleaner air. Smog levels in major cities were dropping and people realised how much better life was without constantly inhaling thick, toxic fumes.

This brings us to the establishment of the California Air Resources Board. In 1967, CARB was given unique authority to deal with serious air pollution in California, which allowed it to apply stricter rules than in other states. It would become a force to be reckoned with, an authority feared by carmakers around the world, because as Ayala told me, 'The way to get into the US market, the only way, is to get through California.'

The reason California has long been so tough on emissions is because it has needed to deal with the specific kind of smog that hung over Los Angeles for much of the twentieth century. This phenomenon is called photochemical smog.

And the main cause of this smog wasn't factories or furnaces.

It was cars.

DEADLY AIR

Photochemical smog forms when volatile organic compounds, VOCs, and nitrogen oxides, NOx, come into contact with sunlight. VOCs are released into the air from many industrial and household products, including paints, cleaning supplies, and glue. NOx, meanwhile, come mostly from combustion, and the hotter the combustion, the more NOx are created. In cities like Los Angeles, NOx come from power plants, factories and – most importantly for our story – cars.

NOx are the leftovers from the explosions that make cars move. Diesel cars are overall more fuel-efficient than petrol cars because their engines' internal combustion happens at higher temperatures and pressures than petrol engines. The fact that diesel engines burn hotter is also the reason why they can produce more torque than petrol engines, which means they are good for pulling heavy loads. These are, however, also the conditions that lead to the increased creation of NOx. From 1970, emissions standards were added to the US Clean Air Act that put NOx firmly on the agenda.

To better understand NOx, I spoke with Dr Harald Frey from the Research Centre of Transport Planning and Traffic

Engineering at the Vienna University of Technology. He explained that 'NOx are responsible for the acidification of soil and water', which means that they contribute to acid rain. This, in turn, damages plants and ecosystems. He also noted that NOx 'are precursors of particulate matter [PM] and ozone, and are indirectly responsible for large-scale pollution'. Stratospheric ozone is high up in the atmosphere and protects us from UV radiation coming from space. But the ground-level ozone that NOx contribute to, otherwise known as tropospheric ozone, is a 'super pollutant' that contributes to global warming and smog.[15]

NOx that come from cars are among the worst because 'in contrast to industrial emissions, traffic emissions are released close to the ground,' Dr Frey explained. While factory chimneys release pollutants high into the atmosphere, cars emit exhaust at the level where people breathe.

As researchers found in the disaster at Donora, air with a high concentration of NOx is particularly bad for our health. Immediate exposure effects are related to the worsening of respiratory diseases such as asthma, including the increase of symptoms like coughing and wheezing. On days with high levels of NOx, there are higher numbers of people admitted to emergency rooms. And even for those of us who take our plentiful lung capacity for granted, NOx are bad news. Long-term exposure may cause asthma, and makes us more susceptible to respiratory tract infections like colds and flu.[16] This is why NOx are particularly dangerous for children and the elderly.

One of the most common kinds of NOx is found in diesel engine exhaust: nitrogen dioxide, or NO2. 'The direct effect of NO2 is particularly harmful to humans,' said Dr Frey.

'Current studies indicate that there is no threshold value for NO2 below which health effects can be ruled out.' In other words, even very low levels of NO2 are still likely to be harmful to health. 'Diesel cars are the main source of NOx emissions in cities. They cause 65 per cent of direct NOx emissions from road traffic.' Given that fewer than one in five cars are powered by diesel, this makes their output utterly disproportional. Frey also stressed that older diesel cars, from before 2022, are often significantly more polluting than newer ones.

And this is partly due to something called a defeat device.

DÉJÀ VU

A defeat device adjusts the emissions produced by a car by changing how the engine runs while it is being tested. Crucially, it only does this for a short period of time. As regulator Alberto Ayala explained to me, it's 'not necessarily just a physical thing that they put on the car. The device is basically software manipulation to say, okay, the car is being tested, so let's make it clean.' But the emissions are only 'clean' for the duration of the test, and then the device is switched off again.

When cars are being evaluated, they get put on a big treadmill and the emissions coming out of their tailpipe are measured. According to Ewing, the test that Volkswagen had to pass in the US mimicked an actual drive in Los Angeles. It went down city streets, onto a highway and up a mountain. Carmakers knew the specific simulated route, because it was public information.

The makers of the defeat device exploited this. In addition to the software noticing other test-specific conditions, like a lack of steering wheel movement,[17] they programmed in the specific curves of the virtual road. Because the software could recognise this unique pattern of movements, it knew exactly when it needed to switch into low-emissions mode. And when this happened, the results were nothing short of miraculous. The cars looked incredibly clean in the emissions tests.

All defeat devices are a bit different, but they do things like temporarily run the engine less hot, thereby producing less NOx. If the car were always in this special mode, it would make the car louder, or make parts of the car wear out faster, or lower the fuel efficiency. That's why engineers need to specifically upgrade the design of the engine or exhaust, so it can run in low emissions all the time. But that costs money. 'For a company like Volkswagen, they were trying to essentially scale back to the bare bones emission control system. Just enough to perform in the lab during the test. But then when it was out on the road? Forget about it,' Ayala explained.

I asked him whether Volkswagen could have built diesel cars that were actually as 'clean' as they were advertised, and he said, 'Yes, absolutely. It wasn't a matter of not knowing how. It was a matter of them deciding that they were going to take shortcuts.' It would have been far more expensive to build cars that only ran in the clean mode and stayed within fuel economy targets.

Underpinning all of this was Volkswagen's commitment to launching their diesel cars in the US. Diesels were seen as dirty by Americans, and Volkswagen wanted to turn this stereotype on its head and wow potential customers with their new 'clean' diesel technology. But regulations in the US were stricter than in Europe, and to create a car that met the stringent US standards, they would have had to spend more money than they wanted to. This led to their decision to use the defeat device.

At first, it worked incredibly well. The cars passed the emissions tests with flying colours, and over the course of about ten years 600,000 'clean diesel'-branded cars were sold in the US alone. Meanwhile, around the world, Volkswagen estimated sales of 11 million of these vehicles.[18]

But in 2012, when Ayala and his team at CARB started looking more closely at the cars, trying to understand how they worked, they had more questions than answers. The following year, two more teams were looped in to help check the emissions results: Ayala's long-time colleagues at the Center for Alternative Fuels, Engines, and Emissions (CAFEE) at West Virginia University, and the centre's funders at the International Council on Clean Transportation (ICCT). When researchers tested the cars in the CARB lab, they got good results. But as soon as the CAFEE team took the same cars on the road, the results were shocking.

On average, the NOx readings were up to forty times the legal limit.[19]

For a while, Volkswagen managed to continue stringing along the regulators, lying in meetings and calling it a technical problem, while trying to hide the deception elsewhere in the defeat device code. Then, the Volkswagen employee chose to tell the truth, and made that confession to Ayala at the 2015 conference in California.

There was something about it all that felt bizarre to Ayala. 'I was probably more than anybody preconditioned not to want to believe that they were lying. Because in my own career at CARB, I had already gone through another major cheating scandal . . . I just couldn't believe that I was going to see this all over again,' he recalled.

Ayala wasn't the only one who felt like it was Groundhog Day. Daniel Carder, one of the researchers from CAFEE who'd found Volkswagen NOx emissions were way out of line, felt the same. Back in the 1990s Carder helped to create portable emissions testing for cars on the road.[20] These tests had exposed defeat devices in heavy-duty diesel engines, the kind commonly found in trucks and construction vehicles.

The resulting Cummins Engine Company settlement, between the US Justice Department and seven major manufacturers, was at the time the largest civil penalty ever imposed for a violation of environmental law.[21] It meant that, in 1998, the manufacturers had to pay $83.4 million. Since then, Cummins has reached two further settlements to resolve alleged violations of the Clean Air Act. In the most recent settlement, agreed in 2024, the company had to pay $1.675 billion. This broke another penalty record, for being the highest civil penalty related to a violation of the Clean Air Act.[22] In that time, they had illegally released an additional 243.5 tons of NOx into the atmosphere.[23]

Rewind even further, and you can see the long history of defeat devices in both petrol and diesel cars. According to the EPA, back in 1973, Chrysler, Toyota and General Motors were caught using a defeat device that involved removing temperature sensors to cheat emissions tests.[24] The following year, Volkswagen joined the club, when they 'failed to disclose two devices designed to alter the emissions controls' for appropriately 25,000 cars.[25] Rather than the industry learning from its mistakes, companies spent decades learning from each other how to lie.

'Volkswagen was a repeat, almost identical to what we saw from the heavy-duty engine manufacturers,' explained Ayala. 'In the test lab, they were meeting the standards, and then the engines would perform on the road and the emissions were several times over the standards. And that's precisely what Volkswagen was doing.' To this day, Ayala feels tremendous remorse for not realising what was happening sooner. But the lie was so massive that it didn't even cross his mind that Volkswagen would try something so egregious.

On 18 September 2015, CARB and the Environmental Protection Agency issued Volkswagen with a notice of violation for having 'manufactured and installed defeat devices' in certain models which had led to NOx emissions higher than the legal levels by 'a factor of 10 to 40 times'. These included their bestselling cars: the Jetta, Golf, Beetle and Passat. Also affected were the 2 litre diesel engines installed in the A3, made by Audi, which is part of the Volkswagen group.

The international press went wild. And people were *angry*. Myself included.

Maybe it's because I'm German. Or maybe it's because I've owned a Volkswagen car, and my family members still do. Perhaps it's because I have always lived in cities, and Volkswagen has forced me and my asthmatic partner to breathe in their NOx all these years. Or . . . it could be the fact that these clever engineers wasted their intelligence on harming rather than helping the Earth.

I can't quite put my finger on it, but I do know that this case got me fuming. And before I introduce you to the people who made me so mad, I want to lean into this storm inside. Just for a moment. Because sometimes anger isn't a problem.

Sometimes angry is exactly what we need to be.

ECO-ANGER

The climate emergency has arrived, and many of us feel it gnawing at the back of our minds. It's relentless, sharp and unyielding, like little claws digging into our conscience.

According to the 2024 results of the UN Peoples' Climate Vote, a survey unprecedented in its reach across countries and backgrounds, climate action is something that 'almost everyone, everywhere, can agree on'.[26] And most respondents said they were more worried about the climate than they had been the year before.

Globally, more than half of people – 56 per cent – think about climate change daily or weekly. Rates of concern are highest in countries most affected by the climate crisis. But even in North America, where concern is lowest, one in five people – 22 per cent – think about it daily.

And when researchers ask people how they feel about the climate crisis, the answer is consistent: *We. Are. Angry.*

In 2021, psychological researcher Samantha Stanley and her colleagues set out to explore this feeling. They hypothesised that distinct 'eco-emotions' exist and that anger might be the key to turning daily climate thoughts into meaningful action.[27] People were asked to rate how depressed and miserable climate change made them feel, a state the researchers called 'eco-depressed'; how much it made them feel anxious and afraid, or 'eco-anxiety'; and how much it made them feel angry and frustrated, or 'eco-anger'.

Then they looked at behaviours, to see whether people were taking actions such as protesting, writing to politicians, choosing eco-friendly products, or fixing things instead of replacing them.

The results were surprising.

People with high levels of eco-anger or eco-depression were more likely to participate in collective climate action. Those high in eco-anxiety, however, tended to disengage. For individual actions, like recycling, only eco-anger mattered. Strikingly, eco-anger also correlated with better overall mental health. 'Our findings highlight that frustration and anger about the climate crisis are adaptive responses,' the researchers wrote. 'The eco-angry recognise the importance of addressing their own daily behaviours as part of the collective goal of mitigating climate change.' To Stanley and her colleagues, eco-anger isn't just healthy, it's a necessary emotion.

In a follow-up research project, Stanley and her team dug deeper into eco-anger.[28] Again, they found that most eco-anger is useful, and is directly related to doing things to help prevent climate change.

Of the adaptive forms of eco-anger, the most common kind was directed at other people's inaction and apathy. As one of the study's participants explained in angry all-caps: 'NOT ENOUGH IS BEING DONE'. People mentioned they were most angry at governments, then individuals, then businesses. A list that feels slightly backwards in terms of who is actually to blame.

Curiously, although many point at governments for doing too little, according to the UN Peoples' Climate Vote most of us also see them as the most effective actors in combating climate change. Clearly, you can think a government is doing better than everyone else, but still be mad at them for not doing more. This tracks with the survey's finding that, globally, 80 per cent of people want stronger climate action from their political leaders.

The second biggest target of eco-anger is climate change deniers. For some, this is fuelled by specific politicians making climate-sceptical statements. For others, it stems from the misconception that climate denialism is widespread. In reality, the UN Peoples' Climate Vote shows that in almost every country in the world the vast majority of people believe that man-made climate change is one of the most important problems of our time.[29]

The third biggest source of anger is big polluters, those who prioritise profits over environmental protection. Like Volkswagen, when they decided to make 11 million dirty diesels in the middle of a climate emergency.[30] They had the technology to reduce their vehicles' ozone-creating emissions, but chose not to use it because, according to regulator Alberto Ayala, it would have cost more. Instead of doing the right thing, they cut corners and lied.

Who does such a thing?

SPILLED SECRETS

The day the world found out about Volkswagen's catastrophic NOx levels was also the day the regulators took a step back from the case. As Ayala explained to me, the investigation now fell to the US Department of Justice (DOJ) and the attorney general of California, Kamala Harris. Of course, Harris would later become the vice-president of the United States and then the Democratic presidential candidate.

This meant the regulators had to go silent. Ayala's role shifted to assisting the FBI and the DOJ's lawyers in gathering evidence. 'These were long sessions that I spent with the FBI and a room full of lawyers from the DOJ talking about the kind of things I'm talking to you about now,' he told me.

Meanwhile, the press seized on the story. This was the dramatic fall of an automotive darling. A company that had spent years aggressively greenwashing while lying relentlessly to the public. It was an infuriating scandal that reached right into people's own driveways, and even their own lungs.

While the investigators in the US worked to piece together *how* this had happened, journalist Jack Ewing started asking *why*. 'Very early in the process, one of the top editors turned to me and said something to the effect of: you'll figure all this out, Jack,' he recalled. At the time, Ewing was based in Germany, covering automotive and business news for the *New York Times*. 'It was just astonishing that this huge company would be capable of such a thing. It was this triple violation: consumer fraud, the environmental violation, plus the cover-up. Volkswagen had basically morphed into a criminal organisation.' In 2017, Ewing would write up his shocking discoveries in his book *Faster, Higher, Farther: How One of the World's Largest Automakers Committed a Massive and Stunning Fraud*.

When the frenzy of daily news coverage subsided, Ewing turned his attention to finding insiders willing to talk. Then, unexpectedly, he got a call. It was 'someone relatively high up at VW' who wanted to meet. But there were conditions. The meetings had to take place in secret locations, and the source's identity would never be revealed.

'We met maybe five or six times,' Ewing told me. 'He was very paranoid about people finding out who he was. He would show me a document, but before I could finish reading it, he would pull it away.' Still, this source provided valuable insights, including details about the culture and mentality inside Volkswagen that had allowed these crimes to happen.

And, over time, Ewing found more people willing to share their stories. These secret meetings, often held late at night, became a regular part of his life. 'Sometimes, I had the feeling I was like their only friend. That they had no one else to talk to.' Some of his sources had been fired and felt 'totally lost'. Others just wanted to tell their side of the story.

One comment from Ewing stood out to me: 'I never actually found anybody who felt that guilty about the environmental stuff.' Given that many of the people who lied were scientists and engineers, it's not like they wouldn't have understood how emissions contribute to climate change. They could not claim ignorance, so instead it appears there was a process of rationalisation and denial. 'One source was always trying to minimise it, saying that on the scale of green crimes, this wasn't that bad. There are other things that are worse,' Ewing recalled. It is precisely because people can choose not to see the harm they are doing that we need regulators who can see it for them.

Ewing also noted that when he spoke with people, '90 per cent of the discussion would be self-justification.' Some people didn't really want to explain what had happened. They mostly tried to convince him that it wasn't really that bad. Little by little, he realised the full scale of the crimes. This was not the work of one rogue individual. The perpetrators were a chain of people, each contributing to the crime and helping to diffuse the responsibility. 'You had one person who would tweak the software and somebody else who did another piece of it. So no one really felt like it was their fault,' Ewing explained. Employees saw their role in the fraud as a task they were told to complete. They seem to have convinced themselves that they had no choice in the matter.

Alberto Ayala gave a similar explanation. 'I think they were just trying to do their jobs. The folks we were dealing with got caught in that whole big lie. But at some point, we all face a fork in the road where we have to decide between right and wrong.'

Why, then, did so many people choose the wrong path?

One reason is that doing the wrong thing can feel right.

A judge later described the first Volkswagen engineer to be convicted as 'loyal. Arguably too loyal.'[31] Another engineer admitted, 'For a time, I was in denial that I personally did something wrong. I justified my bad decisions by telling myself I was obligated to stick to my superiors' instructions.'[32]

This thinking is key to understanding corporate green crime. The individuals who make these crimes happen rarely benefit directly or financially. I have found no evidence that the engineers who were building and implementing the Volkswagen defeat devices, or lying to the regulators, received bonuses specifically for this work. Sure, some people benefitted indirectly, as the company succeeded and sold millions of these cars. People might have been promoted, or kept their jobs as a result of following management's instructions. But it wasn't a simple money-for-crime transaction on an individual level.

I think the motivation for this kind of green crime is rarely just greed. There's something much more powerful at work here: the desire to be good at your job. Wanting the approval of bosses and colleagues, or the satisfaction of beating the competition. 'They wanted to be the number one carmaker in the world,' Ayala said. 'And they were going to do anything to get there.' So much so that they were willing to engage in what researchers call 'unethical pro-organisational behaviour'.[33] In the individual's mind, criminal actions can feel selfless rather than selfish, because they are engaging in harmful acts not for themselves, but for the company. Or, to put it another way, unethical pro-organisational behaviour is when people are too loyal.

And there was another force at play. 'In the background of all this was Volkswagen's culture of "you never say you can't do something",' said Ewing. 'If you told the higher-ups you failed, you were worried that you would get fired or demoted.' Hearing this reminded me of a German phrase: *geht nicht, gibt's nicht*, which translates to 'there's no such thing as can't'. If someone at Volkswagen said they couldn't do something, they were told to make it work.

To lie if they had to.

To just make it happen.

On that note, let's look at the wild ad campaign that Volkswagen ran.

EPISTEMIC MALEVOLENCE

Picture this. It is 2010, and you're watching the biggest event in the US sporting calendar, the NFL Super Bowl, on TV. An ad comes on, and at first you're not quite sure what it's for. On the screen, you see the 'green police' arresting people for all sorts of environmental offences. They confiscate plastic bags and bottles, toss away batteries, fine someone for failing to compost orange rinds, and even bust a person for soaking in overheated jacuzzi water.

A car pulls up to an 'eco-check' roadblock. A green police officer asks the driver, 'You got a TDI here?' – short for 'turbocharged direct injection' – to which the driver responds, 'Clean diesel.' The officer nods in approval: 'You're good to go, sir.' Then the driver speeds away as the screen fades to black, displaying the tagline 'Green has never felt so right'.

The ad from Volkswagen was slick, funny and memorable. It made 'clean diesel' look like the future of responsible driving. But it wasn't just clever marketing. It was a carefully constructed illusion.

This ad was just one of the many examples listed in the 2016 complaint against Volkswagen lodged by the Federal Trade Commission (FTC),[34] which regulates advertising and business practices in the US. Alongside it were various social media campaigns and glossy print ads aimed at attracting environmentally conscious buyers. A TV ad from 2008 ended with the line 'Diesel. It's no longer a dirty word'. Some ads went even further, making very specific claims that Volkswagen's NOx emissions were 90 per cent lower than those of comparable diesel cars.[35] This was, of course, false. Their emissions were actually many times higher than diesel cars that had passed the Californian regulators' tests legally.

And these ads were not aimed at just anyone. They were designed to attract people who genuinely cared about the planet. I think this is what makes the Volkswagen case particularly cruel. Drivers who wanted to make greener choices were seduced into becoming unwitting agents of environmental destruction.

This betrayal is why researchers have called the Dieselgate scandal a prime example of epistemic malevolence, which occurs when an organisation's culture and governance is rooted in a dark disposition that leads to patterns of behaviour and attitudes that undermine knowledge. To put it simply, epistemic malevolence is when organisations harm people by lying to them.

Researchers Marco Meyer from Hamburg University and Chun Wei Choo from the University of Toronto examined eighty high-penalty corporate misconduct cases in the US between 2000 and 2020.[36] One was the Volkswagen emissions scandal. In more than half of these cases, they discovered evidence of epistemic malevolence.

Meyer and Choo found that most epistemically malevolent organisations exploit trust by hiding, twisting or outright falsifying the facts in order to mislead people. 'Sometimes, organizations even set up sophisticated systems that allow them to exercise exclusive control over the flow and interpretation of information, as in the case of Volkswagen,' they wrote. 'By implanting the defeat devices, the company created a "controlled" information use environment, where regulators and customers were fully reliant on the company for information about vehicle emissions.'[37]

Volkswagen knew that by manipulating the flow of information, they could keep regulators, customers and the general public in the dark.

For seven years, these misleading ads helped Volkswagen rake in what the FTC called 'ill-gotten monies'. In other words, profits that they didn't deserve. But by the time the FTC case concluded in 2020, Volkswagen had been forced to pay more than $9.5 billion in penalties for false advertising. The full retail value of the cars had to be paid back to buyers, plus additional compensation for things like registration fees.

Even the time customers had to spend on finding another car to replace their dirty diesel was included in the fines.

Unfortunately, epistemic malevolence is widespread. And lies about the environmental impact of products are dangerously common.

GREENWASHING

Lie detection is one of the biggest areas of study in criminal psychology. I've published on the topic.[38] And, in 2024 I spoke to experts in the field to figure out what exactly we have learned from more than a hundred years of research on deception detection.[39]

It might surprise you to hear that the only thing experts can agree on is that the idea that liars avoid eye contact isn't true. There are no universal signs that someone is trying to deceive. If you think you are a natural at spotting liars, you've probably just forgotten – or never even realised – all the times you got it wrong.

This is also true when it comes to advertising, we find it hard to tell when we are being lied to. Greenwashing is when a business or organisation deceptively exaggerates the environmental credentials of their products or services. It is a common practice, yet research has found that more than half of consumers struggle to identify greenwashing on product labels. This is no accident, because the labels are specifically crafted to misinform. A report by the European Commission found that over 53 per cent of environmental claims on products were vague, misleading or unfounded.[40]

That's why, in late 2023, the European Parliament reached an agreement to ban greenwashing.[41] The new rules prohibit

THE CON MEN

vague environmental claims like 'environmentally friendly', 'natural', 'green', 'biodegradable' or 'climate neutral' unless they are backed up by evidence. Companies must also disclose whether their products are designed for planned obsolescence,[42] which is the deliberate strategy of designing products to fail prematurely so that people need to spend money to replace them. LED light bulbs, for instance, should last for years, but are sometimes designed to burn out in just months.

The fact that we need these regulations in the first place is evidence of our ongoing fight with hostile architects of choice.

Choice architecture is a concept from behavioural economics which refers to the ways in which the presentation of options influences decisions. It can be harmless, or even helpful, when employed ethically. But in the wrong hands, it becomes a tool for manipulation.

Companies study how we think and can use that knowledge to steer us towards decisions that benefit them, not us. Like telling us that their diesel cars are clean, when they aren't.

Another method is to present an option in a way that makes it seem like the default choice.[43] Defaults are one of the most powerful tools in choice architecture. They are the options that feel safe, familiar and easy; the choices we make without much thought. But when hijacked by people trying to sell us things, defaults can actively encourage us to make unsustainable choices.

For example, reducing meat consumption is one of the most effective ways to lower individual environmental impact. Yet plant-based meals are rarely framed as the default choice. Instead, it is common in restaurants to see meat-based options as main courses, the highlights of the meal, while plant-based options are mostly relegated to starters or sides. When this is done deliberately, it may be because meat-heavy meals are usually sold at a higher price.

It's an approach that works incredibly well, because it makes a very clear statement about what is considered the default: in this case, eating animals. It is also effective at selling to us when we don't really want to think at all, on days where we are tired or have decision fatigue. This is how hostile choice architecture operates. It creates an environment where a harmful option is the easiest one to make. Either by manipulating us to see it as the default, or by outright lying to us.

Many people care about greenwashing because they care about the environment, being lied to, or both. This also applies to people within a company that is actively engaging in greenwashing.

Although journalist Jack Ewing found that most Volkswagen employees he spoke with tried to minimise the environmental harm of the company's dirty diesels, this wasn't true of everyone. 'Some of the people who'd gone into this, they went in as idealists. They became emission specialists because they wanted to do something for the environment,' he told me. This makes sense. Fully implementing the clean diesel technology would have improved air quality. So being told it wasn't actually going to happen must have been quite distressing for some of the engineers.

On top of that, although many people in the organisation knew about the defeat device, most probably didn't. It seems unlikely, for instance, that the majority of the people in the marketing and sales departments were aware of what their colleagues were doing. Some probably felt terrible when they realised they had sold these dirty diesel cars.

Research has found that greenwashing is associated with the perception of corporate hypocrisy by an organisation's employees, which is linked with the desire to quit.[44] And the more employees understand about environmental issues, the more likely they are to want to leave when they find out that the company they work for is guilty of greenwashing.

And yet not everyone sees greenwashing as a moral failure. In the case of the emissions scandal, many people did not view the dishonesty as a fundamental flaw of Volkswagen as a company. When deceptive advertising is tolerated in this way, this is called lie acceptability.

When researchers gave people case studies of various kinds of organisations engaging in deceptive advertising, big and small, they found a pattern.[45] If a company is small, people are more likely to see dishonesty as a fundamental trait of the company, whereas with large corporations like Volkswagen, people imagine silos of responsibility. It becomes easier to believe that only a few bad apples are involved, or that key decision-makers at the top have no idea what is happening.

Another factor in the acceptance of greenwashing is emotional attachment. Cars are not just vehicles; they are symbols of success, expressions of identity. People give their cars names, share stories about them, and develop emotional bonds. In Germany, where cars are a national obsession, this connection runs particularly deep.

This relates to something known as national narcissism, which is not quite nationalism but is closely related. It is the belief that your country is both superior to others and inadequately recognised.[46] People high in national narcissism have been found to be less supportive of pro-environmental actions, and more likely to support greenwashing. Particularly as a political strategy for image enhancement.[47] It's easier to justify unethical acts in the vast global market when you believe that your country, or your city, deserves to succeed at the cost of others. And if pretending to be greener than you are is the key, then so be it.

That is, until the green veneer gets stripped back to reveal the truth. And national narcissism morphs into national shame.

WANTED MEN

What does justice look like for crimes against the environment? Is it hefty fines? Prison sentences for those responsible? Mandatory clean-ups? Recalls? Constant oversight? In the wake of the Volkswagen emissions scandal, the US government announced it was not going to choose between these options. It would pursue all of them.

On Wednesday, 11 January 2017, the outgoing US attorney general, Loretta Lynch, stepped up to a wooden podium, framed by two American flags, and delivered a historic announcement. She began by stating the facts: 'Hundreds of thousands of cars that VW sold in the United States were pumping illegal levels of nitrogen oxides into our atmosphere – up to 40 times more than the amounts permitted under federal law.' This was not new information for those paying attention. But what came next was astonishing.

As her final act as attorney general, she wanted to send a message to car manufacturers everywhere. 'Today, the

Department of Justice, the EPA [Environmental Protection Agency], and US Customs and Border Protection have reached a global resolution with VW that carries both criminal and civil penalties,' she announced. 'As part of this resolution, VW is pleading guilty to three felonies.'[48]

The first charge was 'conspiracy to defraud the United States, to commit wire fraud, and to violate the Clean Air Act'. This captured Volkswagen's deliberate lies about their emissions. The second charge, 'obstruction of justice', was related to the company's persistent efforts to mislead authorities, even after investigations into their emissions cheating were underway. The third, 'importation of goods by false statements', held them accountable for bringing cars into the United States under the false pretence that they met national environmental standards.

Volkswagen was ordered to pay a staggering $4.3 billion in criminal and civil penalties, on top of the more than $15 billion in settlements already announced[49] and the $9.5 billion the company was required to pay as part of Federal Trade Commission charges for the greenwashing ad campaign.[50] The FTC's final report marked the end of, at that point, the largest consumer compensation programme in U.S. history.

But Lynch was not done. As part of the guilty plea, Volkswagen would be placed on three years of probation, which meant that an independent monitor would oversee the company's ethics and compliance programme.

Then came the most surprising moment. In an unprecedented move, Lynch announced the indictment of five former Volkswagen executives, and a liaison accused of lying to the regulators. 'Over the course of a conspiracy that lasted for nearly a decade, they seriously abused those positions, and today, they are being charged with a range of crimes,' she declared. If convicted, these executives would face prison terms.[51] A year later, in 2018, another name would be added to the list of indicted people: former Volkswagen CEO Martin Winterkorn.[52] Of course, these were only *charges* against the VW executives. As always, the presumption of innocence applies. To skip ahead to the outcomes of the various legal proceedings, head to pages 45-47.

One of the accused, Oliver Schmidt, had been arrested at Miami airport just a few days before Lynch's press conference, and was already in the firm grip of the US justice system. Like villains in a Western movie, wanted posters were issued for the other five men, who overnight became fugitives.[53] The notices listed all the things you might expect, including what they were wanted for, whether they had any known tattoos, and where they were last seen. The five men were also the subject of Interpol Red Notices. These international requests instructed authorities to locate and arrest the fugitives, with a view to extradition.

In the end, it didn't take long to figure out where the five men were, since they hadn't really gone anywhere. They were presumably living in Germany.

German prosecutors immediately got to work.

For some of the executives, if they are found guilty, this can mean up to ten years of imprisonment.[54]

There is something intensely satisfying about picturing high-ranking executives behind bars for green crimes. But is that really what we want?

MAKE THEM PAY ATTENTION

'I encountered this resistance by people in charge at the very highest level, not at the lower levels – to spending too much money on this environmental stuff,' said Professor Susan Smith. A professor of environmental and natural resources law, she spent years at the US Department of Justice crafting policies and prosecuting federal agencies for violating environmental laws.

Smith is a powerhouse in the field of green crime. Alongside her colleague Susan Mandiberg, she wrote the seminal book *Crimes Against the Environment*, published in 1997 and often referenced since then. And in 2024, she released the *Research Handbook on Environmental Crimes and Criminal Enforcement*.

Realising she had the power to compel agencies to clean up their environmental messes was a turning point. 'We prosecuted some folks, who were civilian employees of the military, for various hazardous waste crimes. And we actually put them in prison.' She paused before adding, 'At that point, I saw the power of the criminal sanction.'

By the time I spoke with her, Smith was teaching at Willamette University and working with the World Council of Churches. Her faith, she told me, was deeply tied to her environmental mission. 'Fundamentally, we are called upon to care for creation. That means we have to think about how we protect the magnificent gifts that we have been given.'

'The United States environmental criminal enforcement programme really ramped up in 1984, and it's been a relatively robust programme ever since,' Smith explained. After years of relying on financial penalties to hold polluters accountable, there seemed to be a better way to protect the planet. 'We ended up with sentencing guidelines that presumed that environmental crimes would send you to prison. An assumption that you would go to prison for two to three years. That's not something that white-collar folks are accustomed to. We started to get more traction with corporate polluters when we started to have a legitimate environmental crimes programme that was going out and prosecuting them and putting people in prison.'

Now, I am not a fan of prisons. I think, generally, that putting people in what amount to very expensive cages often leads to dehumanising treatment, is catastrophic for the lives of prisoners both during their imprisonment and upon their release, and is ineffective at deterring most kinds of crime.

But, in my work as a criminal psychologist, I mostly deal with cases involving violent crime. Violence tends to be impulsive and committed in the heat of the moment, with little thought of the long-term consequences. The threat of prison does not feature in the split-second decision of someone throwing a punch, or pulling the trigger of a gun. But green crimes are different. Criminologists call a lot of it 'slow violence', because the harm unfolds over years, sometimes even decades.[55] And the decision-making involved is completely different too. A large-scale corporate crime is often a slow process, involving a lot of consideration of the minute details and a careful calculation of the risks.

Despite the slow nature of green crimes, however, I think most involve prioritising short-term consequences over long-term ones. Temporal discounting is the psychological process whereby the further away something is in time, the less weight it has in our decisions. An example of temporal discounting is choosing a guaranteed $10 now, rather than a likely $100 in the future. Or choosing $10 now, despite this leading to a likely future *loss* of $100. Or, in the case of Volkswagen, choosing to sell 11 million dirty diesels now with the known risk of having to pay a high amount in penalties if they were caught.

The question is, will sending executives and employees of companies to prison as a punishment for green crimes stop others in their position from making the same choices? In theory, it makes sense that it would. Imagine a boardroom debate where executives are weighing up profits today against the possibility of prosecution years from now. If the prospective punishment was a fine to the company, the individuals in that boardroom might see themselves as having little to lose. But if prison was a possibility, the prospect of ending up in a cell might tip the scales against committing the crime.

But there is a major flaw in this logic. Often, criminals believe they will simply never be caught. This is so common that it has a name, the 'illusion of unique invulnerability', which is the false belief that negative consequences that affect other people won't affect you. In that case, the nature of the punishment might not matter. It is not enough to just put laws in place; those laws must be enforced. For punishments to be effective, people need to think they are likely to be caught.

Without enforcement, laws are just hollow promises of justice.

There has been good environmental protection legislation in places like the European Union, the UK and the US for decades. But the under-enforcement of these laws has led to a sense of impunity among the perpetrators of green crimes. In 2020, the European Parliament published research stating that Europe has long had major deficiencies at all levels of the enforcement chain, and these have made criminal environmental law ineffective.[56]

Regulatory weaknesses make the problem worse. For example, in Europe, companies have long been able to shop around and do business in the countries with the weakest environmental laws. Alberto Ayala explained to me how this played out in the Volkswagen case: 'In Europe, it was a very decentralised process where every member state could certify, but there is no standard for how they do it. In fact, as we found out, most of the Volkswagen diesel cars just happened to be certified in one tiny country, Luxembourg. Like, 70 per cent of them.' The situation outside of Europe is even more grim. 'Regulators are typically understaffed, under-resourced, and do not get the support that they deserve.'

Harsher prison sentences as a punishment for green crimes can only be part of the solution. Regulators must be given sufficient resources to be able to check that the laws are being followed, and people need to know that if they perpetrate green crimes, they will probably be caught.

Luckily, in the Volkswagen case, in both the US and Germany there was a lot of evidence. The case progressed and the threat of individual consequences was real.

PERP WALKS

On 25 August 2017, the former Volkswagen engineer, and Leader of Diesel Competence for VW Group of America, stood in a courtroom in Detroit, Michigan. Shoulders heavy, a simple suit, rimless glasses perched on the bridge of his nose. He had pleaded guilty to his role in the emissions fraud. In return, he was sentenced to three years and three months in prison. The FBI's special agent in charge stepped forward to drive the point home. 'Today's sentencing is significant as it demonstrates there is and will be personal culpability for corporate executives who knowingly cheat American consumers, violate federal laws, and purposely utilize technologies that further endanger our environment.'[57]

The former Volkswagen engineer was the first to fall. But there would be more.

Oliver Schmidt was next, on 6 December 2017. As the former general manager of Volkswagen's Environment and Engineering Office in the US, Schmidt was more senior. He was dramatically arrested in the bathroom of a US airport before he was sentenced to seven years in prison. The Department of Justice made sure the world took note: 'Oliver Schmidt cheated the American people, and today's sentencing shows that such behaviour will be prosecuted to the fullest extent of the law.'[58]

The Americans were cracking down. The press made sure to film those found guilty on their 'perp walks', so everyone could see what happened to those who broke environmental law. Meanwhile, the Germans were conducting their own investigations. And everyone was waiting with bated breath to see whether the whip of German justice would crack as loudly as the American one.

In the US coverage of the Volkswagen case, there is a curious belief that Germany hasn't taken this crime seriously. Even worse, there are theories of corruption, and an underlying sense that the German government didn't *want* to prosecute this big German company and so only half-heartedly pursued it. But that's not what the evidence shows at all.

In 2018, Volkswagen agreed to pay a fine of 1 billion euros in Germany, and admitted responsibility for the fraud. The first to be convicted in Germany was Rupert Stadler, the former chairman of Audi, which is part of the Volkswagen Group. As part of a plea deal, Stadler entered a guilty plea.[59] In 2023, he was given a suspended sentence of one year and nine months for fraud.[60]

Convicted alongside him were a former Audi and Porsche manager who got a two-year sentence, and an Audi engineer who got a twenty-one-month sentence.[61] They accepted plea deals, which meant that in exchange for their cooperation, they were able to serve their time in the community instead of going to prison.[62] In addition to the time spent under the watchful eye of the state, they each had to pay a hefty fine. Surprisingly, Stadler and his co-defendants filed appeals just one week later.[63] In mid 2025, the appeal proceedings are still ongoing, so the verdicts are not yet legally binding.

Then, on 26 May 2025, four more individuals were held accountable, three of whom had already been named back in 2017 by U.S. Attorney General Loretta Lynch.[64] The German Regional Court of Braunschweig sentenced the former head of diesel engine development to four and a half years in prison, and the former head of powertrain electronics received a sentence of two years and seven months. A former head of development and a former department head were each given suspended sentences of three years. At least one of the convicted individuals has filed an appeal, but because of German privacy laws it is difficult to know exactly who.

The question remains: Is this what we want? The planet doesn't care if individuals sit in prison. To me, the only thing that matters is whether imprisonment as a punishment for green crimes actually works. And the answer to that is, frankly, hard to know, because so few environmental criminals have ever seen the inside of a cell.

Alberto Ayala said something on the subject that surprised me. Regarding the Volkswagen case, 'Unfortunately, there were people that I got arrested and went to jail, but I'm sure there were other higher-ups that were in on the lie, including VW's CEO at the time.' It was his use of the term 'unfortunately' that caught me off guard. I had expected an American regulator who spent years cracking this case to be pleased that the perpetrators had to pay the price with their freedom. But he wasn't. There is a fine line in a crime this big between scapegoating individuals just so you can show how tough on green crime you are, and actually helping to save the environment.

And that line – the one between punishment and prevention – is one that is being redrawn across Europe.

EVERY SCREW

'Everybody wants to get criminals into jails,' said Antonius Manders at a European Parliament press conference in 2024. 'We don't want that. But we want to have a preventative approach.' Manders was the Dutch Member of the European Parliament (MEP) and the rapporteur for the environmental crime directive. He was explaining that prison isn't a universal answer to the problem of green crime. Instead, we need a bespoke, but serious, penalty for each case. Included in his speech was the announcement that the European Parliament was extending the list of criminal offences against the environment, and that it would be updated every two years to reflect evolving threats.

What made this legislation unique was its flexibility. 'Normally in criminal law, every article has to describe the offence exactly because people have to know what they do wrong,' said Manders in his speech. 'But now we introduced, also, a kind of dynamic approach.' In practice, judges in each EU member state would decide within their own country whether a specific act constituted a crime.

These new rules aim to make companies and even entire countries pay for the messes they create, strengthening existing 'polluter pays' laws with more serious penalties. Fines could now reach up to 5 per cent of a company's global turnover or 40 million euros, depending on the scale and type of crime.[65] Critics said that these sums were too big for small companies and too small for big companies. But still, it was a huge step forward. And it was adopted with open arms by most European countries. There was only one country that abstained from the vote: Germany.

On top of more companies being held responsible, the legislation meant more individuals could be prosecuted. And if prosecutions failed on the corporate level, 'at least we can hold the CEOs of these companies personally liable at criminal courts,' Manders stated. Within the new legal framework, a CEO of a company would be liable when they knew, or could know, that a green crime was happening, and they did nothing to stop it.

Prison was not the end goal, but in his speech announcing the new measures, Manders made it clear it would still be a necessary tool. To harmonise sanctions across Europe, the commission agreed that the most severe environmental crimes would carry prison sentences of up to ten years.

'We had the question, is the car industry exempted?' Manders said, his facial expression hinting at the absurdity of this. 'Criminal law is for everyone,' he emphasised, before offering a pointed hypothetical example. 'For instance, the case in Germany, Volkswagen . . . Mr Winterkorn, he even motivated his technicians to introduce the fraud of diesels. And then in this case he is liable and might be sentenced to jail. But it's always the judge who decides on this. And I'm happy that I'm not in the seat of a judge.' Manders was just exploring a hypothetical scenario. Winterkorn has not been convicted of any crimes.

Martin Winterkorn was the CEO of Volkswagen when the Dieselgate scandal broke. When he resigned on 23 September 2015, he denied any knowledge of the fraud. He has consistently denied all charges brought against him. The German press has been critical of his answers regarding this lack of knowledge.[66]

As I write this, in July 2025, Winterkorn still maintains that he did not know anything about the deception. His trial has been postponed indefinitely for health reasons. The judges may eventually get to decide whether Winterkorn is guilty, but by then, the court of public opinion has potentially already reached its own verdict long ago.

Meanwhile, Europe's new environmental laws may be imperfect, but they mark a shift in accountability. CEOs can no longer hide behind the company that employs them, and companies cannot treat environmental destruction as the unpaid cost of doing business.

'Anecdotally, we know automakers go through the calculus of the cost of compliance versus the cost and risk of cheating and getting caught and paying fines,' said Alberto Ayala. 'Here is where the new European law can really help, if the equation now must include the chance of jail time for CEOs.'

As Manders put it: criminal law is for everyone. And that includes other car companies. After the news of the Volkswagen lies broke, emissions researchers and law firms around the world started asking questions. If Volkswagen's diesels were fraudulent, others might also be breaking or bending the rules.

The results of the subsequent investigations were staggering. When tested under real-world conditions instead of controlled labs, nearly all European diesel cars manufactured before 2017 emitted far more NOx than was legally allowed. 'Suspicious' emissions were recorded for 100 per cent of these cars, suggesting the likely use of defeat devices.[67] In more than 1,400 official government tests, 42 per cent of cars were found to have 'extreme' NOx emissions, which researchers claimed indicated definite cheating. It wasn't just a Volkswagen problem. It was an industry-wide deception.

Epistemic malevolence had gripped the entire sector.

'Everybody copied Volkswagen,' journalist Jack Ewing explained to me, referring to other car manufacturers who had also cheated on their emissions tests. 'They saw Volkswagen was having success with these diesels, and they started doing the same thing. And I think they all realised that Volkswagen had to be cheating, because they could all buy stuff from the same suppliers, and they couldn't make the cars compliant. In the end, almost all cheated at one level or another . . . And that all came to an end.'

When a market leader cheats, it influences norms within an industry and dictates the price of the thing being sold. To not get left behind, other companies must either carve out their own niche or let themselves be ethically dragged down in order to compete. Volkswagen fired the starting shot for a race that only other cheaters had a fighting chance in.

Further lawsuits began to roll in, one after another. Some would drag on for years. In the UK, group litigation was still ongoing in 2025 against sixteen major car manufacturers.

I asked emissions researcher Dr Harald Frey what this means for diesel cars today. His response was blunt: 'Many modern diesel cars do not meet the air pollution standards.' In the EU, new cars need to pass an on-road test in order to meet the Euro 6d emission standards. But these were only introduced in 2022, and the vast majority of diesel cars on the road today are older and thus far dirtier.

The numbers are brutal. 'Diesel cars with older standards exceed the pollutant limits in practice by more than six times on average,' said Dr Frey. 'And in individual cases, these exceedances are even higher.' Around the world, the levels of acceptable emissions differ, including being different between the EU and the US, so it's hard to say whether Volkswagen was the worst polluter or just one of the most brazen.

This is not a problem of the past. Every time you drive on the road, cycle along a bike lane or walk on a pavement, you likely pass one of these dinosaurs of destruction. They are still out there, rumbling along at full speed and belching out their NOx legacy.

But at least there have been consequences. Volkswagen

has been forced to pay enormous sums of money. And in situations like these, a company's reputation is damaged and, almost always, sales decline.

The era of impunity is fading. And a message rings out for the next generation of polluters: if you poison our air, we will come for you.

THE SIX PILLARS OF EMISSIONS CRIME

As mentioned in the Introduction, in each chapter I will present a 'six pillars' profile of the case to decipher the key motivations. The six pillars model is loosely inspired by situational crime prevention theory from criminology, which has benefitted from decades of research demonstrating its effectiveness. It is a very useful way to think about how we can change the circumstances in which crime typically occurs, to prevent it from happening in the first place.

According to situational crime prevention theory, we need to: (1) increase the effort it takes to commit a crime; (2) increase the risks of committing it; (3) reduce the rewards of committing the crime; (4) reduce the provocations that tempt people to commit crime; (5) increase incentives to adhere to the law; and (6) remove excuses for criminal acts. My six pillars – ease, impunity, greed, rationalisation, conformity and desperation – are effectively the psychological antecedents to these. For example, to counteract the tendency to choose ease, we need to increase the effort it takes to commit a crime. Here is the six pillars breakdown for the Volkswagen case:

Ease seems to have driven Volkswagen to cut corners. The company had the knowledge and tools to build cleaner diesel engines, but doing so would have been time-consuming and expensive. Instead, they developed their defeat device. As regulator Alberto Ayala explained, Volkswagen opted for the 'bare bones emission control system'. It was easier to fake it than to do it properly.

Impunity for emissions crimes had long plagued the car industry. Defeat devices were an open secret, and Volkswagen probably assumed they could get away with it because others had. For a long time, they were right.

Greed probably motivated the people at the top, who stood to gain the most from the company's success. It seems that Volkswagen's leaders were focused on becoming the world's top car manufacturer. 'Clean diesel' was their ticket to breaking into the US market and outpacing their competitors.

Rationalisation emerged in how the perpetrators spoke about their actions, downplaying the harm. Some even tried to convince journalist Jack Ewing that what they'd done wasn't so bad, arguing that the environmental impact was negligible in the broader context of climate change.

Conformity played a key role in recruiting many people into the conspiracy. Responsibility was diffused throughout the company, so no single individual felt accountable and, saying no to leadership felt like it wasn't an option.

Desperation intensified as regulators began asking questions. As the people in the company were backed into a corner, Volkswagen's lies spiralled. They desperately tried to dodge the legal consequences they could see coming their way, prolonging the environmental damage even more as they doubled down on their deception and continued selling dirty diesel cars.

The Volkswagen emissions scandal illustrates how an industry can be riddled with charlatans peddling fake environmental promises. It also shows how the green crimes we think are a thing of the past can resurface elsewhere. Like when defeat devices that appeared in trucks were installed into cars. To prevent this, we must keep scrutinising the greenwashing done by polluting companies and support our local regulators, who are the unsung heroes of the climate crisis.

UNSUNG HEROES

After Dieselgate, something unexpected happened.

Regulator Alberto Ayala found that he was approached by several Volkswagen executives. 'They came up to me, they shook my hand, and thanked me. Some of them said they were just on the wrong side of history, and it took something like this to set them back straight.'

There is something deeply revealing about this response. Green crimes do not rely on evil masterminds; they rely on silence. They rely on people following orders, keeping their heads down, and convincing themselves what they are doing is not so bad. But lies are heavy. They demand a constant effort to keep them hidden, with more lies, more cover-ups. When the truth finally comes out, it is not just good for the environment, it can also be a relief for the people who were involved in the crime.

'It took an outsider like us [the regulators] to essentially call it like we saw it,' Ayala explained. Having regulators inspecting a company's work can awaken its employees to the moral realities of what they are doing. Pull them out of the corporate fugue that obscures the harms lurking behind the sales figures. 'I think some people were very uncomfortable with what the company was doing. But they were just not in a position to do much about it,' Ayala told me. By revealing the truth, he managed to help the whole company, and then the whole car industry, travel a less harmful path.

Volkswagen's use of a defeat device forced people around the world to breathe more toxic air, endangering public health and contributing to climate change. None of that happened by accident. It was the result of deliberate decisions, made over and over again. And yet eventually the chain was broken.

Breaking the chain starts with one person putting their foot down. One person asking the difficult questions. One person calling out the harm.

As Ayala put it to me, this was David against Goliath.

Precise acts of resistance can bring down giants.

2

THE MURDERERS

When Laísa arrived at the scene, she pushed her short curly hair behind her ear and stared at the ground. From under permanently indented dark brows, her eyes scanned for clues of what had happened.

The blood was still pooling, soaking into the brown palm leaves below. The wind smelled of the last days of May; the ground was spongy from the recent rains, and a temporary stream flowed along the edge of the dirt road. Glittering through the tangle of trees and ferns, the morning sun was waking up for another hot and humid day.

Laísa had been pulled out of bed around 7.20 that morning, when she groggily opened the door to find her neighbours outside her house in tears. They had come to take her to the crime scene where her older sister, Maria, and her sister's husband, Zé Cláudio, had just been found. Both were in their fifties. After having lived life at full speed, they had only recently started to slow down.

At the crime scene, Zé Cláudio and Maria's motorcycle, toppled over on the road, was easy to identify. But the familiar banana-yellow stripe running down the middle of it was now splattered with blood. Laísa could also make out Zé Cláudio, although his body was twisted in unnatural ways.

Laísa walked slowly towards the widening pool of blood, reluctantly taking one step at a time until she reached the edge of it. She went a couple of feet then stopped again. Death comes to everyone, she thought to herself, but sooner to those who fight these environmental battles. She looked closer, and recoiled when she saw that one of her brother-in-law's ears had been ripped off.

Laísa's eyes searched through the mess as she suppressed a wave of nausea. She was struggling to differentiate the various red shapes. Where was her sister? Hadn't they been together? Perhaps her mind wasn't letting her see things for what they really were, or maybe she was mistaken.

Laísa asked her neighbour who was standing beside her. 'Where is Maria?'

But just as she let the question escape, she saw Maria's bloodied foot, right in front of her.

This chapter explores how entangled human and environmental rights are. My reconstruction of this scene is based on a filmed interview with Laísa, who in poetic detail recounted discovering her sister's tragic death. The interview was part of a submission to the International Criminal Court by Brazilian environmental lawyer Paulo Busse and his colleagues. Busse and his colleagues believe that the Brazilian state's inaction in the face of ongoing killings and other inhumane acts against environmental defenders is a crime against humanity. I spoke with him to get a better understanding of the issues currently faced by those on the front lines of environmental justice.[1]

In South America, the killing of Maria and Zé Cláudio is one of the most well-known crimes related to the environment. Their deaths have inspired people to mobilise for the rights of Indigenous peoples, to fight for the protection of those who continue to protect our environmental heritage when no one else will. It has become symbolic of the thin green line. The fight between those who are protecting nature and those destroying it. But without Paulo Busse's help, I might never have known about the case, because the media coverage of it is almost exclusively in Portuguese and Spanish.

In this chapter, I wrestle with issues that form a key part of the current debate about how best to protect our fragile ecosystems, and whether concepts like ecocide are part of the answer. It brings us to the fundamental question: should nature have inherent rights, like a person? And if so, what would that actually look like?

Having these kinds of discussions can fundamentally reframe how we think about humanity's relationship with the Earth. A relationship that has historical roots in ideas about land ownership, colonisation, and exploitation. Psychologically there is a key issue here too, for if we are to ensure the protection of the shared resources that we all need in order to survive, we need to understand why people so readily destroy things they feel entitled to.

This case involves a man who bought land rights that couldn't be sold, a scuba diving mask that formed a key piece of evidence, and a criminal who evaded justice for years under a false name.

And all it began in one of Earth's last ancient forests.

MASKED KILLERS

In the early hours of 24 May 2011, Maria do Espírito Santo's arms were gripped around José Cláudio Ribeiro, better known as Zé Cláudio. Riding their yellow motorcycle, they rumbled down the remote dirt road in the middle of the Amazon rainforest.

Zé Cláudio manoeuvred the motorcycle to accommodate every familiar bump and turn, and slowed down as they came up to the weathered bridge they had crossed thousands of times before. But on this dewy pre-dawn morning, hiding in the thicket just beyond the bridge, were two men who had been patiently waiting there in a stake-out, watching intently for this specific motorcycle.[2]

As they reached the bridge, Maria and Zé Cláudio were ambushed. One of the men, armed with a hunting rifle, sprayed bullets at them. Then he bent over Zé Cláudio's bleeding body on the ground and, while he was still alive, cut off his ear.

The killers got away, leaving the two of them to bleed out on the road. It didn't take long for the crime scene to be discovered, and just hours later Laísa stood there, identifying her sister's foot in the pool of blood.

Police quickly began to investigate the crime. The missing ear was a clear sign of a hitman in need of evidence for his employer. 'Certainly, it was a contract killing, ordered by someone. The characteristics are typical of an execution,' the local police chief said at the time.[3] But initially the police didn't have any clear leads. This wasn't because they couldn't find anyone with a motive. The problem was quite the opposite.

After their deaths, Zé Cláudio's mother, Raimunda Santos, spoke with the press about how her son would go to the houses of those cutting or burning down trees and try to convince them to stop. He would tell them about how beautiful and abundant the forest was, and that it should be preserved. Together with Maria, he also organised protests and campaigned against illegal deforestation and the eviction of local farmers. Through these kinds of tactics, 'he enraged some people', his mother said, even though 'he didn't want to'.[4]

'Many farmers and loggers were interested in my brother and his wife not getting in the way anymore,' said Zé Cláudio's sister, Claudelice Silva dos Santos, who told the press on the day of the murder. The couple had recently gone to the local police to report the death threats they'd been receiving. According to Claudelice, Maria and Zé Cláudio's home had been broken into and ransacked more than once. In fact, just weeks before they were killed, there had been a failed assassination attempt. But despite these clear threats to their safety, the police hadn't offered Maria and Zé Cláudio any protection.[5] Laísa, Maria's sister, was having a similarly horrific experience, with constant threats of violence.

Zé Cláudio, who regularly gave public talks, had even voiced his fears to huge audiences. In a TEDxAmazônia talk just a few months before they were murdered, he had proclaimed solemnly, 'I live off the forest, I protect it in every way I can.' Standing in front of the bright red TED talk logo in his favourite soft black hat with a Che Guevara signature on the front, he continued: 'That's why I live at gunpoint all the time. Because I don't just stand around, I denounce loggers, I denounce the charcoal burners, and that's why they think I shouldn't exist.'[6] With the press quick to cover the case, the pressure was on the police to figure out which of the people making the threats, if any, were involved in the murders.

A breakthrough came when a black neoprene diving mask was found floating in the water near the crime scene. It was immediately treated as evidence, and hairs were found inside the mask.[7] There was also a witness. A man who would later testify in court that he had been putting up a fence that morning, on the road where the murder happened. He had seen two men driving by on a red motorcycle. While he hadn't been able to make out the man on the back, he knew that the broad, stocky man driving the motorcycle was Lindonjonson Silva Rocha, who he'd recognised because they had spoken before. He gave a sketch of Silva Rocha to the police, portraying his protruding ears and deep-set eyes. The police followed up on this lead.

Worn and weary, Rocha was taken into police custody. Now the question was whether the DNA from the hair samples in the diving mask matched his. Samples were sent off to the forensics lab and came back positive.[8] The police now had clear evidence linking Silva Rocha to the crime. At some point, presumably after the witness working on his fence had seen him, Rocha must have pulled on the mask. After the murders, he had either intentionally ditched or unintentionally dropped it.

The police then managed to track down the other man on the motorcycle: a lanky, red-eyed man named Alberto Lopes do Nascimento. He too was brought in for questioning.

The question now was, who exactly were these two men,

and why did they want Maria and Zé Cláudio dead? Were they recipients of Zé Cláudio's door-to-door campaign to make loggers change their ways? Men with a vendetta against environmental defenders? Farmers? No. It turned out that they weren't any of these things. They were just two out-of-work day labourers. Work was short, and they had been willing to take on a horrible job.[9] They were hitmen. And they weren't the only ones getting their hands bloody for bosses who wanted environmental defenders dead.

In order to understand how we got here, and why, we need to go back. Way back. To 1500, when the mentality that would psychologically underpin these gruesome murders was born.

MOTHER EARTH

For thousands of years, the Amazon has teemed with people who have cut down its trees, hunted and fished its animals, and plucked the berries off its bushes. Because of this, and because of the emergence of agricultural societies, people have been fundamentally transforming the Amazon for a long time.[10]

Archaeologists have estimated, based on human burial sites, that the first settlements in the Amazon were formed between 4,000 and 10,600 years ago. One region in Bolivia, known as Llanos de Moxos, shows evidence of an extensive landscape transformation that began 2,500 years ago, resulting in hundreds of miles of roads and thousands of hectares of fields. It's here that staple crops like sweet potatoes, wild rice, chili peppers, and peanuts are thought to have been first domesticated.

In 1500, Brazil became part of the land owned by the Portuguese crown by right of discovery. The first European arrivals would have seen blue waters, golden sands and the yellow blossoms of the brazilwood trees along the edge of the Atlantic rainforest. These trees would soon become prized exports as their wood was used in the production of stringed instruments.

Back home, Portugal had implemented the 'sesmaria system' to help deal with a severe food crisis it was experiencing, by putting an obligation on landowners to use their soil productively.[11] In other words, if someone owned land, they were expected to do things like cultivate crops or rear animals on it. The Portuguese settlers brought this concept with them to Brazil. Except, by then, the food shortage in Portugal had ended, and these laws were used as a lever for colonisation instead. If people did not make productive use of the land in Brazil within five years of it being allocated to them, it was returned to the crown. Even if people were still living there, perhaps having lived there for as long as they could remember, it was deemed vacant land, or 'terra devoluta', and could be given or sold to somebody else. The new owners would usually then kick the existing inhabitants off the land.

From today's viewpoint, it could be argued that the Portuguese colonisers were the first large-scale environmental criminals in Brazil. The act of clearing the Amazon for agriculture and settlements not only displaced Indigenous peoples but also destroyed vast ancient ecosystems. Their actions, driven by a philosophy of modernisation, set in motion the widespread environmental destruction that continues to threaten the Amazon today.

The arrival of the Portuguese also marked the beginning of the fight for nature. At odds with Indigenous ways of life, colonisers followed economic and social ideologies in which the Earth belonged to individuals, and nature was a resource to be exploited for immediate human gain. Once they had taken the land for themselves, the colonisers began to tame and shape the wilderness around them, to the dismay of the Indigenous peoples.

This was all before Indigenous peoples had rights on the global stage, in the way we legally mandate them today. In 1986, a landmark UN report was published by José Martínez Cobo that became known simply as 'the Cobo report'.[12] One of the main questions he sought to answer was: who, and what, counts as Indigenous?

The Cobo report determined that Indigenous communities, peoples and nations share a historical continuity with the pre-invasion and pre-colonial societies that developed on their territories. They also consider themselves distinct from other sectors of the societies currently prevailing in those territories, or in parts of the territories in which they live. Additionally, Indigenous peoples are often, but not necessarily, linked by a shared language, group consciousness, culture, belief system or religion, or type of dress, and may live in a tribal system. Another common aspect of Indigenous peoples is how they earn their livelihood, often using specific hunting, fishing and agricultural practices that are a manifestation of their culture.

The report criticised the public authorities of many countries for seeing Indigenous practices as primitive, marginal and undeveloped. This is an example of ethnocentrism, which is a key psychological driver in the dehumanisation and devaluation of groups of people. Ethnocentrism is when people treat their own norms as superior to those of others, and assume that their own way of life is the correct or best way to live. It can lead to a racist outlook where Indigenous lives are seen as simple and backward, and therefore less important.

Talking broadly about Indigenous attitudes, Cobo wrote: 'For such peoples, the land is not merely a possession and a means of production. The entire relationship between the spiritual life of Indigenous peoples and Mother Earth, and their land, has a great many deep-seated implications. Their land is not a commodity which can be acquired, but a material element to be enjoyed freely.' This is an overgeneralised, but still valuable, statement about Indigenous ways of thinking.

From an environmental standpoint, the idea that we should not treat land as a commodity is a radical one. If we all treated the Earth as a shared resource, we would probably not be in the climate catastrophe we find ourselves in today. But it seems this philosophy of nature having intrinsic value is not a universally welcome one. It has tragically put a target on the backs of Indigenous environmental defenders like Maria and Zé Cláudio.

The Cobo report brought to light centuries of large-scale violations of the rights of Indigenous peoples, as well as the unlawful dispossession and plundering of their lands. 'One cannot really speak of respect for Indigenous cultures when powerful States and gigantic companies are allowed to destroy that relationship whenever they wish to exploit the resources of Indigenous lands,' Cobo wrote in the conclusion.

In 1988, the year after the report was published – and

three years after the end of Brazil's military dictatorship in 1985 – the rights of Indigenous peoples were finally recognised under Brazil's federal constitution.[13]

Today, Indigenous peoples and their land have the highest level of protection under Brazilian law, and unlicensed or unauthorised commercial activity is illegal in reserves and Indigenous territories. But just because there are laws in place, it does not mean these rights are being respected or policed.

The rights of Indigenous peoples around the world continue to be treated as a niche issue, an afterthought in environmental conversations. Indigenous peoples have comparatively limited visibility in mainstream media and online channels, which is a major disadvantage. Just think of how many politicians live in an always-on world, where the issues they focus on tend to be those they see get the most traction. This highlights the importance of creating bespoke spaces where conversations about Indigenous issues are facilitated, like at the United Nations Permanent Forum on Indigenous Issues.

Limited mainstream cultural visibility also means that it is easy to underestimate the amount of land that Indigenous peoples inhabit and protect. Despite the centuries of domination, violence and dispossession, Indigenous peoples occupy about 20 per cent of all land on Earth. If the territories of Indigenous peoples were a country, it would be, by far, the largest country in the world. It would also be the world's third-most populous nation, with 370 million citizens.[14]

Since the Portuguese colonisation, Indigenous peoples in the Amazon, like Maria and Zé Cláudio, have faced persecution as they are pushed into an ever-smaller corner of the vast forest they consider their home. As Zé Cláudio explained, when he was young, the logging trucks arrived, and deforestation began.

Trees are seen to be in the way of open pastures, and fires are intentionally caused to grant quick access to empty land for the cattle.

Cattle ranching is yet another legacy of the colonisers, who by the seventeenth century had brought over their farm animals from Portugal. But today, it's not just the cattle that need space; it's also the soybeans that are grown to feed them. Greenpeace has estimated that cattle rearing for the production of meat and dairy products is responsible for 80 per cent of the destruction of the Amazon. They also found that about a fifth of the rainforest has already been destroyed, with 'almost all of the deforested areas being turned into cattle ranches'.[15] In 2023, Brazil was the world's largest beef exporter, sending much of its meat to China.[16]

Modern Brazilian cattle farming practices can be traced back to the 1960s. At that time, Brazil ushered in a brutal economic modernisation project, enforced by the military government, which further displaced Indigenous peoples. That's when the first big access road was built in the Amazon.[17] By 1966, Operation Amazonia was underway. It was a government initiative put in place to attract private investment and raise Brazil's GDP by offering massive tax cuts to certain industries, including for those raising cattle.

Slowly, political resistance formed against these forest clearances, often with the help of the Catholic Church, and unions emerged for those in traditional industries such as rubber tapping. The members of these unions relied on the survival of the trees for their livelihood. Strategic alliances were also formed with high-profile environmentalists, after the Cobo report helped to bring the plight of Indigenous peoples out of the shadows.

Throughout the 1990s and 2000s, new proposals for land use based on collective land rights were drafted, and more than 500,000 square miles of rainforest were reserved for the use of traditional communities.[18] These areas are called Extractivism Settlement Projects – or, in Portuguese, *Projetos de Assentamento (PAEs)*. They are a way to redress the social and economic injustices against Indigenous peoples in Brazil. It is on one of these projects that Maria and Zé Cláudio were living when they were murdered.

Before I get back to the case, and the wild story of the man who hired the hitmen, we first need to understand the importance of what they were protecting. Why should we care about the rainforest?

BIODIVERSITY HOTSPOTS

In order to understand why deforestation is such a threat to our future, I spoke with National University of Colombia professor of landscape ecology and ecosystem modelling Dolors Armenteras, who has published extensively on the impact of human activities on the environment.

She explained to me that deforestation 'results in forest loss, meaning the complete removal of forest cover and the conversion of forested land to non-forested uses. This is different from forest degradation, where some forest remains but its quality is diminished.' If forests were people, and trees were hair, then deforestation would be a buzz cut, and degradation would be like someone leaving random patches of hair.

I asked Armenteras what was special about the Amazon specifically. 'Deforestation in the Amazon is significantly different from deforestation in Europe,' she explained. 'The Amazon is a tropical rainforest with unparalleled biodiversity and plays a vital role in regulating the global climate. In contrast, forests in Europe are often more managed, have less biodiversity, and were extensively deforested in the past, with only a fraction of the original forest cover remaining.' That's why, today, 'the loss of the Amazon's forests has far-reaching consequences for the planet, affecting global weather patterns and contributing to climate change on a scale not seen with smaller, more temperate forests.'

Although most people have probably heard of deforestation, 'there is often a lack of understanding about its full impact,' said Armenteras. For example, 'a common myth is that replanting trees or the restoration of forest can easily and rapidly offset the damage caused by deforestation. However, those "restored" forests rarely replicate the complexity of old-growth forests, which are a legacy of the past and crucial for today's biodiversity and carbon storage.'

This complexity is why forests like the Amazon are biodiversity hotspots. Biodiversity hotspots have areas with at least 1,500 endemic species of plants. There are currently thirty-six of these hotspots in the world, and between them they are home to almost 43 per cent of Earth's mammals, birds, reptiles and amphibians.[19] In thirty-one biodiversity hotspots there are documented Indigenous territories, with

Indigenous lands covering 22 per cent of the hotspots in total.

Biodiversity hotspots are vital carbon sinks, which draw CO_2 out of the atmosphere and sequester it away safely in plants. What makes news of fires and other destruction in biodiversity hotspots like the Amazon so galling is that, not only does this mean we are losing some of Earth's ability to absorb and store carbon, we are also releasing even more of it into the air. 'When forests are cleared, this stored carbon is released into the atmosphere, exacerbating climate change,' Armenteras explained. 'It's estimated that deforestation accounts for about 10–15 per cent of global carbon emissions.'

Trees also act like natural air conditioners, dramatically reducing the surface temperature near them. Their roots pull large amounts of water from the ground, more than the trees themselves can use, and the excess is released into the atmosphere through their leaves. This water vapour combines with microbial spores that grow on the leaves and moves up into the atmosphere, a process that plays a crucial role in cloud formation. It's how rainforests literally make their own rain, and thereby affect global weather.

Another worry about the continued degradation of biodiversity hotspots is an increase in climate velocity: the measure of how quickly and how far organisms have to migrate to keep up with climate change. All species need certain amounts of water, eat certain plants, and have temperatures they survive best at. If the temperature rises, fish need to find cooler areas. If the rains stop, frogs need to figure out how to get to new ponds. If the sun gets more intense, trees need their seeds to be transported to cooler areas.

This means that, when weather changes, entire species need to move hundreds or thousands of miles to stay alive. Over the next few decades, there will be a massive redistribution of organisms. Those species that don't, or can't, move in accordance with our new world will go extinct.

Globally, climate velocity is affected by climate change, but it can also be affected at a local level by human activity. Logging and burning parts of rainforests changes the temperature of the forest and impacts things like water retention and rainfall. Climate velocity is one of the primary concerns around biodiversity loss, and is a useful metric for understanding which species are most at risk of extinction and which biodiversity hotspots are most at risk of collapse. It can also help researchers plan for problematic and invasive species arriving in new places.

In 2022, Earth's highest climate velocity on land was in South America, particularly in the Amazon.[20] It affects the trees, mangroves, rivers and streams. The resources that Maria and Zé Cláudio dedicated themselves to protecting. Their fight to preserve these resources is also why they were killed. Before we return to the case, I want to ask one more fundamental question: psychologically, what is it that differentiates those who destroy nature from those who protect it?

RECKLESS ENTITLEMENT

The tragedy of the commons is the idea that when individuals have access to a shared resource, each individual has an incentive to selfishly exploit that resource as much as possible. If everyone follows this logic, the resource will eventually be depleted, and everyone loses. If we all selfishly cut down parts of our local forest, we will be left with an uninhabitable Earth.

There is a notion that underpins this, and it is one that a lot of people fundamentally believe in: that humans are inherently selfish. Some research supports this belief. For example, in 2021, a major article reinterpreted the results of 237 experiments that tested how people deal with things that are shared. These are also called public goods, and the research found that, in general, people are not altruistically motivated to help others, but rather learn over the course of experiments how best to help themselves.[21]

But, public goods experiments have also shown that there are specific factors that change whether someone will behave selfishly. For example, when people see someone else leading by prosocial example, so behaving in a way that helps others, they are more likely to cooperate.[22] Similarly, when people lead with selfishness, others often follow suit. Researchers have also found that labelling behaviours as 'good' or 'bad' can have a strong effect on promoting cooperation and the maintenance of public goods.[23] For example, reprimanding people for littering by calling it a moral failing can have a big impact.

Another solution that has been proposed for the tragedy of the commons is ownership. With the idea being that, if people own their own piece of land, then they will take care of it. But while this may be true for a small plot of land where you eat and sleep, is it really the case for land ownership in general? It's not. In fact, environmental psychologists have found that legally owning land can even make people more likely to destroy it, rather than less.

That's because land is often bought, and its resources are extracted, in a purely transactional way. Many of those profiting from a patch of land don't live there; they might never even have seen, visited or touched the earth they own. Land thus acquired becomes reduced to a concept, acres recorded on a spreadsheet.

There is no feeling of loss if there was never a connection to the place that is being destroyed in the first place. This is a problem. We generally think that it is important for criminals to do more than just logically understand that they broke the law. They should feel remorse, regret, even grief. We want this because we assume that if those psychological minimums aren't met, the person will surely reoffend. People need to *feel* that what they are doing is wrong, not just *know* it.

In the Amazon, what has happened is a systematic selling-off of land, both legally and illegally. For decades the destruction of the Amazon was state-sanctioned, with presidents like Jair Bolsonaro taking a deliberate pro-profit stance and encouraging big business to move in. International meat and animal feed companies were invited to strip the Amazon of its resources and sell their products to multinationals, which they continue to do to this day. It isn't just the tragedy of the commons that has burned down large parts of the Amazon; it is the tragedy of short-sighted economic policies that have sold off irreplaceable resources. Short-sighted because you can only cut down an ancient forest once.

When it comes to understanding criminality and conflict in the Amazon, a lot of it centres around land disputes and 'ownership insecurity', which is when people are not confident that the land they bought and see as theirs is legally recognised as such. Researchers have found that insecure land property rights contribute to deforestation and homicides.[24] That's because buying land makes it feel like it is yours to destroy or repurpose as you like. It can foster reckless entitlement.

But it doesn't have to be like that. Fostering a personal or emotional connection to a place can help counterbalance this problem. This is called psychological ownership. A plot can be a special place that we want to take care of and maintain, whether or not we actually legally own the land. A beautiful public park that we often visit, for example, can feel just as much like ours as our own garden. And that feeling can make us want to tend to it, fight for it, even chain ourselves to trees to stop people from cutting them down.

Experimental research has found that *legal* ownership increases a sense of 'mine-ness', and increases the desire for control and to keep other people out.[25] On the other hand, *psychological* ownership increases our willingness to protect a place, and oppose exploiting it. People are more willing to safeguard land they love and more likely to exploit land they feel they own. When psychological and legal ownership converge, we often treat that place as our home.

A core tenet of many Indigenous cultures is psychological ownership, and an opposition to destroying nature. Many Indigenous peoples who extract valuable resources from the Amazon to eat, use or sell, do so with a profound sense of symbiosis. Living not *off* the land, but *with* it. That's one reason why granting collective property rights to Indigenous peoples has been shown to decrease deforestation in the Brazilian Amazon.[26] Giving legal ownership of nature to people who already have psychological ownership over it is a great way to fight the climate crisis.

Another argument that is often made in climate research is that we would also benefit from giving more land to women. A UN report published in late 2023 found that women are champions of the environmental rule of law, working on the front lines of conservation and environmental protection around the world.[27] But because women are such effective environmental advocates, they can face violent backlash. Some women who protect nature are subjected to gender-based harassment, persecution and even sexual violence. Female-run environmental initiatives also receive significantly less support and funding than those run by men.

In order to create safer places for women to organise their environmental activism, eco-feminist exchanges have been created. These are places where women can share knowledge and adopt sustainable practices in informal settings. In Brazil, for example, the Guerreiras da Floresta (Warriors of the Forest) is a group of Indigenous women promoting environmental and land rights who travel around villages to discuss the importance of forest and ecosystem conservation.

Claudelice da Silva Santos was also heavily involved in environmental activism. Alongside her brother, she fought against those who were trying to take Indigenous land in Pará. She became a renowned human rights lawyer and an environmental celebrity after her brother was murdered. She has travelled the world raising awareness of the resistance shown by Indigenous peoples in the Amazon, and the dangers they face as a result. She has also set up an organisation called Instituto Zé Cláudio e Maria, which works to support environmental defenders whose lives are in danger and seeks to keep alive the memories of those who died in the battle.

As she explained in an interview for the evidence bundle that human rights lawyer Paulo Busse and his colleagues collected for their International Criminal Court submission, 'Exploitation and destruction continue, and together with the destruction of the forest and the environment, people who live there are also being destroyed. Doesn't that touch you? Doesn't that touch the rest of the world? To know that whilst you are buying meat, whilst you are buying wood, minerals, all of those commodities are soaked in blood.' She challenges us to feel something for the harm we have caused, to accept responsibility, asking: 'Doesn't that hurt?'[28]

It probably hurts the most if we see nature as an extension of ourselves. If we think of nature as having inherent value and inherent rights, like humans. If we feel, in other words, psychological ownership of the Earth. Before he was murdered, Zé Cláudio expressed what it means to feel this: 'When I see one of these trees on top of a truck going to the sawmill, it brings me such pain. It's as if I were watching a funeral procession taking the dearest person I've got.'[29]

This idea of viewing trees and animals on the same level as loved ones is revolutionary. Many people see humans as superior to all other life on Earth. But what would happen if we stopped thinking that way? What if, instead of exploiting nature, we treated it as the magnificent self-sustaining life support system that it is?

UTOPIA

'Actually, this is utopia,' Maria says in Portuguese, straight to camera. 'Here in my piece of land we can show society that it's possible to live with forest resources in a sustainable way.'

The video interview which was filmed just months before she was killed was being shown in 2012, when she and Zé Cláudio were posthumously awarded the United Nations Forest Heroes (Heróis de Floresta) Award.[30] Her expression in the footage is tired, her eyes red. Maria's black earrings dangle pleasantly as she speaks; her bright green T-shirt is the same colour as the rainforest behind her. The two of them lived in Pará in the eastern Amazonian region. Specifically, in Praialta-Piranheira, the Extractivist Settlement Project they helped to establish in 1997. The people living there are activists who extract sustainably from the land. This is a model known as extractivism.

It is clear from her surroundings that life in the rainforest doesn't divide as starkly between the natural and the human world. A simple wooden wall gives way to the trees beyond. Two pieces of laundry hang outside, just out of focus, catching the muted sunshine. Next to Maria is a pile of books, their spines facing away, with various papers and notes sticking out of random pages.

When her husband Zé Cláudio comes onto the screen, he is walking through a densely leafy part of the forest. He is wearing his signature beret, with fluffy grey tufts of hair sticking out from underneath. On his face is a pair of sunglasses. His plaid vest, left unbuttoned in a deep V, reveals a long knotted string necklace with a tooth-like pendant. He stops in front of an enormous tree that looks like it is from another time, and stretches out his arms. The trunk is far wider than his wing span.

'This is majesty, the pride of our forest,' he says, smiling. The camera turns upwards, towards the crown of the tree, and the trunk is so long that it appears to never end. 'If it's up to me, this will be here for many years.' As he explains that this is his place of meditation. To him, this is a cathedral to nature, a shrine to Mother Earth.

Before they were murdered, Maria and her husband were living off the forest. Zé Cláudio had been a nut-gatherer since he was seven years old, digging through the leaves amidst the tangle of the Amazon's roots to collect chestnuts to sell. Whenever the value of the nuts dropped, Zé Claudio would instead use his talents as a craftsman, weaving baskets out of liana vines.[31] Both he and Maria engaged in community organising and protests, defending their land against over-exploitation and destruction. In the late 1990s, logging trucks started to roll into the area where they lived. 'That's when the attack on the forest began,' Zé Cláudio says in the video, 'along with my fight against them . . . That's when people started coming after me.'

Pará is a dangerous place, with a long history of land conflicts, aggression and murder. Zé Cláudio had proclaimed solemnly in his TEDxAmazonia talk: 'The same thing that was done to Chico Mendes in the state of Acre, they want to do with me.'

ENVIRONMENTAL DEFENDERS

Chico Mendes was a famous environmental defender who advocated for sustainable development in Amazonian extractive communities and settlement projects, and worked to strengthen the rights of the peoples of the forest. He also penned the famous *'Carta aos Jovens do Futuro'*, or 'Letter to the Youth of the Future'. This was composed on an airplane in 1988, the same year he was murdered for his activism.

Written as if from 6 September 2120, in this letter Mendes praises those who have saved the world and mentions a revolution 'which unified all the peoples of the planet in a single ideal'. In this imagined future: 'Here remains only the memory of a sad past of pain, suffering and death.' Although this future was one he would never see, 'I have the pleasure of having dreamed,' wrote Mendes.[32] His letter would be an inspiration for generations of activists.

When Zé Cláudio invoked the comparison between himself and Chico Mendes, it was part of his talk titled 'Killing Trees is Murder'. One of his main arguments was, perhaps surprisingly, an economic one. 'The forest has to be preserved at all costs, because everything it contains generates profit, money. And the forest is there, providing for me. Whenever I want, I just go there and get it. Now, some people think that it can only provide resources if it is cut down.' He urged his audience not to refrain from buying things made of trees, but rather to check the sources of those products, and avoid buying things that might come from the illegal logging of the Amazon. This includes the beef and cheese made from the cattle raised on these lands.

To some this might come as a surprise, because the fight for environmental protection is often framed as a fight between consumerism and austerity. But buying things can directly help protect the environment too. When there is money to be made from plants that are especially good at sucking carbon out of the air – like bamboo, cork, hemp and flax – this can motivate people to sustainably plant more of them, which is generally a good thing for the planet. The problem isn't the products people make, or that they want to make money. It's how they choose to do it. Maria echoed this thought in her interview with the UN, saying: 'Environmentalists are seen as the people that hold back progress. That's what makes it difficult.'[33]

Indigenous people like Maria and Zé Cláudio aren't advocating for leaving natural resources untapped. They just have the long-term economic vision to recognise that the sustainable use of natural resources means that the planet will continue to feed and house us. Hence the common allusion to Mother Earth. Our mother gives us life, and provides for us as her children. If we kill or maim her, she will no longer care for us. Why would we be so cruel to our mother – and ourselves?

The UN defines environmental defenders as 'individuals and groups who, in their personal or professional capacity and in a peaceful manner, strive to protect and promote human rights relating to the environment'.[34] The environment they protect includes water, air, land, plants and animals. Some environmental defenders are Indigenous peoples fighting for their own land, while others are allies, including non-Indigenous journalists, lawyers and politicians.

In 2020, a large group of international academics published a global review of environmental conflicts, analysing 2,743 cases contained in the Environmental Justice Atlas – the world's largest database on environmental conflicts – that included people resisting or reacting to projects that caused environmental harm. For example, land-grabbing by a palm oil company in Indonesia. Or toxic soda ash being dumped on a beach in Italy. Or turning a large plot of wild land into a golf course in France.[35]

In 11 per cent of these cases, it was found that environmental defenders had contributed to halting environmentally destructive and socially conflictive projects. This meant they were defending the environment, as well as the livelihoods of the people who lived off the land.[36] The researchers also found that when certain strategies were implemented, the success rate of environmental defenders more than doubled, to 27 per cent.

The recipe for a successful environmental defence is threefold: preventive mobilisation, protest diversification, and litigation. Preventive mobilisation includes things like early campaigning, and raising formal objections before construction on projects starts. Protest diversification involves using different tactics for the same fight, including formal petitions, public campaigns and street protests. Other methods include the creation of collective action networks, or non-cooperation actions such as strikes, boycotts or the refusal of compensation payments. Combining these with litigation, like lawsuits, can create a force powerful enough to stop the bulldozers.

But effective environmental defence is something that many states are trying to thwart. The 2020 review also found that, in 20 per cent of cases, environmental defenders faced criminalisation. This means enforcing laws designed to limit the freedoms and rights of individuals and organisations, preventing them from being able to participate in environmental activism. It can also include the creation of new laws that make certain aspects of activism a crime, such as making specific peaceful protest tactics illegal. Consequences can include prosecution or imprisonment without clear charges.

For instance, in the UK, where I live, a new public order law was introduced in 2023 that made 'locking on' a specific crime.[37] This is a peaceful protest tactic used by many environmental activists. It's where people attach themselves, using strong glue, to another person, an object, or a building, in order to disrupt operations. Other countries, including Germany, sometimes prosecute these acts through legislation related to property damage or trespassing laws.

A widely covered example of locking on is protestors attaching themselves to the wall beneath a famous painting in a museum, often after throwing paint onto the glass that protects the art. One protestor who glued his bald head to the painting of *The Girl with a Pearl Earring*, while another protestor poured a can of tomato soup on him, said in 2022: 'How do you feel when you see something beautiful and priceless being apparently destroyed before your eyes? Do you feel outrage? Good. That is the feeling when you see the planet being destroyed before our very eyes.'[38] 'Apparently destroyed' because the painting, behind the glass, was fine. But such incidents draw attention to the divide between people who think such civil disobedience is a legitimate protest tactic, and those who think that disruptions like this should be crimes.

As an aside, I have been asked why I didn't include a chapter on environmental activists who commit crimes in this book. The answer is simple: I am focused on the people who perpetrate green crimes. Whatever you think of their tactics, even environmental activists who commit offences – usually property crimes or breaches of the peace – are not the people who are intentionally destroying the Earth. And to put them into the same group as those who are would be a categorical error.

In 18 per cent of the Environmental Justice Atlas cases analysed by the researchers, there was physical violence used against environmental defenders. And in a startling 13 per cent, environmental defenders were assassinated. According to the human rights watchdog Global Witness, 1,910 land and environmental defenders were killed between 2012 and 2022. That's one person killed every other day. Of these murders, 88 per cent took place in South America, many in the Amazon rainforest.[39] In 2024, Global Witness published another report, in memory of the 196 people murdered the previous year. Almost all the killings had taken place in Central and South America. Ranked second-highest in the list of countries, with twenty-five dead, was Brazil.[40]

The psychological consequences of this are stark. It's not just the killings that are harmful, it's the insidious forms of violence that are perpetrated alongside them. Researchers have stated that environmental defenders suffer from marginalisation, poverty, surveillance, threats, and assassination attempts, and this can lead to sleep disorders, anxiety and panic attacks, loneliness, depression and even suicide.[41] There is a climate of fear and a persistent atmosphere of violence.

A climate of fear is also what Maria and Zé Cláudio were living in as they received death threats before they were murdered. In the investigation into their deaths, when the police found hair in the diving mask, they found hair from not just one person, but two. The first was the man driving the motorcycle, Silva Rocha; the second was his brother, a landowner called José Rodrigues Moreira. The two brothers were notably different in their appearance. While Rocha had round features and a pout, Moreira's face looked like a bow pulled back tightly, waiting to be shot.

Police searched Moreira's house, and found the matching diving set to the black neoprene mask discovered at the scene.[42] This was bad news for Moreira. And it didn't take long for the police to dig up his past and establish a motive.

Moreira was a local fazendeiro. Fazendeiro is the Portuguese term for a landowner who has a large farm or plantation. He'd been looking to expand his cattle business, so he'd bought 144 hectares of land on which to farm.[43] Or so he thought. What he had actually bought was land in a protected settlement area. Moreira wanted to chop down the forest, sell the timber and plant grass for cattle. However, on this protected land, such extractions of resources would have been a crime.

There was another problem: there were people already living on the land. Maria and Zé Cláudio reported to the federal land-reform agency, INCRA, that Moreira was trying to kick three 'settlers' – as they were called because they had rights by way of already living on the land – off their plots in order to take over the land.[44] Maria and Zé Cláudio were helping the farmers to keep their homes and had denounced both INCRA and Moreira in the press.

In response to this, it was believed, Moreira hired his brother, and his brother found an accomplice. The two hitmen ambushed then killed Maria and Zé Cláudio and left them to bleed out on the side of the road.

The evidence seemed pretty damning. But was it enough for a conviction?

It was certainly enough for a flurry of news coverage and protests to accompany the case as it unfolded. But before I get into that, I want to discuss the psychology of impunity.

EXPERIENTIAL EFFECTS

People usually get away with their crimes.

The rate of crimes that go unreported to the police is called the 'dark figure'.[45] Generally, the more remote and sparsely populated an area is, generally the higher the dark figure.

For green crimes, the dark figures are likely to be astronomical. Most people couldn't identify an environmental crime even if it was happening in front of them, never mind know who to report it to. And the pathway to justice is far from clear. This is a major problem that the people I interviewed kept bringing up: that the risks of perpetrating green crime are far too low.

Impunity is the lack of adequate punishment for a crime. This can be down to failures at various levels, including the police inadequately investigating crimes, the courts not finding perpetrators guilty, or the lack of proportionate sentences.

When people are able to commit crimes without being caught or punished, they update their internal risk calculation. This is known as an experiential effect. It means as people get away with more crimes, they think they can go unpunished if they commit even more.[46] For example, if people start by thinking of deforestation as risky, but then cut down huge numbers of trees and go unpunished, they update their risk calculation and think of it as something they can get away with without consequences.

Psychologically, the feeling of impunity, then, has two components. One is the reality of punishment, like being caught and put in prison. The other is the perception of whether you will be caught. For crimes in general, the perceived certainty of getting caught has been found to have even more of a deterrent effect than the severity of the punishment.[47] Instead of being tough on crime, we need to be consistent on crime. Because as long as people have a sense of impunity, they will continue committing crime.

How do we reduce actual and perceived impunity? Based on crime research, step one to diminishing the feeling of impunity is the improved monitoring and policing of nature. There is strong evidence that a more visible police presence deters crime, because it increases the perceived risk of getting caught. This is true even if the police aren't catching more criminals; it's just the perception that they can.[48]

That being said, while ramping up cameras, or police, has a big effect initially, it does weaken over time if people notice that they aren't actually getting caught. It can also carry other risks, like communities being – or feeling like they are being – spied on by people who are there to control rather than help them.

It's also important for people to be aware that certain laws exist, and posters and signs can help to educate people on what counts as illegal. But we need to be careful, because awareness measures can backfire. Perhaps the worst thing you can do to increase the feeling of impunity is to have under, for example, a no fishing sign, a row of people fishing without consequences. If you aren't going to enforce a rule or law, it can be better not to have it in the first place.

Brazil has long had problems with impunity.[49] And impunity has consequences beyond the crimes themselves, on a societal level. If people see criminals blatantly disregarding laws and getting away with it, this leads to the widespread fear of crime, distrust of police who are often thought to be corrupt and paranoia that those you know are committing crimes.

When Moreira was deciding whether or not to hire hitmen, he probably figured that, like so many others who had killed environmental defenders and gone unpunished, he too would benefit from impunity. But, having killed such prominent environmental defenders, Moreira couldn't just slip away.

Or could he?

VILE MOTIVES

The Maria and Zé Cláudio double homicide trial was a high-profile case from the beginning.

It started on 3 April 2013, and outside the courtroom, hundreds of people gathered. Protestors held wooden crosses with wispy pieces of black cloth wrapped around them, representing murdered environmental defenders.[50] Extra police had been brought in to secure the perimeter. Inside, the courtroom was packed with journalists and relatives, leaning forwards eagerly in the gallery's soft blue chairs. The three defendants were brought in through the back door in the early morning, hours before the trial was due to begin, in order to avoid drawing the attention of the crowd.[51]

Witnesses had to present their evidence through the night and into the morning, because the judge needed to fit all their testimonies into the two days that had been set for the trial.

On the stand, the witness who had been working on his fence that morning recounted how he saw the men whip by on their motorcycle. As he did so, the lawyer for the defence started to put on quite a performance. At one point, he shouted, 'You are lying!'. The judge had to repeatedly reprimand him, calling his behaviour ugly. At one point the judge felt the need to remind the jury, 'Do not take into account such phrases. No one here owns the truth.'[52]

When Maria's sister, Laísa, took to the stand, she explained that Maria and Zé Cláudio had lived under a constant threat. Maria had told her she'd spoken to Moreira before he even made the deal, telling him that it wasn't land he could legally buy. But he had disregarded Maria's warnings. And when Zé Cláudio and Maria told officials about the illegal land deal, they had been ignored by them too.

Laísa also testified about the ongoing campaign of intimidation against herself that had started after the suspects were arrested. Threats were coming to her via circuitous routes from the family who had ordered the killings. They were passed on through her friends, her daughter, and the children who attended the school where she taught. They had even shot her dog. Just days before the trial began, their last message had arrived in the form of reverberating gunshots from Zé Cláudio and Maria's former house, and on her own doorstep. She had gone to the police, worried they were going to kill her to prevent her from attending the trial. 'The danger here is the path, the road, each movement, where an ambush could occur,' she testified.[53]

After a marathon of testimonies and cross-examinations, the members of the jury were sent to deliberate.

The verdict for the two men on the motorcycle came back: guilty and guilty. They were convicted of homicide for vile motives. This is a charge of murder in Brazil, reserved for crimes that are especially immoral, cruel or despicable, motivated by factors such as greed and revenge. In this case, the judge clarified that the motive was the dispute over land ownership. The cruel means included cutting off one of Zé Cláudio's ears while he was still alive, and it was noted that victims had no possibility of defending themselves because the crime was committed in an ambush.[54]

Lindonjonson Silva Rocha, who was driving the escape motorcycle, got forty-five years. Alberto Lopes do Nascimento was sentenced to forty-two years in prison. When the verdict for Moreira came back not guilty, those watching in the courtroom were shocked. The result made the headlines and there was a widespread public outcry.

'I define the end of the trial as the worst day of my life,' Laísa said shortly after to the press. She continued to fear for her life and expected the worst. 'They are sealing three coffins,' she said, meaning one of them would be her own.[55]

While the two hitmen left in handcuffs, Moreira walked out a free man. But, very quickly, the judgement was annulled, which meant it was declared to be invalid. Moreira was an important fazendeiro in the area, so there were concerns about the impartiality of the jury. His preventative detention was ordered, but by this time he was already gone. He had, immediately after his release, fled the province, maybe even the country. We don't know, because no one has seen him since. He is still on the run.

Despite Moreira being nowhere to be found, a retrial was organised, and the court proceedings against him were moved to a different area where his family had less influence and therefore less ability to intimidate witnesses or trade favours with judge and jury. At this second trial, held in 2016 without Moreira present, the court found him guilty of having orchestrated the hit. According to the judge's ruling, Moreira had 'planned, organized and financed the double homicide'.[56] He was sentenced to sixty years in prison. To some, this feels like a success. But until he is imprisoned, that's not how Zé Cláudio and Maria's families see it.

In a weird twist of this story, Moreira wasn't the only one of the three men to go missing. His brother, Lindonjonson Silva Rocha, managed to escape from prison in 2015. The police immediately sent out a notice saying they were looking for him, but he was on the run for almost five years.[57] Finally, in 2020, police received a tip that he was hiding in a small village, under a false name. There were allegations that he had committed other serious crimes while he was there. He was arrested and sent back to prison.

This is one of the rare cases where some justice was served for crimes committed against environmental defenders. But not everyone thinks it was a success story.

THIN GREEN LINE

'Zé Cláudio and Maria, it is a very symbolic case,' Paulo Busse, the environmental and human rights lawyer who introduced me to this case, told me. He explained that, actually, the case 'shows how Brazilian justice doesn't work properly'. Busse said that protecting the Amazon is not only about protecting the forest, because 'there is always a person in front of a tree in the Amazon'.

In November 2022, Busse and two of his colleagues filed a communication to the International Criminal Court, alleging that the murders, persecution and other inhumane acts against rural land users and defenders in Brazil constitute crimes against humanity. Their complaint included the killing of Maria and Zé Cláudio as just one example.

'Every single one of these cases has problems,' Busse told me about the court cases involving people being prosecuted for murdering environmental defenders. During our video interview I could see, behind him, through a window, dense green trees lit so brightly by the Brazilian sun that they were almost white. 'Justice is not delivered properly in any of these cases.'

Busse has worked as an environmental lawyer for decades, after initially being hired by Greenpeace to defend activists who had been arrested. It was sheer luck that Greenpeace approached him, fresh out of law school, and it profoundly shaped the rest of his life. In his early days, he told me, the focus by the public was exclusively on deforestation rather than on human rights abuses: 'It was as if there were no people living in the Amazon.'

Many Indigenous peoples in the Amazon spend their whole lives amongst the trees. For them, stopping the destruction of nature is fighting an immediate existential threat. This makes Indigenous peoples both more vulnerable and more powerful than people who don't, or can't, see first-hand the extent of the damage being caused to the forest. 'They are the real guardians of the forest. Because they are there, impeding, blocking other people from entering,' Busse said. Their enemy is a supervillain-sounding group he calls 'the Network', which has given Brazil a particularly devastating version of capitalism.

At the top of the Network are the politicians, policymakers and lobbyists who hold the rigid view that rural land should be used for commerce only, and are trying to convince everyone else that this is the only sensible path. 'The Brazilian government always has to consider the agribusiness in every single decision. But that doesn't mean they should defend anti-environmental agendas,' Busse said.

While politicians and the media treat big business as the country's saviour, Indigenous peoples are depicted as selfishly blocking access to jobs and profit-churning opportunities in the Amazon. Their struggles are infantilised and delegitimised. Turning public opinion against Indigenous peoples is key to people stealing their land with impunity.

Busse also told me about the ruralist caucus. It is a group of politicians, including congress members, who form a huge parliamentarian front in defence of agribusiness. They include soy producers, beef producers, and those interested in Brazil's timber and gold. These industries dominate Brazil's economy, with agribusiness accounting for between a quarter and a third of the country's GDP, and about half of its exports.[58] In 2024, the two dominating exports were soybeans (which are mostly intended for animal feed) and meat.[59]

The ruralist caucus is aligned with private corporations. 'What they have in common is they are completely against the forest. Because it is the biggest obstacle they have,' Busse explained. Then he added that, actually, 'The people are the first, the main obstacle. Because in order to destroy the forest, one needs to get rid of the people first.'

The second tier of the Network is middle management. This includes local officials, business executives, and organised crime bosses. The money for large-scale operations to get rid of those pesky trees that stand in the way of short-term profit is typically provided by criminal groups.

Then there are the bottom dwellers, the people who actually do the dirty work. Like the hitmen. They are an essential part of the Network, and the most obviously criminal. They tend to be armed men who threaten and kill those who live in the Amazon. They are often members of gangs or militias, and many are active or former police officers.

Brazil has allowed over a decade of impunity when it comes to killings linked to land and environmental disputes. Paulo Busse told me that fewer than 10 per cent of cases between 2011 and 2022 made it to court, and only about 1 per cent of the killings resulted in a conviction. That's what makes the case of Maria and Zé Cláudio special; at least there were convictions, even if the man who organised the murders ultimately got away.

Given the ways in which environmental defenders are often killed in Brazil, this impunity is particularly distressing. Victims are often bound and gagged, and common murder methods include throat slitting, drive-by shootings, execution-style shootings, hacking people apart with machetes and beating people to death with sticks, followed by the mutilation or burning of the bodies.

Is the murder of an environmental defender a green crime? Not directly. But the killing of people specifically because they are defending the environment is certainly part of the broader issue of green crime.

Part of the cycle of impunity is also the lack of adequate and timely reactions. Police let threats slide, organisations ignore requests for help, and ministers fail to intervene when communities say they fear an imminent attack. Within this lies an indifference to the suffering of Indigenous peoples. Sometimes there is also collusion between businesses and the police.

The simple reason why people continue to see the Amazon as an obstacle between themselves and money, according to Busse, is that 'they are old-fashioned capitalists who don't want to wait, they just want to grab profit as fast as they can'. A classic problem of the tragedy of the commons. As he pointed out: 'And it's kind of stupid. If they keep destroying the Amazon, they will end the rain, the rain they need for the soy and other crops . . . In the medium and the long term, it is suicidal.'

The problem with impunity is also something that professor of landscape ecology Dolors Armenteras touched on when we spoke. 'Environmental regulations can be effective, but they often fall short due to weak enforcement, corruption, and the pressures of economic development. For regulations to truly protect forests like the Amazon, they need to be part of a broader strategy that includes economic incentives for conservation, strong monitoring systems, traceability of products and commodities, combating crime and corruption at all levels – demand and supply – and the protection and empowerment of Indigenous and local communities.'

She added that, because of their importance in sustaining

life, 'tropical forests like the Amazon should be recognized and managed as global common goods'.

The privatisation of nature has failed. We need a fundamentally new relationship with our forests, otherwise we will continue to lose them at pace.

One way this can happen is to see nature as having inherent rights. But before we get to the rights of nature, I am going to summarise the psychological drivers of crimes against environmental defenders.

THE SIX PILLARS OF CRIMES AGAINST ENVIRONMENTAL DEFENDERS

The murders of Maria do Espírito Santo and José Cláudio Ribeiro reveal how the six psychological drivers of green crime come into play.

Ease was evident in the ambush. The remote locations where environmental defenders live make murder and other crimes in the forest terrifyingly easy.

Impunity permeated the justice system. Maria and Zé Cláudio had reported threats, endured home invasions, and survived a prior assassination attempt. Yet their concerns were dismissed. Even after their deaths, the system failed them: Moreira walked free, and Rocha escaped prison for years.

Greed probably drove Moreira's desire to turn occupied land into a cattle ranch. His logic reflects a broader pattern in the Amazon, where short-term profits outweigh ethical concerns.

Rationalisation was evident in Moreira's actions. It seems that he believed that, as the landowner, he was entitled to do whatever was necessary to use the land as he pleased.

Conformity normalised the violence. In Pará, where Maria and Zé Cláudio lived, murder was a routine tool to silence opposition.

Desperation shaped the lives of the hitmen. As out-of-work labourers in a region marked by poverty, they were easily exploited to do Moreira's bidding.

This tragedy highlights a fundamental clash of values. On one side, entitlement frames forests as commodities, and violence as a tool of ownership. On the other, defenders see nature as something to protect.

Perhaps it's time to extend legal protections to nature itself.

RIGHTS OF NATURE

Can a forest have inherent rights, like a person?

Many Indigenous knowledge systems value the interconnectedness of all life on Earth. Sometimes this is achieved by associating nature, including animals, with emotional and spiritual traits. Other times it centres around the belief that humans are part of nature, rather than being hierarchically superior. In this model, nature is more like a supportive family: the trees are like our relatives, the animals our cousins, and the Earth our mother.

This conceptualisation means that many Indigenous epistemologies are incompatible with treating nature as property. And there have already been legal cases which have successfully leaned into this, officially granting nature its own rights.

For example, Māori peoples in New Zealand successfully fought for the right of an ecosystem called Te Urewera to own itself. In the 1950s, without Māori consent or consultation, this beautiful area of mountains, forests and lakes was turned into a national park. The purpose of the 2014 Te Urewera Act was to create and preserve in perpetuity a legal identity and protected status for the area, because of its intrinsic worth.

The landmark act starts with a beautiful sentence which shows this is a legal document that is in many ways different from business as usual: 'Te Urewera is ancient and enduring, a fortress of nature, alive with history; its scenery is abundant with mystery, adventure and remote beauty.' [60] Te Urewera is now officially a legal entity, with all the rights, powers, duties and liabilities of a legal person. These rights are exercised by a board of trustees appointed as Te Urewera's guardians.

The law is a tool to help us guide behaviour, and safeguard things we think are important. Of course, people can still go and burn down sacred forests. The law isn't necessarily going to stop them. But creating social and legal barriers that make it clear that such behaviour is unacceptable, and that it carries negative consequences, has power. There is also a psychological impact. As research has shown, labelling behaviours as bad or illegal can be very effective.

When I met David Boyd, an environmental lawyer on the front lines of the fight for nature rights, he spoke to me from the idyllic evergreen landscape of southern British Columbia in Canada. He is a professor at the University of British Columbia, which is where I got my PhD.

Boyd has a bright smile and a bushy moustache, and a

friendly demeanour. 'The rights of nature include respect for nature's existence, for the maintenance of life's systems,' he explained. 'The right to be restored when it's been damaged. Making sure the conditions of life are adequate.' When nature is given rights, there are obligations on humans and businesses to respect and protect those rights.

An example he gave of where the rights of nature have already been enshrined in law was the 2008 constitution of Ecuador, in which Article 71 states: 'Nature, or Pacha Mama, where life is reproduced and occurs, has the right to integral respect for its existence and for the maintenance and regeneration of its life cycles, structure, functions and evolutionary processes.'[61] Pacha Mama means 'Mother Earth', and the law was inspired by Indigenous ways of thinking about nature. It was the first time that any country had set out the rights of nature as law.

Article 71 also states that people can rely on public authorities to enforce the rights of nature, that incentives should be given to people who protect nature, that nature has the right to be restored, and that there need to be preventive measures to restrict activities that could lead to the extinction of species or the destruction of ecosystems. Ecuador really set an example for other countries by legally treating nature not just as property, but as an entity with its own rights.

The concept of property has changed many times throughout history. It wasn't all that long ago that we decided that humans couldn't be property. Slavery is something that we look back on as morally reprehensible, but at the time there were laws in place that permitted some humans to treat others grotesquely. Around the same time that we started to enshrine in law that humans possess inherent rights, we also extended the idea of legal personhood to non-human entities, like corporations and states.

'We have a legal system that's incredibly flexible and we are the masters of that universe,' Boyd told me, explaining that the idea of granting legal personhood to forests isn't as absurd as it may sound. 'We have historically used it in different contexts: like municipal rights and corporate rights. And now we are applying it in terms of ecosystem rights. Ecosystem rights are analogous to the rights of a municipality.' Still, 'Nature rights are distinct from human rights,' he told me, adding 'No one is proposing that trees should have the right to vote.'

In addition to being an environmental lawyer, David Boyd has also served as the UN special rapporteur on human rights and the environment. Part of what inspired his work in this area was a famous 1960s US court case where lawyers argued for giving rights to a natural entity in California called the Mineral King Valley. The case failed in the US Supreme Court and the valley was not granted rights, but 'there was a really powerful dissenting opinion by a judge named William O. Douglas that sparked this modern movement to recognise the rights of nature,' Boyd explained.

Then he smiled, adding: 'I say "modern movement" because another thing I've learned through my work with Indigenous peoples in Canada and beyond is that we have these Indigenous legal systems that have recognised nature's rights for millennia. So it's just the Western legal system which is late to the game.'

Fortunately, there are people and organisations who are

pushing the system to catch up, and one recent conversation that has aimed to drive the narrative on the rights of nature further is the fight for the legal concept of ecocide.

ECOCIDE

In 2021, an international panel of independent experts proposed a consensus definition of ecocide, defining it as 'unlawful or wanton acts committed with knowledge that there is a substantial likelihood of severe and either widespread or long-term damage to the environment being caused by those acts'.[62] Stop Ecocide Now is perhaps the organisation most well known for advocating for the adoption of ecocide as the fifth core international crime, pushing it to one day sit alongside the crime of genocide, war crimes, crimes against humanity and the crime of aggression.

In late 2023, I attended a symposium at Queen Mary University in London on the politics of ecocide. It was hosted by professor of climate justice David Whyte, and many internationally renowned experts had travelled to be there for the event. It allowed me to formulate a greater level of understanding regarding a legal concept of ecocide and its possible positive and negative impacts, which can be broken down into four categories.

First, ecocide could be a threshold trap. Making ecocide a core crime means that it can only be applied to a few, very severe cases. This would be problematic because it would be missing the point that environmental destruction often happens as the result of many smaller crimes.

Second, ecocide could be beneficial as a risk amplifier. Even with a high threshold, the law can still deter harmful practices by increasing the financial, legal and reputational risks for those involved.

Third, it could falsely make environmental destruction seem like it is primarily the responsibility of individuals, when it should be companies or groups of people being held accountable.

This third point was stated by the most eagerly anticipated guest at the symposium, Richard Falk, an international law and international relations scholar who taught at Princeton University for forty years. Back in 1973, Falk proposed an international convention on the crime of ecocide, urging the global community to adopt it as a crime.[63]

He has changed his tune quite dramatically since then, however. He now argues that laws need to be directed towards states and businesses rather than individuals, as is the case with the International Criminal Court. 'If one can't reach and control corporations, the game is over,' he said at the event.

The fourth potential impact is symbolic. Legislating ecocide brings important environmental issues into the realm of public debate and reflects society's values regarding what actions should be condemned, even if the law may not be easily implemented around the world.

I spoke with French environmental lawyer Sophie Lemaître about her views on ecocide. And she said something related to this that I thought summarised it well: 'You need words. Sometimes there are behaviours we don't think are morally okay, but we don't have words in law . . . Before ecocide, we didn't have a term for it.' What she means is that language shapes our thoughts and provides the scaffolding for morality.

These debates show that there are very different viewpoints on the answer to the question of how we should craft rights that protect nature. Personally, I think that pursuing ecocide as an international crime is immensely useful in strengthening the conversation around green crime, and I hope that the campaign succeeds. Setting the bar high – even unrealistically high – can mean that even if you fail to reach your target, you still land on useful terrain.

And as the legal debates continue, so does the front-line fight by Indigenous people.

CRACKDOWN

Some very positive news about the Amazon is that, after the election of left-wing president Luiz Inácio Lula da Silva in mid-2023, the part of the Amazon in Brazil got far more protection. Lula promised to end deforestation of the Amazon by 2030, and he got to work immediately. I virtually attended the United Nations global climate summit, COP28, in December 2023. There, the president of the Brazilian Institute of Environment and Renewable Natural Resources, Rodrigo Agostinho, presented some astonishing results from police investigations.

'It's incredible what's happening,' he said, tugging his bright blue chequered tie energetically as he spoke to the crowd. He explained that Brazil was using satellites to locate environmental criminals. In 2023 alone, law enforcement had stopped 100,000 trucks from entering or leaving the Amazon. The trucks were filled with wood, minerals and other precious stolen resources.

Part of the crackdown on forest crime involves destroying

the tools the criminals need, which means burning the equipment in huge fires. Burned items even included the logging trucks and chainsaws. 'It's very ugly, this, because we are producing carbon. But if we don't destroy, they still destroy the environment,' said Agostinho, pulling up pictures of a small plane on fire, with a huge plume of black smoke coming from it. He explained that this kind of intervention works really well, despite the optics. But at the end of his presentation, he also uttered an explicit plea: 'We really need to stop the crime. We really need to stop deforestation. We need help.'

Brazil has continued to fight hard to shut down green crime. For example, in 2025, Brazilian environmental agents announced Operation Maravalha, a year-long crackdown on illegal logging in protected areas and Indigenous lands. The operation confiscated illegally logged trees, seized sawmills, and issued heavy fines both to loggers directly and through financial audits that exposed fraud.[64]

Meanwhile, by taking up the case for environmental defenders, and presenting the International Criminal Court with a list of people they have found to be guilty of crimes, Paulo Busse and his colleagues are making violence against people in the Amazon visible. Busse is also directly connecting these violent crimes with deforestation and climate change. For him, it's all part of the same fight. And that's because humans aren't separate from nature; we are part of it. In Zé Cláudio's words, 'Those who lose are those who live in the forest. And you, who won't have the forest later, because it will be gone one day. And if it's gone, how are people to survive?'

We are not *in* nature, we *are* nature.

Most of all, we need to keep fighting, even in the face of threats. Maria and Zé Cláudio's family members, and the activists and lawyers they have inspired, continue the fight for the Amazon today. As Zé Cláudio's sister, Claudelice, put it: 'If I don't do it, who will? If I do not resist, who will resist? Who would I wait for?'

3

THE TRAFFICKERS

THE UNDERCOVER AGENTS were being taken to a warehouse of death.

As they drove down ever-narrower, remote roads, through the disorientating inky darkness, the knots in the gnarled tree trunks on either side looked like leering eyes. The car smelled musky.

It was already past midnight, and the two Chinese agents hadn't expected to be out here this late. They also weren't supposed to be in the car of one of the men they were trying to catch red-handed. But Ou, the trafficker who picked them up, had insisted. It felt crowded with the three of them in the car. One of the agents was wearing a hidden body camera. Its presence made him conscious of every movement.

After more than an hour of driving, there was light ahead, and the car pulled into the driveway of a two-storey house. White paint peeled off the facade in small flakes, guards keeping an eye out for trouble. If they searched the undercover agents and found the wire, they would be done for.

In their charade as interested buyers, the two agents swung

open their car doors and stepped out onto the gravel path. This was the moment they had worked so hard to arrange. Now all they needed to do was keep cool. Then, an old phone went off in someone's pocket, the Nokia ringtone unmistakable. Their hearts skipped a beat. Had someone tipped off the traffickers? All the last-minute adjustments had been strange. What if this was a trap?

But the call was ignored, and Ou chatted through it as though the ringtone was just background noise. He pointed the agents to one of his associates, Wang. The agents nodded at Wang in recognition. As he smoked his off-brand cigarettes, he told them that his family members were the ones keeping watch outside the house.

The agents were led to a small room, a white-walled storage space containing precisely the evidence they were looking for. Sixty, maybe seventy, enormous elephant tusks. The tusks looked simultaneously impressive and underwhelming because they were stacked so lovelessly on top of one another, with just a thin layer of cardboard separating them from the ground. To the untrained eye, this might as well have been a stack of branches harvested from birch trees, rather than an expensive pile of teeth brutally cut off elephant faces with chainsaws.

Ou motioned to the tusks and explained that this was half a ton of the best-quality white ivory on the market. The agents nodded along and picked up their conversation from lunch the day before, discussing price, payment and logistics. Ou and Wang made it clear that the sale needed to be quick. They were already preparing the next order.

The agents kept pushing them to say more. To give specifics about the deal they thought they were making.

Meanwhile, every statement, every movement, every aspect of this negotiation was caught by the watchful gaze of the hidden camera. In this elephant tomb the traffickers continued to dig their own graves of incriminating evidence.

This chapter asks how we can protect wildlife from the ever-present threat of extinction at the hands of organised criminals. It covers the story of a dangerous operation that offers an intimate glimpse into the heart of one of the largest ivory trafficking groups ever to be unmasked, known as the Shuidong syndicate.

I spoke with one of the agents who worked the case: Environmental Investigation Agency (EIA) campaigns director Julian Newman. The EIA is a non-governmental organisation that investigates and campaigns against environmental crimes and abuse.

Newman told me that of all the cases he has worked on, this was one of the most interesting and important, forever changing how the world deals with ivory. He sent me official reports and videos from the investigation, and his colleague, wildlife campaigner Ceres Kam, provided me with unique access to translated Chinese documents. I crafted the opening scene of this chapter by watching the original body-camera footage captured by the undercover EIA agents in 2016.

To really immerse myself in the world of wildlife crime, I also met with rangers in South Africa who are using military-grade tech to defend their animals in the war against poachers. And, I spoke with a UN researcher who spent years unravelling the complicated web of international wildlife crime. It all helped me to build an answer to the big question: why are people willing to hunt wild animals to extinction? And the related question: who is buying these specimens of endangered animals?

The Shuidong syndicate case is a thrilling and devastating example of a type of criminal evasion that is happening in every country in the world. Where shadowy recruiters descend upon isolated villages, tempting desperate people to kill by flaunting fistfuls of money. Funded by underground criminal networks whose dirty dealings cross continents.

In the case of the Shuidong syndicate, it all began in China.

OWN THE ROAD

When they were children, Ou Haiqiang and Xie Xingbang watched with big eyes as their uncles moved into mansions and bought expensive German cars. They seemed like modern-day emperors, sitting on a magic mountain of money. The village where they lived, Shuidong, wasn't far from the coast of the Yellow Sea, and the boys' uncles were known for the large containers that arrived for them at the docks. They claimed the deliveries were plastic pellets, seashells and seafood. But some of the locals knew better. Those containers were filled with ghosts.

When they were old enough, Ou and Xie were told by their uncles that it was time to join the family business; they were to learn the ways of the Shuidong syndicate. The boys quickly discovered that the plastic pellets and seashells in the shipments concealed body parts ripped from endangered animals. They had been trafficked from Africa to be eaten as delicacies, ground into traditional Chinese medicines, or intricately carved into opulent ivory artworks. While ivory can also come from walrus or narwhal tusks, or ancient mammoth tusks emerging from the permafrost, it almost always refers to the tusks of elephants.

The family had spent many years painstakingly forging the necessary trade routes. This, despite the fact that ivory trafficking wasn't what the uncles had originally set out to do. It had just sort of worked out that way. Back in the 1990s, they had run a successful import business. One of their biggest imports was an underwater creature called the sea cucumber. A sea cucumber is a simple animal that looks like a fat caterpillar. The uncles shipped these creatures in from Zanzibar, where they were mostly ignored by the locals, to China, where they were sold as a delicacy. Sea cucumbers were already overexploited in the 1990s, but police and border guards didn't really care about these shipments. So, most got through without much fuss.

This is what made their business such a perfect fit when a new opportunity came along. Why not use this same means of smuggling for a few elephant tusks, or pangolin scales? Maybe some shark fins and totoaba swim bladders too, through a roundabout route from North America? By that point, since they were already going through all the hassle and danger of importing illegal wildlife from abroad, why not add in some elusive rhino horn? With every container of dead animals that made the long journey to China, the uncles' wealth grew. They even recruited others to help them expand their empire, including a man named Wang Kangwen.

Ou and Xie learned everything they needed to know to follow in their footsteps. Most importantly, that they needed to 'own the road'. Which meant managing their accomplices at every stage of transit. They needed to keep up relationships. Pay bribes on time, and never, ever, touch the goods. Fingerprints were too easy to track. These criminal practices were passed down like an heirloom.

By 2012, Xie was running the business, having even learned how to haggle with the Tanzanians in Swahili. Business was good, with profit margins for ivory being bigger than they had ever been. By 2016, Tanzania, where Xie had set up his network, had stepped up the enforcement of laws against elephant poaching. He realised he needed to find easier hunting grounds or he might soon face arrests and fines.

Meanwhile, Ou was also quickly becoming an ivory kingpin. His uncle provided him with some start-up capital and connected him with an established network of customs agents willing to look the other way. His early shipments paid off, which meant that Ou made $8 million in profits in just the first few years. But his luck didn't last long. Two shipments were seized, setting him back financially. He was also arrested twice, and he managed to pay his way out. But it was all getting a bit too risky. He needed to find a less precarious route.

That's how Ou, Xie and Wang found themselves setting up a new network, in Pemba, Mozambique. This relocation would prove to be a big, big, mistake.

But before I explain why, I want to talk about our psychologically complicated relationship with wildlife conservation. And try to answer a fundamental question: What is it that makes us care about some species of animals more than others?

PASSING FASHION

Our love of animals is a curious and temperamental thing.

As a species, humans have long taken it upon ourselves to decide which animals get to live or die, be cuddled or tortured, be admired or eaten. And exactly what makes us decide a species is worth saving is somewhat spurious. Right now, conservation efforts tend to have what has been referred to as a charismatic megafauna bias. This means we are more likely to care about the conservation of large, striking animals like pandas, elephants, rhinos and lions.

But it hasn't always been this way.

As British historian Helen Cowie has chronicled, the history of conservation can actually be traced back to a very different kind of animal: birds. In the late nineteenth century, humans were slaughtering birds by the millions. It started in Britain with local birds – robins, wrens and goldfinches. But the trend quickly extended to more exotic species, such as hummingbirds. Most of the bird bodies and feathers ended up in New York, Paris and, most prominently, London.

Trade catalogues and newspapers from the time give a sense of the number of birds killed. 'In 1892, one London auction room sold "6,000 birds of paradise, 5,000 Impeyan pheasants, 400,000 hummingbirds, and other birds from North and South America, and 360,000 feathered skins from India" in a single week,' writes Cowie.[1]

And what was all that bird death for? Hats, mostly.

When people realised the scale of the killing, they started to worry about what it meant for the future of these delicate and beautiful species. Their extinction at the hands of humans looking for fluttery fashions would be sad, and was seen by some as a moral failing. In 1872, one of the first laws in the world aimed at saving a vulnerable species was passed. It was called the British Wild Birds Act, and it protected birds during their breeding season to help populations recover. But it wasn't enough and birds continued to be killed in huge numbers.

In 1895 bird conservationist Margaretta Lemon wrote: 'The common sense of every thoughtful woman must at once tell her that no comparatively rare tropical species, such as the Bird of Paradise, can long withstand this appalling drain upon it, and that this ruthless destruction, which merely panders to the caprice of a passing fashion, will soon place one of the most beautiful denizens of our earth in the same category as the Great Auk or the Dodo.'[2] Both of the birds she mentions, the greak auk and the dodo, were by this time already extinct. In 1889, together with Eliza Phillips, Lemon founded what would later become the Royal Society for the Protection of Birds.

Around the same time, on the other side of the Atlantic, the Audubon Society was born. It too wanted to protect birds from going extinct. Raising public consciousness around conservation also led to the Lacey Act of 1900, one of the first major wildlife protection laws in the US. In 1918, the Migratory Bird Treaty Act further strengthened the protection of birds. These were some of the first laws of their kind in the world, and are still in place today.

The people involved in the bird societies were mostly women – birds for birds, if you will. But even though it was only because of these women that the plight of the birds was understood in the first place, it was also women who were being blamed for the killing. The bird societies found themselves having to counteract hostile statements about how women didn't care about cruelty as long as something was fashionable.

Luckily, ferocious campaigning and educational campaigns on the part of the bird societies managed to significantly change public perceptions about the acceptability of wearing feathers. Eventually, the bird trade was one of the first animal-based industries to generate – and maintain – widespread disapproval.

The reason that people wanted to save the birds was the fear of species extinction. But it wasn't about saving a species in the wild for its own sake, as much as keeping pretty and interesting animals alive for us humans to marvel at. As Cowie writes, 'The underlying assumption here was that animals were put on earth for the benefit of mankind . . . and that the survival of a species depended on its surrendering to human control.'[3]

Speciesism involves perceiving animals as subordinate to humans, which often comes with the assumption that they are less sentient than humans and less capable of suffering, and therefore less worthy of ethical treatment. It is particularly an issue in factory farming, where animals are treated as commodities rather than as sentient creatures.

Speciesism opens up big ethical questions about whether animals have an inherent right to life. Should they be protected from torture and cruelty, like humans? Is it morally justifiable to enslave and exploit animals?

During the Enlightenment, more than a hundred years before the bird societies, thinkers like Jeremy Bentham argued that animals' capacity to suffer deserved moral consideration. 'The question is not, Can they reason? nor, Can they talk?

but, Can they suffer? Why should the law refuse its protection to any sensitive being?' he wrote in 1789.[4]

If we accept Bentham's argument, then we might run into problems in our minds. For example, many people who eat meat also love animals. This can make people suffer from what is known as the meat paradox. The fact that so many people who feel this way continue to eat meat is something that psychologists have been trying to understand for years. Researchers have found that it is mostly because people are excellent at morally disengaging from issues of animal welfare.

Moral disengagement is a psychological mechanism that reduces the discomfort of behaving in a way that contradicts a person's own moral standards. It's when we decide not to think about something too hard. When we choose not to care.[5]

That being said, meat eating has decreased significantly over the past decade in places including the UK and Germany. But this is not primarily driven by people deciding to align their morality and their eating habits. Rather, it is driven by drops in the economy, and an increased realisation that eating meat every day is bad for your health.[6] Environmental factors and animal welfare are also taken into consideration by many consumers; they just don't seem to matter as much as personal factors.

There's another interesting psychological phenomenon associated with this issue: 'meat attachment', which is people's emotional connection with meat. Research in this area often talks about the '4Ns' that people use to justify their meat consumption: it is normal, necessary, nice and natural to eat meat. By framing meat eating as something that everyone does, it's easier not to think about the animals it comes from. To morally disengage.

In the nineteenth century, this moral disengagement was made more difficult when the British Wild Birds Act was brought in, and public campaigns alerted people that their fashion choices were endangering whole species.

Fast forward to today, and we have the UN Convention on International Trade in Endangered Species of Wild Fauna and Flora, known as CITES, which does this on a much larger scale.

ENDANGERED

CITES aims to ensure that trade in animals does not threaten the survival of wild animal and plant species.[7] Every year, all the countries who have signed the voluntary agreement meet up to discuss which wildlife can be captured and traded, and which needs to be protected.

CITES puts species into three categories. Species listed in Appendices II and III can be traded with the appropriate permits, though an eye is kept on their global populations. But, Appendix I includes species threatened with extinction, and the international trade of these plants and animals for commercial purposes is not allowed. When a species is moved to Appendix I, it is a big deal, and it is often opposed by countries that sell these plants or animals as well as their business allies. I find it interesting to see the issue of extinction reframed in commercial terms like this.

Creating a sustainable world is not about stopping the killing of wildlife entirely. We will need to keep fishing and harvesting from the wild to continue being able to feed and house the now 8.2 billion people in the world. Some of the conservationists at the CITES meeting I attended in 2023 spoke about how it is essential for us to harvest the maximum amount of a species without depleting its population over time. This is a utilitarian concept called maximum sustainable yield. Sustainability is simply about using resources, including fish, mammals and trees, in a way that ensures we continue to benefit – and financially profit – from their abundance.

The states that have signed the CITES agreement are bound by a number of rules, including that all import and export of CITES-listed species has to be authorised through a permit system. Member states must have their own laws that penalise those who do not have permits and move endangered animals into, or out of, their country. Countries also need to have at least one scientific authority to advise them on the effects of trade on the status of each listed species. In this way countries are expected to hold each other accountable when it comes to engaging in the sustainable use of wildlife.

In addition to local laws that can criminalise or at least issue fines to people who don't have the necessary permits, CITES is also able to publicly reprimand a country when they threaten the survival of a species. If, after being reprimanded, shipments of endangered species are still being seized at borders, full investigations are launched by CITES members to assess the scale of the problem of poaching and other illegal activities.

All of this is specifically designed to make it very difficult for organised criminals in the wildlife trade to move their contraband across borders.

Unfortunately, there are loopholes, and porous borders that are taken advantage of by groups like the Shuidong syndicate.

HOT AFTERNOONS

Back in Mozambique, traffickers Ou, Xie and Wang had started to scout local business prospects. They knew that the only way their plan could work was if they were able to 'own the road' like their uncles had taught them. But initially, things weren't going so well.

In one of their first shipments from Mozambique to China, they opened their long-awaited cargo only to find that they had been ripped off. They were short-changed with bad-quality tusks. They couldn't exactly go to the police and cry about how their order of illegal goods wasn't up to standard, so this had to be accepted as an expensive setback. But this loss was not enough to deter the three new kingpins of the Shuidong syndicate.

Determined not to be taken advantage of again, for the next ivory order they flew to Mozambique to supervise the shipment personally. This was risky, because sourcing and interacting with the tusks made it easier to directly connect them with their illegal goods. But they figured they knew how to navigate the risks. They were, after all, from families with decades of experience dodging the police.

Together with a contact they had from their previous trafficking endeavours, Ou, Xie and Wang drove around in a black car with tinted windows, working to create a new network of poachers, fixers and corrupt officials. It wasn't easy to rebuild in this new place, to know whom they could trust in a world where their contacts were limited. It took months of work, but eventually they managed to organise a new shipment. Three tons of raw ivory were acquired for them. And, when the tusks were ready for inspection in

Mozambique, the traffickers went to the secret storage facility and meticulously sorted through the tusks, checking each for colour, quality and size.

Elephant tusks are incisor teeth that grow with the elephant. This means that the smaller the tusk is, the younger the elephant. The average weight of ivory that an adult elephant carries is about 10 kilograms, between their two tusks.[8] Ou, Xie and Wang rejected 700 kilograms of tusks for this second shipment. This means about seventy elephants were killed for their ivory, only for their teeth to be tossed into a rejects pile. The rest of the tusks were given the go-ahead to be loaded onto ships and sent on a route through ports chosen for their lax checks and corruptible officers. Everything now was just a matter of strategic shipping.

It was in the town of Pemba, where they were inspecting the tusks before shipping that Ou, Xie and Wang met the two undercover EIA agents.

Pemba is a port city in northern Mozambique, and is known for having one of the best natural harbours on the East African coast. There were rumours that ivory traffickers had moved into the area, and the agents had arrived in Pemba to find out more. They happened to meet Ou, Xie and Wang, after picking them out from the locals for being Chinese and for their specific dialect.

The undercover agents spent hot afternoons chatting with the traffickers and drinking together, building trust while they posed as interested ivory buyers. With each drink, the traffickers spilled a little more information, and the agents' nets tightened around their oblivious prey.

But the agents needed more than just drunken words. Direct evidence was required to place them in the middle of the illegal ivory trade. Otherwise, the police wouldn't have enough to go on. But this work was dangerous. And even if they got more evidence, the police in Mozambique and China might still brush them off and see this case as unimportant.

This is how the undercover agents ended up in the warehouse of death.

Before I get back to that opening scene, why should police take time out of their day cracking murder cases to care about wildlife crime? Is it really such a big problem?

WILDLIFE CRIME

Wildlife crime is any activity related to the illegal exploitation of wild plants and animals. This includes poaching, transporting and processing wildlife. It also includes related crimes that allow these creatures to change hands, like document fraud and corruption.[9]

Every four years, the UN Office on Drugs and Crime publishes the *World Wildlife Crime Report*, and it really makes it clear just how pervasive this problem is. The 2024 edition provided a breakdown of the most seized items, based on how much each was estimated to be worth. Of all confiscated animal goods, three came out as by far the most valuable: rhino horn, pangolin scales and elephant ivory.[10]

Ivory is mostly sold for decorative purposes. And while rhino horn has applications in traditional Chinese medicine, 'We are seeing rhino horn increasingly used decoratively. It is usually sold whole,' Ted Leggett told me. Leggett is a research officer for the UN Office on Drugs and Crime, and he has been involved in the research and writing of two editions of the *World Crime Wildlife Report*. Pangolin scales

– along with dried seahorses and big cat bones – are also used in traditional Chinese medicine, which is sold all over the world.

Although referred to as medicine, scientifically speaking, consuming rhino horn or pangolin scales is about the same as eating your own fingernails. There is often no empirical support that the treatments advocated by traditional Chinese medicine work at all. It's one of the aspects of animal poaching that I find the most saddening. Not only are endangered species being decimated; many are being driven to extinction for products that don't reliably do anything.

It is not only the remains of animals that are confiscated. The black market in exotic pets is huge. Smugglers have stowed away turtles, raptors, parrots and snakes in odd places when trying to get them through customs. They are shipped in falsely labelled boxes, tied into socks, stuffed into hair curlers, and even hidden inside toilet paper rolls. Then there are crocodile parts, regularly smuggled for their leather. And live glass eels, which are eaten as a delicacy or taken to be farmed into adult eels.

Even your house probably contains at least one illegally sourced material. The UN report highlighted illegally harvested cedar wood, mahogany and rosewood. One of the most expensive tree products confiscated at borders is agarwood, a fragrant resin harvested by wounding *Aquilaria* trees.[11] It is used for one of my favourite scents in perfumes and candles: the hearty scent of oud. Finding this out has made me look at my own purchasing habits more carefully.

Even houseplants aren't safe. Orchids, succulents, cacti and aloe are all commonly poached plants. These are illegal when they are stolen from nature reserves, or moved across borders without the right permits. Some plants are poached rather than grown, like certain cacti, because they take decades to reach a desirable size. Others are very hard to propagate, or are endangered and impossible to find in legal markets.

But there was something else that bothered me when I first started engaging with the issues of wildlife crime. There are so many humans who don't have their basic needs met. Should we really be spending so much money and time on protecting endangered animals and plants?

Ted Leggett explained to me that dilemmas around priorities are a constant issue in the world of international conservation. When it comes to the global discussion around the trade of endangered species, 'there's kind of a neo-colonial aspect about it that sits really uncomfortably with me,' he said. Countries in Europe and North America are often trying to regulate what countries in the global south can do with their wildlife. This is sometimes seen as hypocritical, because the global north spent centuries killing off their own wildlife. This shouldn't undermine efforts to conserve wildlife, but there is a historical element of environmental injustice that needs to be acknowledged.

In late 2023, Interpol estimated that the black market for illegal wildlife products was worth about $20 billion per year.[12] This widely reported number suggests that wildlife crime is one of the most lucrative criminal sectors. However, Leggett has some of the best access in the world to date on the profits made by wildlife criminals, and he has disputed the accuracy of the figure. 'We calculated the value of the trade of ivory and rhino horn, two of the largest wildlife markets. At their peak in 2011, they were worth $300 million. If you include timber and fish, this number can be higher, but I don't think it is anywhere near $20 billion.'

Before he started working on wildlife crime, Leggett spent years researching brutal gangs in South Africa and international drug smuggling. I first met him at a UN environmental crime course in 2024, where he passionately debunked some of the myths that have crept into the well-intentioned world of animal conservation.

'Even if you look at the stuff the EIA has done, they showed the Shuidong connection, where they traced back these people's houses in China that are associated with trafficking huge amounts of ivory. They are big houses,' he told me. 'But they are not making billions.' Compared to drugs, he said, the financial value of confiscated wildlife is low. But looking purely at the money involved doesn't account for the harm to nature that these crimes cause. Or the threat they pose to our future.

FLAGSHIP SPECIES

Our forests are much quieter than they have ever been. The reason you might not have noticed is that you live in a city, like more than half of the global population.[13] In urban landscapes, there are few animals that can thrive. Sure, there are the mice and rats under our feet, and squirrels up in the trees. The occasional bird that thwacks into the window of a high-rise, or sings from the bushes in a park. Late at night we sometimes encounter the bigger mammals, like foxes in London, raccoons in New York, possums in Sydney, leopards in Mumbai, and baboons in Cape Town. But that's about it. Most of us have become accustomed to living alongside a startlingly small number of animals.

When those of us who live in cities visit the countryside, or the wilderness, we easily feel spoiled by the comparative prevalence of wild creatures. It's like when someone is starving, and they perceive even the smallest assortment of food as a feast. Even slightly more regular animal sightings can give the illusion of abundance.

As we continue to degrade nature, the threshold for what we think of as acceptable environmental conditions drops. Most of us lack our own memories of a more richly diverse natural world. And each new generation accepts the nature in which they were raised as normal, an example of shifting baseline syndrome.[14] This is a major obstacle in getting people to mobilise on environmental issues, because it's hard to miss a past you never had, and even harder to get up and fight for it.

But the reality is that we have lost a shocking amount of wildlife in the recent past. To better understand how much, I contacted Oscar Morton, conservation scientist at the University of Cambridge. 'Herds of large herbivores in sub-Saharan Africa were on a scale we can barely comprehend today,' he explained. 'Equally, bison herds in North America – in the millions. And flocks of passenger pigeons, populations of billions.'

We are currently experiencing a biodiversity crisis, including the collapse of the world's largest herbivore populations.[15] Experts believe we are in the midst of the sixth mass extinction.[16] The fifth was when the dinosaurs were wiped out by an asteroid 65 million years ago, long before humans entered the picture. But today's extinction event isn't a natural disaster. It's man-made. It is also not inevitable that we continue on this catastrophic path. 'If the biodiversity crisis continues throughout the century, it won't be because we lack knowledge on its drivers, it'll be because we lack the will to act on it,' said Morton.

So why are so many big animals dying? The first major reason is the repurposing of wild areas for food. Mass land conversion, particularly for cattle farming, kills off huge amounts of wildlife. The second reason is that wild animals are being hunted.

Many people around the world rely on hunting to feed themselves. This is often referred to as 'bushmeat' by experts, although this term has been criticised for having racist connotations because it is almost exclusively used to describe people of colour hunting in developing countries. When Americans and Europeans hunt, the animals and their meat are normally referred to by a more cutesy, morally innocuous term: 'game'.

Responsibly hunting animals that exist in the wild is widely considered an important part of sustainable food practices. While cases of, mostly, American hunters going abroad to kill lions may capture our indignation, most hunters are not looking to put heads on plaques in their living room. And, as researcher Ted Leggett told me, 'Hunters are big contributors to wildlife preservation.' This includes culling animals to make sure populations don't grow too big, as well as killing off species that are harming or threatening local biodiversity. 'We humans have messed with their world irreparably, and it is now our responsibility to regulate it. There is no longer a world where we can just leave animals alone.'

But hunters who are killing illegally are a problem. Poaching is often by definition unsustainable, because it puts stress on species that are already endangered. And poaching is even more likely to be problematic if the animals are being sold rather than eaten by the hunters themselves. When herds or populations are thinned out too much, their numbers can start to drop irreversibly. In 2021, Morton and his colleagues found that in areas where animals were killed to be sold as meat, or caught to be made into pets, or for other reasons, species declined in abundance by more than half.[17] This meant that it wasn't just the hunting that was the problem, but the knock-on effects of it which led to the animals failing to reproduce at the same rates as before. This is a level that is hard to recover from. In the worst-case scenario, a whole species can die out.

And it does matter if species go extinct. The fact that animals are disappearing isn't just a problem for those animals; it's an existential issue for the whole planet. Morton spelled it out: 'Make no mistake, a world devoid of even just the animals with backbones would be the collapse of society as we know it.'

Big animals have a particularly important role in the natural world, as they act as ecosystem engineers. As Morton explained, 'Large herbivores, like elephants, have the ability to structure and impact their ecosystem on a scale that other species simply cannot.' Elephants smash down trees, which allows more sun to hit the ground and more diverse plant species to thrive. They make paths for other animals to use. With their big tusks, they dig out watering holes that are crucial for the survival of other species, particularly in dry areas. Their dung is also a great fertiliser, which they spread around as they walk. And in their poop are seeds, which they spread across wide distances. This seed dispersal is critical for the survival of forests.[18]

There is also the simple argument that losing species is inherently bad. That animals should be valued in their own right. For me it became particularly easy to understand this viewpoint when I found myself in an open jeep right beside an elephant. The tennis-ball-sized eye looking curiously into mine. The unique enormity of its wrinkled grey body. Encountering nature's giants makes you feel like you have stepped back in time, to when dinosaurs roamed the Earth.

'Failing to save one of the most charismatic and emblematic flagship species of global conservation efforts would really be an unbelievable catastrophe,' said Morton. 'If concerted global efforts fail to save that one species, it bodes really poorly for thousands of other threatened but less well-known species.'

That's why tracking down and stopping ivory poachers is so important. In fact, when the EIA was first founded in 1984, elephant poaching was the very first issue they threw themselves into.

WHOLESALE SLAUGHTER

'Pressure from environmental groups, including from us [the independent researchers working on the *World Wildlife Crime Report*], from the UN, from a lot of people, resulted in several major legal markets shutting down. Which tanked the ivory price,' Leggett said with pride. 'That was a big victory. And for sure we have fewer elephants killed as a result of that.' And the raid on the Shuidong syndicate was part of this. 'The closure of the domestic market was key.'

Despite its popularity, the trade in ivory is an industry that has been criticised for more than 150 years. Back in 1874, a

German botanist named Georg Schweinfurth was calling hunting for ivory a 'wholesale' and 'indiscriminate slaughter'. 'It may be easily imagined how year by year the noble animal is fast being exterminated,' he commented accurately.[19] And yet, rather than slowing down, the ivory trade ramped up to meet the increasing global demand. It was used for piano keys and billiard balls. Combs and trinkets. Religious statues and furniture inlay. Even after the invention of pretty plastics that could serve the same decorative function, elephants were being pushed to the brink of extinction.

Until 2017, ivory that was already in China was allowed to be legally traded within the country. Today, there continue to be some countries, including Thailand, which have a legal domestic ivory trade. One problem with domestic markets is that it can be difficult to track exactly where a specific piece of ivory came from, and whether it was brought to the country before or after the CITES international trade ban in 1989. Traffickers can launder their tusks into legal markets by faking import dates and certificates, or claiming that a tusk came from a domestic stockpile.

A more recent, and bizarre, loophole is that ivory traffickers can pretend that their tusks come from mammoths retrieved from the recently thawed permafrost in places like northern Russia. Although mammoths are long extinct, it is very difficult to verify that a tusk is from a mammoth or an elephant. This is something that ivory traffickers can exploit when they want to move elephant ivory across international borders, because mammoths aren't listed under CITES.

As of 2024, it was estimated that there were around 415,000 elephants left in the wild in Africa, and only about 50,000 in Asia.[20] For comparison, it has been estimated that in 1800 there were more than 26 million elephants in Africa alone.[21] All species of elephant are currently either endangered or critically endangered.

That's also one reason why poaching hotspots have moved over the years. Dwindling populations and tougher enforcement mean that organised crime groups, like the Shuidong syndicate, have to try their luck elsewhere.

In their case, in Mozambique.

UNDERCOVER AGENTS

The EIA had been following the illegal trade in ivory for decades. Around 2014, they realised that the trade was shifting out of Tanzania and were trying to figure out where the organised crime syndicates dealing with ivory had moved to. The rumours were that Mozambique was the new hub of the illegal ivory trade. Chinese undercover EIA agents were sent to Pemba to pretend to be buyers, with the goal of finding out any useful information.

By chance, the EIA agents met Ou, Wang and Xie, who were in town to supervise their next shipment of goods. When they heard the men speaking in the Qingdao dialect, the agents immediately clocked that they were from Shuidong. Shuidong was already known to the EIA as a landing spot for illegal ivory. They worked to win the traffickers' trust, initially in person. Then, through months of communication, mostly through text. The more they learned about the men, the more important keeping in contact with them became. 'They claimed they were the experts in trafficking elephant ivory tusks,' Julian Newman told me about the traffickers Ou, Wang and Xie. 'They claimed 80 per cent of ivory tusks entering China from Africa came through their hands,' he added. Back in 2016, Newman was working on the Shuidong syndicate case in his role at the EIA.

The EIA is like a detective agency for the environment. Many of its members work on investigating green crimes remotely, but some also do ground-breaking undercover work. These are highly skilled jobs, and the agency continually needs to adapt to changing global crime trends. 'I used to do that back in the day,' Newman said about his own experience going undercover. But by the mid-2010s things had changed, 'If I turned up as an ivory dealer, they'd be suspicious,' Newman told me. Had he, as a white man with silky blond hair, shown up in Mozambique in 2016 and started chatting up three suspected Chinese wildlife traffickers, he would not have got very far. If anything, it might have rung alarm bells and derailed the whole project. For the Shuidong mission therefore, Newman worked from the London office, providing intel and support to the Chinese agents on the ground.

The agents in Pemba had to string the traffickers along with promises of a big order, in the hopes of being shown tangible evidence of the tusks. Orders from buyers are often made before the animals are killed, so managing this can be delicate. 'Of course, we are very careful not to trigger incidents by showing interest in a product that they might then go away and poach. So that's always quite a skilled job,' Newman explained. 'We don't put money down. That's clear rules. So we need to try and be good enough to convince them we are worth talking to, and get sight of the goods. Even if it's remotely. To prove what they are saying is true.'

The key was for the agents to pretend to be very discerning, and untrusting, ivory buyers. They asked for names, documents related to transactions, proof of deliveries. But, still, there was nothing to stop Ou, Xie and Wang from forging these documents in order to scam the alleged buyers out of millions. To make sure that the Chinese dealers weren't all talk, the agents needed to see for themselves that they actually had ivory.

In-person meetings were organised when Ou, Xie and Wang were back in China. Back on their home turf, the traffickers felt more comfortable explaining the specifics of their illegal operation. After all, they thought they were speaking to kindred spirits. As Ou told one of the undercover agents, 'Now we are back in China, I can tell you whatever I want!'

After a couple of hangouts in China, it was finally time to see the goods. Which is how the undercover agents ended up in a room full of tusks in a random house in the middle of the night, as described at the beginning of this chapter. That moment, as recorded on the agent's body cam, would be a key piece of evidence.

'We put together an intelligence briefing and we sent it to various authorities,' Newman explained. He even went to a meeting at the Chinese embassy in London and gave them his dossier in person. It had everything they would need in order to bust the world's biggest ivory syndicate. Names, photos, texts, receipts. And, of course, the incriminating video footage.

But then, nothing more seemed to happen. It was like telling the police there is a serial killer on the loose, and the police taking no steps to stop the spree. The EIA later found out that China Customs had started to act on the information, but weren't yet letting outsiders know of their investigations.

In the meantime, as the EIA team worked to get law enforcement to pay attention, wildlife rangers were waging their own war on poaching on the frontlines. A war that continues today in many parts of the world, including in South Africa.

MILITARY GRADE

In 2023, I moved to South Africa for three months. While I was there, I visited a game reserve dedicated to helping populations of endangered species recover. I managed to convince two of the rangers to speak with me about their work protecting the wildlife, although they made me promise to keep the reserve, and their names, anonymous. We met outside in the warm sun, at a table overlooking a field of wild cacti.

'The shape and the face of anti-poaching has changed so drastically over the last twenty years, it's frightening,' one of the rangers told me. 'You know, if you are catching a subsistence poacher with a spear, you take the dog away that he uses to hunt and you give him a warning and he goes home.' He contrasted that to 'guys shooting herds of elephants out of military gunships. It's a totally different ballgame.' This has forced the anti-poaching efforts to also scale up so they can match the new armoured threat.

The ranger explained that even after the 2016 discovery of the Shuidong syndicate the war over the animals had escalated. This was a major survey of wildlife rangers conducted by the World Wildlife Federation which found that about just under 85 per cent of rangers said they found their job to be dangerous because of encounters with poachers.[22] And in 2022, the International Union for the Conservation of Nature declared that in recent years, on average, forty-three rangers were killed by poachers annually.[23] Criminal networks were to blame, and they were kitting out poachers in unprecedented ways. The rangers needed to keep shifting strategies in this arms race.

Rangers will speak in code on their walkie-talkies, making it difficult for people intercepting the radio frequency to know what animals they are tracking on their safari runs. Elephants, rhinos and wildcats are intentionally not fitted with long-range trackers, because these could make the animals easy prey if they were hacked into. The rangers use physical observation points on hilltops to keep an eye out for poachers who can come both from the ground and the air. They also have gunshot detection tech. Like microphones with integrated software that alerts rangers if a shot has been fired. Radar can help them detect when someone crosses an invisible fence.

'It's military-grade stuff. The type used in modern-day warfare,' one of the rangers told me. But the rule is to assume that any tech the rangers have, the poachers have too. So, any signal that the rangers receive can be intercepted.

While the tech is important, the people are still vulnerable. Research has shown that it is social infrastructure that guides the ivory trade.[24] Anyone can be threatened or bribed into spying for poaching syndicates. And that makes every colleague a potential threat.

This constant state of suspicion must be exhausting.

But vigilance is important. One of the rangers told me

how his friend had been offered 10,000 rand, or about $570, for a single text message of poaching intel. That's nearly half of the median monthly salary in South Africa. The colleague declined the offer, but also felt that she couldn't report it to the police as she was worried about what the gangs might do to her two children. Disobeying the syndicates is dangerous, but reporting them is dangerous too. This can put people in tricky situations and often gives poachers the upper hand.

'These things are so interlinked with other organised crime,' one of the rangers explained, 'If you start diving into the syndicates and how it works, and where the products go, and who is involved, then it becomes really quite intricate.' The rangers made it clear to me that for the wildlife crime perpetrators, it is all about the money.

But is this true?

It's time to meet the people who actually do the dirty work. The poachers.

SKULL PIERCERS

The two men were an odd sight, sharing a single soldier's uniform. The one wearing the beige camo jacket, the sleeves rolled up past his strong biceps, cradled an AK-47 assault rifle. He wondered how much longer this would take. A week in the forest was okay. Two weeks was a problem. Three weeks? A disaster. He was hungry and tired, his cracked heels were sore, and his cargo shorts were still heavy with ammo.

The other man, wearing the uniform trousers and a jarring pair of lavender Crocs, clutched a bright yellow jug of water under his right arm. Out here, water was life. A hunter could go for weeks without food, but only days without water. He also hadn't quite realised when they first set off how much more difficult it would be to find the elephants now that there were so few left.

The men froze as a noise from beyond the tangled bush ahead of them caught their attention. The thick white thorns of the branches shook and the waxy green leaves made a noise like rain. There was a quick snapping motion, and the unmistakeable exhale of an elephant.

The man in the purple Crocs put down his water jug and lifted his hunting rifle. The two poachers exchanged a glance. It was time; they had finally caught up with her. They started to move closer to the bush, their guns pointed forward like spears.

Then, bouncing through a gap in the greenery, came a plump baby elephant. Slightly unstable on its chunky legs, it leaned into the bush and almost tumbled into it, sending up a cloud of dust. It pulled out a decisive trunkful of leaves and then bounded back to its mother.

Once it was out of sight, the men exhaled and continued to push forward. A machete was unsheathed and used to create a small peephole through the bushes. The rest of the herd was probably nearby, but for now this female elephant was on her own with her baby. It was perfect.

Seizing the moment, the man with the AK-47 pulled it against his right shoulder and launched a spray of bullets into the bush. It wouldn't be enough to kill her, but it would slow her down.

A horrible bellow came from the other side, followed by a frantic thundering. The poachers walked around the thorny bush towards the noise. Once the screaming elephant was clearly in the crosshairs of his long wooden hunting rifle, the man in the purple Crocs used two of his special skull-piercing bullets to take her down.

Gasping for air, the elephant collapsed to the ground. Bright blood gushed from the bullet wounds. Her baby had disappeared while the men were focused on the attack, but it didn't matter anyway. The poachers didn't have any use for the little ones. It would be years before they started to grow tusks, so they had little commercial value.

The man in the Crocs nodded at his accomplice, who pulled out a walkie-talkie to tell the others to come and get them. Shots tended to attract unwanted attention, so they had to be quick. Looking into her slowly blinking, deep black eyes, they put the chainsaw against the top of her trunk and started slicing downwards, her blood turning the ground into a rusty mud. The elephant took her last laboured breaths as they cut off the front of her face and dislocated her tusks, grabbing every gram of ivory they could and tossing away the handfuls of flesh they carelessly cut along the way.

Shivering behind a tree, her baby watched in horror. The herd would later come to this very spot to mourn its mother's violent death, performing their elaborate rituals of grief.

Such is the horror of the hunt. Poachers who kill elephants are rarely there because they enjoy the thrill. There is no sadistic psychological motivation. No perverse hatred of these wrinkled grey giants.

As with most high-risk crimes, poachers are often young men with low levels of education, limited options for employment, very little money, and no assets such as land or animals.[25] A major study published in 2023 by the Royal Society reviewed more than 10,000 records of poached elephants in thirty African countries between 2002 and 2020. They found evidence that as poverty increased, so did elephant poaching.[26]

The poachers hired by the Shuidong syndicate had been approached by a Black man we will refer to as Mr K, from a neighbouring country. Mr K was working with Ou, Xie and Wang and had been tasked with getting the traffickers three ton of tusks. The syndicate had placed an order in Pemba for a 'one dragon service', which meant they expected everything to be taken care of. They didn't care how they got their ivory, as long as they did.

To stay off the radar of any banks, the syndicate had hit the black market and gone to moneychangers back in China. After converting their yuan to US dollars in shady back rooms, the cash was used for all payments in Mozambique.

In order to get the goods, Mr K was given money to deal with all the logistics and payments on the ground. For each kilogram of ivory, the poachers were paid between $80 and $100. They also received money for supplies, including guns, ammo and food. And they got money for bribes in case a pesky ranger, police officer or border official needed to be silenced. After shipping it to China, the ivory would be sold to the next level up the chain by the syndicate for an average of 4,059 yuan (about $610) per kilogram.[27]

One of the only studies where elephant poachers were interviewed was designed by Ted Leggett, the researcher on the *World Wildlife Crime Report*, working with a field researcher, João Salgueiro, who conducted the interviews. They found that many of the hunters were farmers and took poaching on as supplemental work. These poachers seemed to care as much about the elephant meat as the ivory. During a hunt, elephant meat would often be smoked on the spot and divided up between the poachers, the bosses, and the porters who were hired to carry the big loads.

In fact, while most of the poachers were paid an amount of money for the tusks, almost all of those interviewed were also paid in elephant meat. Some of it they would eat themselves, but a lot was sold at local markets for a remarkable price. At the time of the study, in 2015, elephant meat was four times the price of beef. It could fetch the poachers more money than the tusks. Probably because the meat isn't traded across borders, this facet of elephant poaching is often forgotten. At the same time, it's also true that comparatively few elephants are killed just for their meat. The much bigger problem for elephant populations is those who hunt with an investor arming them and paying for the tusks. Only money and the influence of crime syndicates can explain why Africa's elephants are disappearing so fast.

Leggett found that 'bosses' like Mr K would actively seek out villages known for elephant hunting. They would find willing poachers, arm them, give them food, and cover various other small expenses.

What's interesting about the psychology of poaching bosses is that they see themselves in a rosy light. A study by the AQ, or TRAFFIC, found that bosses often believe they are doing good. This comes from the rationalisation that they are providing employment for others, helping to put food on the table and money in their pockets.[28] In their eyes they are, effectively, doing the poachers a favour by bringing this foreign money into their small villages.

Newman told me that in some African countries, this view is shared by many locals, especially in impoverished communities. Some of the poachers and bosses will use the money they are paid to help build roads, schools and other key infrastructure that the government has not invested in.

Poaching is opportunistic. Without the bosses waving easy money at them, most of these farmers would not turn to killing endangered animals. That's why efforts to stop poaching need to specifically target recruiters. Removing the corrupting forces is much more efficient than trying to reach every single farmer to convince them not to accept poaching jobs.

Ted Leggett has also raised concerns about imprisoning or fining poachers. If you give a poor farmer a hefty fine, it can actually lead him or his family to go and poach more elephants, in order to pay it. Fines are counterproductive for crimes that are so tightly tied to poverty.

So, what can we do to stop poaching?

For one, we can use psychology to change what people are buying.

BEHAVIOUR CHANGE

'People don't understand how ivory is harvested,' Ceres Kam told me. 'People don't know you have to kill that elephant and you have to cut open its face. A lot of people are under the impression that you can just shave it all off and then it will grow back.'

As a psychiatrist, Kam has worked on emergency wards helping people in crisis. She is also heavily involved with anti-poaching efforts, and works as a wildlife campaigner at the EIA. She was part of the Shuidong syndicate case, which allowed her to flex her Chinese language skills. She shared some translations of the court records with me, which I would never have been able to find otherwise.

Kam told me about growing up in Hong Kong. 'When I was school-aged, ivory would be sold openly in department stores.' You could walk into a high-end store and find a whole floor selling precious goods with 'a whole quarter of the floor with just ivory. Huge carved tusks, just like, one after another, lined up.'

China only banned the domestic sale and trade of ivory in 2016, with a grace period for companies to sell their existing stock before December 2017. Kam recalled the frantic scramble at the end. 'There were sales posters put up by department stores: *Final sale, Ivory 20 to 30 per cent off. Last chance!*' Today, despite the ban, China remains one of the world's biggest ivory markets. 'Even though one of the main slogans in China is "without buying, the killing can stop too", I don't think people really understand.'

For those in many parts of the world, where ivory has long fallen out of fashion, it might be hard to accept that there is still demand for it. So, who is buying ivory?

Between 2017 and 2022, the WWF conducted a series of surveys to profile ivory buyers, and the results were unexpected. The average Chinese buyer was found to be a high-earning, highly educated woman aged 25–34. Many bought ivory while travelling, either within China or in countries where ivory was easier to buy. These young women weren't buying the ivory for themselves, but as presents. In China, ivory is still seen as a high-status gift.

Once they had the profile of the typical buyer, the WWF sought to counteract this behaviour via an elaborate campaign, called Travel Ivory Free. It was one of the first-ever conservation campaigns on such a large scale to be aimed specifically at demand reduction. The campaign worked alongside the controversial Chinese social media giant WeChat, and managed to get 300 million impressions. Geolocation was used to push digital ads, targeting people who were at airports and near ivory hotspots. Part of the campaign was also physical, with information about elephants included in leaflets in back-seat pockets on airplanes headed to and from China, on billboards in airports, and on posters in souvenir markets in Thailand, Laos, Myanmar, Japan and China. The campaign included photos of baby elephants, and celebs holding up a curved pinky finger to represent their tiny trunks. It was cute, it was educational, and it was huge.

Psychologically, the message was clear: buying ivory is unethical and unacceptable. Unless you want these adorable floppy-eared baby elephants to die? Which, of course you don't, because you're not heartless.

More random factors have also had an unexpectedly large influence on the public perception of buying ivory. 'It was when [the UK's] Prince William raised it through his platforms that people in China started to take it more seriously,' Kam told me. 'It really showcases how important it is to not just leverage voices from the charity sector organisations side, but also the government side through international platforms.'

Kam herself prefers a different approach. She tries to figure out how to get the people in power to pay attention. 'Our behaviour-change targets are usually government stakeholders, finance-sector stakeholders and so on,' she explained. And the way she does this is not by showering people with as many facts as possible, or presenting them with photos of dead elephants with their faces cut off, or with influencers holding up fingers symbolising baby elephant trunks. Instead, Kam taps into their deep-seated psychological and professional needs. 'You need to establish rapport and a relationship first, and then understand what they need.'

This is the opposite of how most people approach messaging about conservation. Often, scientists and activists create information based on what they think people need to hear, which usually involves telling people what they should do. Instead, Kam first asks people in power what they actually want. She then tailors the EIA's intelligence and messaging to help these individuals meet their goals. Goals like getting re-elected. Or impressing shareholders. Or creating a positive global image. It's a much more tailored approach. 'This is really about putting forward our material for them, to say that we think you should step up your law enforcement efforts because this will, for example, influence your reputation on this international platform.'

In a world where government officials have to justify deploying police to join anti-poaching efforts instead of, say, violent crime units, they must have very strong arguments to convince voters that this is the right call. The key is to find the right angle. Which is what Kam does. She is constantly translating what is happening on the ground into something that can be used for individuals' political or professional gain.

This is also important to counteract the effects of the downlist brigade.

DO NOT DOWNLIST

Whenever a species gets moved to the CITES Appendix 1 – species banned from trade – there are those who argue that a ban will make things worse. That, actually, legal trade is what keeps the animals safe, because it keeps things transparent and eliminates the need for criminals to get involved.

I was first introduced to this concept in a very weird context. I was on the famous Garden Route in South Africa, a lush green area following the winding southern coast, with its dramatic cliffs and small colonial towns. Long stretches of road contain back-to-back farms, mostly owned by the Afrikaans white minority. It's a place that feels, at times, stuck in South Africa's not-so-long-ago racially segregated past.

In this peculiar place, I stayed overnight on a buffalo farm with my partner. We arrived when it was already pitch-black and had to drive our tiny car around what was clearly a body of water. When I woke up to the sun streaming through the big windows across from our bed, I saw two chonky rhinos there, peacefully grazing. After my conversation with the rangers about their anti-poaching war I half expected to look up and see a helicopter keeping watch. But there was nothing. I was dumbfounded to see the rhinos on a private farm, without any obvious security. Wasn't this a big risk to the farmer? And – the even bigger question – why were they here?

Over breakfast I would learn that the white Afrikaans farmer collected animals like others might collect trinkets for a curiosity cabinet. In addition to the two rhinos, he had some naughty zebras, a very handsome oryx, and a few frisky kudu. When asked why, his answer was effectively 'because they're cool'. Unprompted, he also lamented that when the rhinos died of natural causes, he would not be able to legally cash in on their horns.

He was pro-downlisting, but as EIA agent Julian Newman told me, open trade in endangered species and wildlife is bad today for the same reasons that it was bad when the EIA submitted their first ivory report to CITES in 1989. He explained that southern African countries often come to CITES meetings and 'try to downlist elephant populations'. Downlisting means moving a species out of CITES Appendix I, the list of species that are endangered and whose trade is severely restricted, to Appendix II or III, the species that are monitored but can be more easily legally traded internationally.

As Newman explained, people who want to downlist species 'believe that the answer for elephant conservation is to allow ivory to be traded. But to my mind, it's a no-brainer that when you start legalising these products, then of course they flood into it [the market] and that brings us back to about 2010.' And this isn't just true for elephants and rhinos, but for other endangered animals too. Including those that will be facing difficult times in the future, as climate change and urbanisation continues.

Ceres Kam also told me about an important psychological aspect of legal trade. Not only does it open up channels to sneak illegally poached animals into countries, but also 'you are confirming for potential traders and consumers that this is a commodity. It's great. It's a market. Keep doing it.' We only need to look at China for an example of how this can pan out.

Despite the global ban in the international ivory trade coming into effect in 1989, it took China and Hong Kong another twentyseven years to shut down their domestic trade. While it was clear that the domestic market was driving poaching abroad, China often disputed this and pointed to stockpiles of ivory from before the ban. Their argument was that they weren't importing any ivory; they just had a lot left over from the days when it was legal. But the existence of the Shuidong syndicate is a clear indicator that this wasn't true, even if Chinese officials may have wished it to be.

This touches on another issue that is often brought up at CITES meetings. That there are warehouses that are full of ivory, just collecting dust. Their argument is if it is all from endangered animals that have already been killed, why can't it be sold? The reason why selling the stock is a bad idea is because it normalises the ivory trade again, and traffickers are able to launder fresh ivory amongst the stockpiled ivory, which leads to killing more elephants.

Ceres Kam told me that storing ivory in stockpiles is in itself a huge problem in terms of demand reduction. Because that's basically the government saying that we don't want you to trade it, but it's worth a lot of money.' People are going to think ivory is still a good investment if their own government is treating it as such. Sitting on it until they can, perhaps, sell it. And the scarcity in the market that comes from banning ivory can make it feel rare and exclusive, reinforcing this idea.

In addition to sending the wrong message, it takes time and money to guard the stockpiles. And governments rarely succeed in preventing 'leakage', which is when ivory disappears from warehouses that are poorly guarded, or whose guards are willing to look the other way for a fee. The advice is generally to burn existing ivory stockpiles in order to get around all of these issues and to send a clear message that ivory is not an investment. Only then will the demand drop.

Since implementing its domestic ban in 2017, China has successfully cracked down on ivory at customs points and markets. But it hasn't made the demand vanish entirely. Kam explained that some people still buy ivory chopsticks to give to newlyweds, or pick up the occasional ivory earring or small trinket. But for the most part, the government's strict enforcement has worked incredibly well. As Kam said, 'There will surely be diehard buyers . . . but if a hundred people were doing it before, maybe now it's ten or twenty.'

And one reason why this change in China happened was because of the EIA's report on the Shuidong syndicate. It was a watershed moment, after which officials could no longer deny the role of Chinese ivory buyers in the extinction of African elephants.

THE RAID

When Julian Newman first presented the EIA report at the Chinese embassy, he had expected swift action. The undercover EIA agents had managed to extract themselves from the fake ivory sale unharmed, and their body-camera footage was passed on as crucial evidence. But the report, which had taken a year to pull together, seemed to disappear into a black hole. And so, because the EIA's investigative team knew that the Shuidong syndicate was actively planning to import yet another consignment of tusks, the decision was made to go public.

When the regular pathways of communication fail, public shaming can be a powerful lever to force people into action. And that's exactly what happened.

The EIA released the report online, and, two days later, Chinese Customs took action. 'Our initial report triggered the raid,' Newman told me proudly.

Now it was a race against time, as there was the risk of

the poachers and their loot disappearing if the police in Shuidong didn't act quickly or decisively enough. 'They were in the town doing the raid as we were communicating via email,' Newman elaborated. He spent the next few days working remotely with Chinese officials, and then flew to China to help in person.

On 6 July 2017, the police raided the home of one of the suspects and seized four phones. The next day they searched a silver Mercedes, which had eighteen pangolin scales scattered inside, like an incriminating trail of breadcrumbs. This confirmed what the EIA had suspected: that the syndicate was smuggling multiple species of endangered wildlife.

Things then continued at pace. That same day, police searched two homes, finding multiple phones and SIM cards along with a USB stick loaded with incriminating files. The following day, they searched two more cars. Yet more phones were confiscated, along with fourteen different bank cards. By this time, the police were on a roll. They already had a heap of incriminating texts, documents and suspicious money transfers.

But they hadn't found any ivory.

That changed on 10 July, when they followed a lead to an unsuspecting backyard hut. There, hidden in three cheap woven bags, were eighty-nine tusks. That same day they searched a plastics company that had acted as the Shuidong syndicate's import-business cover story. They confiscated the plastic beads that were used to hide the tusks during shipping, along with more damning documents. Confessions started to spill out too, and people began implicating others in the crimes.

The syndicate had scattered their ivory, and other evidence, all over town. Not just in backyard huts, but in a craft shop and a tourism centre, where a man nicknamed Grass Turtle was caught with at least eight tusks.

Then came the pig farm.

As some of the suspects confessed to their crimes and cooperated with the authorities in exchange for more lenient sentences, a disused pig farm in a small village near Shuidong came up repeatedly as the place where the ivory deals were made. On 26 July, almost three weeks after the initial raid, the authorities physically took one of the men suspected of purchasing ivory to the farm for an on-site visit. There, he told the investigators exactly how and where he'd bought the ivory. A few months later, they repeated this on-site interrogation method with another suspect, who also confessed to buying ivory at the pig farm.

It should be noted that this is a highly unorthodox police interviewing technique. At least one of those convicted in connection with smuggling the ivory would later say that he had been pressured into falsely confessing. And the two suspects who continued to maintain their innocence were sentenced most severely. But in most cases, there was so much other evidence that the confessions just served to help the authorities make sense of it all.

Over the next few months, the police would raid several homes where they found ivory tusks, ivory products and pangolin scales. By the end of the raids, more than twenty people had been arrested. Many were sent to prison, including Ou Haiqiang and Xie Xingbang, who were convicted of smuggling precious animal products and each given a six-year prison sentence. Wang was given a higher sentence of fifteen years, which reflected his role managing the money.

It was a major win for Newman and the Environmental Investigation Agency. 'We are pretty sure that the network has been effectively dismantled,' he told me. 'Not saying it'll solve everything. But they were major traffickers. We don't often get that. And I think that there's been a big impact on the ivory trade globally, and also on our relations with China Customs, who have really done a good job and tried to crack down on wildlife crime.'

THE SIX PILLARS OF WILDLIFE CRIME

The Shuidong syndicate's ivory-trafficking operation demonstrates how the six pillars of green crime can enable devastating wildlife crimes.

Ease was evident in the syndicate's established trade routes. Originally used for legal goods like sea cucumbers, they were repurposed for smuggling ivory and other illegal wildlife products. The existing infrastructure allowed goods to flow smoothly from Africa to China with minimal interference. Syndicate members also avoided physical contact with the contraband, delegating tasks to accomplices at every stage to minimise their own risk.

Impunity was pervasive in this case. Corruption allowed ivory shipments to pass through ports with lax oversight and bribable officials. Even when shipments were seized, traffickers like Ou and Xie paid their way out of legal trouble, enabling them to continue operations seemingly without fear of lasting consequences. The bosses in charge of recruitment, as well as the poachers themselves, were even given money specifically for bribing police and any officials who got in the way.

Greed drove the syndicate's pursuit of profit at great

environmental cost. They wanted bigger houses and flashier cars – a lifestyle that other kinds of business would not have as easily afforded them.

Rationalisation flourished particularly among the bosses, who framed their actions as entrepreneurial, claiming they were creating jobs for the poachers and supporting poorer communities.

Conformity normalised illegal activity within the syndicate and the communities they operated in. Ivory trafficking was seen as a family business, to be passed down through the generations. In villages known for poaching, participating in these crimes could feel like just another job.

Desperation was most evident among the poachers. Lured by promises of cash, young men with few alternatives took on the bloody work of killing elephants. Poverty and inequality drove them to risk their lives, highlighting the systemic vulnerabilities exploited by the syndicate.

The Shuidong syndicate's downfall was a critical win for conservation, and the investigation illustrates the firm grip that organised crime groups have on some of our last remaining wild spaces and the desperate people who live near them.

Since the Shuidong case, there has been a push towards a new strategy that doesn't involve paramilitary-style interventions or endangering rangers. It's more subtle and can often be done from a distance. This new frontier of catching wildlife crime perpetrators isn't confrontation, it's disruption.

BREAK THE CHAINS

'When I'm at a party and I tell people I work on corruption and tax evasion, that usually kills the mood,' French researcher and legal adviser Sophie Lemaître told me. One of her specialties is illicit financial flows, an area that has only recently been applied to green crimes.

'If we take, for example, a wildlife trafficking case,' she explained, 'I look at all the actors involved. I'm not just looking at the traffickers or the person who poached the pangolin, but the entire ecosystem of actors.' To do this, following the money is important. 'In a financial investigation, we will be looking at where the money went, from A to B to C.'

This relates to something that comes up often in conversations about preventing green crime. We need to break the value chains.

In standard business settings, a value chain is the full lifecycle of a product. The term is often used to explain how costs increase as more people handle a product. Every link in the chain, from sourcing raw materials to creating a product, shipping it, packaging it and selling it, means someone is getting paid.

The same applies in the context of organised crime. Between the poachers and bosses, bribed officials and permit forgers, and the syndicate members themselves, many people in the illegal wildlife trade are making money. And that's before we even get to the lawyers who set up shell companies, the accountants who launder the proceeds, the artists who carve the goods, and the retail outlets, galleries and market stalls selling illegal products to consumers. If you stop any one of these actors, you can break the chain.

As Ou, Xie, and Wang might have said, it's hard to 'own the road'. Forging these chains takes time and trust. If you break one of these chains, it can be very difficult for another to be forged to replace it. And if you break enough of these value chains, eventually the stakes get too high and the perpetrators move on to other ventures.

'To map the network, we look at locations, like houses and physical addresses, assets they own like properties and luxury goods. But we also examine countries to identify the jurisdictions involved in the wildlife trafficking case,' Lemaître explained. 'It's about tracing the money – where it ended up, who received it and how it was transferred, whether through banks or other means.' Investigating the entire ecosystem of organised crime and using this information to seize and confiscate the proceeds can make a big difference.

While getting people locked up for their crimes can be one useful outcome, to stop green crime making their lives more difficult is key. One way to do this is to erect financial roadblocks. 'If you only seize the pangolins,' said Lemaître, 'they'll just return to the protected area and kill another. But if you seize their bank accounts, houses and cars – confiscate everything – how will they fund their crimes?'

One major problem in her work is that money often moves across borders, requiring cooperation between governments. 'Mutual legal assistance requests are a big issue,' Lemaître told me. And navigating different legal systems and languages can be a slow and complicated process. However, once a law enforcement agency has the data, they can take the appropriate measures to ensure green crime does not pay. Lemaître and others like her can convince banks to freeze suspicious accounts, or prompt police to begin investigations. Hers is quiet investigative work, but it makes it clear that there are people in all sorts of professions who can help track down and disrupt those who are stealing our natural resources.

Disruption as a deterrent is something that also came up in a conversation I had in the UK, when Charlotte Milton, a senior environmental crime officer for the Environment Agency, told me about her work tackling waste crime. 'I'm a waster,' she joked. 'I just find waste really interesting.'

Waste crime, such as illegal dumping, trafficking or improper processing, is a huge global issue. It's well known that the e-waste of discarded electronics is shipped to poorer countries, where it is stripped for parts and recycled. But illegal dumping isn't just something that happens in faraway places, or that just applies to our electronics. Everything from paper and plastics, cars and clothes, to furniture and building waste, is regularly dumped in places where it is both a nuisance and a biohazard. Chances are, there is an illegal dump site not far from where you live, contaminating your own neighbourhood.

Milton often comes across unexpected waste crime scenes. 'These illegal landfills can exist for years, and no one reports them,' she said. And it's not just household rubbish either; it's bigger than that. 'I'm shocked at how much abuse there is of packaging regulations and the extent of cash-based money laundering around scrap sites.' For example, the practice of 'comingling', which involves mixing legally sourced waste with rubbish from companies trying to skirt proper processes, makes it very difficult to track whether money at the scrap sites is earned through legal or illegal financial pathways. Ironically, dump sites are a perfect place to clean dirty money.

Organised crime groups play a significant role in these kinds of waste crime, but penalties are low, and laws often lag behind the evolving industry. So what can Milton do to deter these waste mafias?

Like Lemaître, she focuses on disruption.

Once she spots a crime scene, Milton's aim is to intervene before environmental damage escalates. The key is to 'be visible'. This can mean conducting random inspections at dump sites in high-visibility vests, sending multiple warning letters to suspected offenders, or installing surveillance cameras around a site. But of all the disruptive techniques she uses, my favourite is the most literal kind of barriers. 'Concrete blocks can make a surprising difference, stopping access to popular dump sites,' she explained.

While Milton focuses on waste crime, the same principles apply to all organised environmental crime. Disruption, whether financial or physical, can cause the entire value chain to snap. As Julian Newman put it: 'That's one less group of baddies in the world.' As for the elephants, the takedown of the Shuidong syndicate is one reason why their future looks good. In fact, the decline in ivory poaching is one of the biggest triumphs in conservation since we helped save the world's prettiest birds from the hatmakers. Elephant populations are recovering, and some species have been saved from extinction.

It shows that targeted work to infiltrate organised green crime groups can do more than just expose harm. It can disrupt and dismantle the dangerous criminal networks that criss-cross the world and threaten our future.

4

THE OUTLAWS

THE HEMP ROPE ladder bit into the three men's hands as they climbed aboard the sinking ship. A ship that others had said couldn't be found.

For 110 gruelling days, the crew had pursued the *Thunder* through the unforgiving Antarctic waters. The chase had pushed them to their limits. Icy winds, unrelenting storms, isolation. Now, they had followed the ship into the warmer waters of the Gulf of Guinea, and time was running out. A small plane circled above like a vulture, capturing every morsel of action on camera.

As their boots hit the deck, the ship groaned. Water hissed into the hull. The *Thunder* was leaning, dipping deeper into the sea with every passing second. Constant radio contact with the captain of their own vessel kept them informed about how quickly they were taking on water. How much time they had left before it would be too perilous for them to continue.

First, they searched the wheelhouse. They were in luck. The three men tore out the hard drives and took mobile phones. They grabbed the ship's certificates, nautical charts, the binders that held the registration information. They were hoping all of it would provide a trail that could be followed, to build a case in order to take down these criminals.

But they weren't done yet. They wanted more concrete evidence. Something bigger.

As they made their way through the ship, nothing seemed to make sense. The captain had put out a mayday call, but this wasn't how you were supposed to secure a ship that was taking on water. Instead of sealing everything to maintain buoyancy, all the doors were lashed open, ensuring water could flow freely from one section of the ship to another.

The three men shuffled quickly through the narrow halls, deeper and deeper. The ship's groaning was becoming louder, more desperate. When they got to the engine room, it was full of water. If they didn't move fast, the evidence would soon be deep below the surface. And they would be too.

Then they lost radio contact with the captain of their own vessel. The thick steel hull had walled off their signal. But they kept going, until they reached a room with rows of freezers. Slamming open one of the metal doors, they found the first freezer empty. The next one, empty; the next, empty. Then, bingo. It was there, in the belly of the sinking ship, that they found what they were looking for.

An ugly brown-grey fish, about the size of a human leg, with tiny and irregular pointy teeth. Its mouth gaping, as though frozen in shock.

This chapter tries to understand whether it is possible to stop people from taking advantage of environmental enforcement vacuums. Using the thrilling case of the longest maritime pursuit in history, the chase of the *Thunder*, we head out into the vast oceans of the world where illegal fishing is rampant.

I spoke with Peter Hammarstedt, the captain of the ship that followed the *Thunder* until it sank to the bottom of the sea. Hammarstedt is part of a non-profit ocean conservation movement called Sea Shepherd. With a logo strongly resembling a skull and crossbones, which flies from the bows of their long-range fast ice chaser boats, these aren't your average heroes. Sea Shepherd is a direct-action organisation, which means its members get physically involved in catching ocean criminals. As the self-appointed police of the seas, they are the last, and often only, barrier that stands between illegal fishermen and their prey.

I also spoke to Mario Alcaide, the Interpol agent on the *Thunder* case, who took me through the details of what is needed to police green crimes on a global scale. He explained that often both thoroughness and creativity are required to make sure cases don't fall through legal cracks.

This chapter raises fundamental psychological questions about deviance. If we think of the oceans as a lawless place, does that perception of freedom change us? It also leads us to consider the question of how other people shape our ethics, both when we are being watched and when we aren't.

The chase of the *Thunder* involves the most wanted boat of all time, hunted and investigated by twenty-six countries. It involves a bizarre task for the German police in Bremen, who had to store their fishy evidence. And an unfolding drama in a pink courtroom in one of the smallest and most remote countries in the world.

But most importantly, it is a story of outlaws stealing our last truly collective resources.

And it all began with a fleet of ships ready to scour the high seas.

110 DAYS

The small Sea Shepherd fleet was ready to go out and patrol the Antarctic waters. 'I'd come across illegal fishing gear down in the Antarctic before,' Captain Peter Hammarstedt told me. 'This was an opportunity to actually do something about that problem.' He was speaking to me from his office. A shelf behind him contained books and a model of a silver ship, with a sharp bow and a tall hull. From my angle, the ship was right above his head. As though he was dreaming of it.

'It's a model of the *Bob Barker*,' he said when I asked. That was the ship he'd captained a decade earlier when he pursued the *Thunder*. Since then, the ship had been retired and turned into scrap metal. Now, all that remained of it for Hammarstedt was this tiny model. And his memories.

It was no accident that the ship was named after the host of the longest-running television show in US history, *The Price Is Right*. The ship had been donated by Bob Barker himself. The sister ship was the *Sam Simon*, named after the co-creator of *The Simpsons*. Both men were animal rights activists.

Under the command of Captain Paul Watson, the co-Founder of Greenpeace and founder of Sea Shepherd, they turned to fighting the notorious poaching of Patagonian toothfish, more commonly known as Chilean sea bass. These fish were being relentlessly targeted by poachers because there was a big market for them, and Patagonian toothfish were difficult to find in the overfished waters elsewhere. In order to protect this species, it was hard to get the necessary licence to legally fish in Antarctic waters because of worries that this slow-growing species was being extracted to extinction. But that setback didn't stop the Bandit Six, a gang of six ships that had evaded international law enforcement for years.

The most notorious of them all? The *Thunder*.

There was even an Interpol Purple Notice out for the vessel. 'I would constantly refer to it as an international arrest warrant,' Hammarstedt recalled. 'Which it isn't. In Interpol terms, it is essentially a request for information.' Purple Notices are used to collect information about the methods used by criminals, the tools they use to commit their crimes and the ways in which they hide their contraband. The notice for the *Thunder* included key details in order to help people spot the vessel if they came across it, including its various previous names.[1]

The Sea Shepherd team were eager to get back out to sea. So, they set out on their two celebrity ships to find any of the Bandit Six fishing vessels, who were in the Antarctic Ocean. Frustratingly, Captain Watson had to stay on shore in France, so he had to serve in an advisory capacity rather than heading out himself. He delegated the mission to Captain Peter Hammarstedt on the *Bob Barker*, and Captain Sid Chakravarty on the *Sam Simon*. The two ships, each with their respective crews, had to work together to catch the illegal fishing vessel. The role of the *Bob Barker* was to pursue the *Thunder* the role of the *Sam Simon* was to retrieve the abandoned fishing nets. Collaboration was key.

Over the next two weeks, Hammerstedt and a crew of thirty sailed south on the *Bob Barker*, with its grinning shark teeth painted on the hull, going deeper and deeper into the ice floes. They were heading to the edges of the Earth. To the most remote body of water in the world.

'I set up a search grid. Looking at the radar, it was like a like a vegan pepperoni pizza. There were a hundred possible targets of which most of them, if not all of them, were icebergs,' Hammerstedt explained. But then one of the dots started moving, and he knew they had discovered one of the Bandit Six.

The chase was on.

The *Bob Barker* sailed full throttle towards where the other boat was showing up on the radar. Just off the ice edge of the Antarctic, where the ice meets the water, they knew from the scanners that it had to be close. But they couldn't see another vessel. In fact, they couldn't see much of anything because of the dense blanket of fog.

Then, like a ghost, a ship materialised before them.

Hammarstedt's heart was pounding. He had to find out which one of the Bandit Six they had found. 'I had a binder of, essentially, vessel mugshots,' he said. 'We had pictures of all six of the ships and their various paint schemes over the years.' He flipped through the binder and stopped on one of the laminated pages. The ship they had tracked down was, without a doubt, the *Thunder*. It was a perfect match to the photo; they hadn't even bothered to repaint the hull. He almost couldn't believe it. 'It showed how brazen and confident they were that they could get away with their crime.

And that kind of brazenness is ubiquitous among these boats,' he told me, referring to fishing vessels that are known to engage in illegal activities.

For the next 110 days, Hammarstedt sent twice-daily updates to the authorities, charting every move in the unfolding chase. The *Bob Barker* tailed the *Thunder* like a shark hunting its prey. Together they battled bitter storms, and dodged through an ice field of dangerous islands.

Most days, the two ships were so close that the Sea Shepherd crew could make out the people on the *Thunder*. They could see that the men on the illegal fishing vessel were trying to hide their identities, wearing balaclavas whenever they headed up on deck to take their smoke breaks. In the control room, orders and insults went flying across the airways, with Captain Hammarstedt telling the captain of the *Thunder* to head back to shore and surrender, and the captain of the *Thunder* yelling various insults in return. This went on for several weeks. Realising that the *Bob Barker* was not going to give up or go away, the *Thunder* turned off its engine and just began to drift, to conserve fuel. The situation had turned into a waiting game. A question of who could endure these waters the longest.

The ships drifted together. But with the *Thunder* showing no signs of heading back to port, the Sea Shepherd team didn't know how long this would go on. Another day? Another month? Years? It didn't feel fair to ask those on the *Bob Barker* to put their lives on hold indefinitely, especially since most of them were volunteers. So, a couple of months into their chase, Hammarstedt offered his crew a choice. 'I said, look. Here's the reality. We have enough fuel for two years. We don't know how long the *Thunder* will drift. We have no guarantee of outcome here . . . only thing we can say with any certainty is that every day we're with them, they can't fish.' For anyone who wanted out, now was the time to say. Their sister ship, the *Sam Simon*, was nearby, and could take them back to shore.

Remarkably, of the crew of thirty, only four decided to head back. 'I still think back to that and am blown away by the fact that twenty-six people were willing to remain on board a ship for two years to save a bottom-dwelling fish with an unappetizing name,' Hammarstedt told me. 'To save a species other than their own' and catch these criminals. Cold, remote, vulnerable. Stuck in the confines of the ship, day in and day out, for an indefinite amount of time.

Luckily, they would be rewarded for their efforts.

But how is it that the crew found themselves in this situation in the first place? Why was the *Thunder* even out there in the waters of the Antarctic? And what is it about the seas that seems to attract criminals? To answer these questions, we need to rewind to the seventeenth century. When a fundamental idea took hold that has driven how we think about the Earth's oceans.

NEGATIVE FREEDOM

It all started with a man who has been called the father of international law, Hugo Grotius.[2] In 1608, Grotius wrote his famous essay *Mare Liberum*, which translates to *The Freedom of the Seas*. It was originally published anonymously, and people only figured out a couple of hundred years later that it was a follow-up to his larger work, *Commentary on the Law of Prize and Booty*.

Mare Liberum was written about a very specific dispute.

Portugal had just colonised Brazil, and was trying to monopolise certain trade routes, particularly around Africa and the Indian Ocean. The Portuguese were effectively trying to do on water what they had just managed to do on land. These, they decreed, were now *their* waters.

But the Dutch were having none of it. They wanted access to this lucrative shipping highway too. And they believed they were entitled to it. Grotius was arguing the Dutch side, saying that the seas couldn't belong to anyone, because they inherently belonged to everyone.

The sea was too 'limitless' to be owned by any one nation, wrote Grotius, so it must be a common resource. This wide open, ever-changing space, which flowed between the shores of every continent on earth, couldn't be owned. To try to split it up would be doing 'violence to Nature herself'.[3]

How can you turn a belief like that into law? By making it more practical. In the words of Grotius, 'that which cannot be occupied, or which never has been occupied, cannot be the property of any one' – as in any one nation or any one person. In other words, if you can't put your house on it, pop up a fence or cultivate it, it can't be yours.

Notably, he argued this only for remote waters. Shorelines and waters that were easily accessible could be cultivated and occupied, so they could be owned. This is how people can have fisheries just off the coast that still belong to them, or own a beach and the port that's just off it. But this idea left the vast majority of the Earth's seas unownable.

And that's how many still see the high seas today. As everyone's, and no one's. A place of complete freedom.

This is where the problem starts. Because everyone has

a different idea of what this freedom should mean. The most basic version is that people can do whatever they want. That's called 'negative freedom' because it's a freedom *from* rules. It involves the absence of external restrictions, like laws, or those who enforce them, like the police. This is a libertarian idea that emphasises limiting government interference in our lives and maximising individual autonomy. Negative freedom sees the ocean as a blue no-man's land, the wet wild west, where anything goes.

Imagine you are in the middle of the ocean. And you can do anything without consequences. You can dump waste into the ocean and no one will know. You can push someone off your ship and easily pretend it was an accident, and others can do the same to you. You can pull up sea creatures from the depths and torture them. You can use and exchange drugs, weapons and enslaved people, without any authority realising it has even happened. If no one was watching, would you become a criminal?

Undoubtedly, people being watched tend to behave differently than those who aren't, self-monitoring actions and decisions that are normally automatic. This is called the observer effect, and it can cause people to overthink their movements. Changing where they look, how they speak and how they behave. And that's because people who are aware of being watched tend to see themselves through the eyes of the watcher. Because of this, observers estrange the familiar. There is also something at work here called the social desirability bias: people who are being watched tend to change what they say and do in a way they think will make them look good. They might even say things that they don't believe, just to be liked.

Scientists tend to find this annoying, because it makes it harder to know whether what we see in research settings translates to how people behave normally. But for society, the observer effect is crucial. We want people to think about how others will morally assess them, and to change their behaviour to be more socially responsible. We want them to be more mindful of their actions, rather than letting their standards slip. To continually ask themselves: Am I a good person? Is my life an ethical one? What would someone say if they saw me?

For seventeenth-century Grotius, unowned international spaces were governed not by a nation, but by two abstract 'courts': 'Conscience, or the innate estimation of oneself, and Public Opinion, or the estimation of others'. He called these personal ethics a 'conceptual tribunal'. The conceptual tribunal is a place inside each person's mind that helps them make the right decisions about what to do. Where our own ethics and the ethics of those around us come together to decide how we should behave.

Fundamentally, the negative freedom of the seas was captured, somewhat ironically, in a set of international laws. To keep the sea free, it had to be ringfenced with legislation.

The biggest attempt to formalise what is allowed at sea was the Geneva Convention on the Law of the Sea in 1958 which was adopted by eighty-six countries straight away. The parties agreed that each state had control over everything up to twelve nautical miles from their coastline. It was also agreed that all ships would be allowed through these waters as long as they weren't taking any resources or spying. This is also known as innocent passage.

But there were immediately a number of problems. The

rules were ambiguous about how far out into the ocean a state could claim control over its fishing zones. Conflicts broke out between nations, who were fighting over the fish. In the Cod Wars, for example, Iceland forced UK fishing vessels out of the North Atlantic by expanding territory they claimed as rightfully theirs. These disputes made people realise that the laws weren't really working.

That's how we got the United Nations Convention on the Law of the Sea (UNCLOS), signed in 1982. After more than a decade of negotiations, it came into force in 1994. It is often described as the constitution for the oceans, because it provides a legal framework for everything from territorial waters and navigation to marine resources and environmental protection.

Today, countries have what is called an exclusive economic zone (EEZ), generally extending up to 200 nautical miles from their coastline. In the EEZ they have exclusive rights to explore and exploit marine resources, such as fishing and oil extraction. Anything beyond that is considered the 'high seas', which are international waters where no one country has sovereign authority. They belong to everyone.

But even the high seas aren't quite the vacuum of laws, the negative freedom utopia, that people might think. UNCLOS has guidelines for managing resources and protecting the marine environment in international waters. States are legally required to conserve fish stocks, in particular making sure that highly migratory species like tuna don't run out. UNCLOS also states that every country needs to have regional fisheries management organisations to prevent overfishing, and must monitor the impact of their activities on the high seas with regular environmental impact assessments. Almost all coastal countries have ratified UNCLOS – and those that haven't, most notably the US, have their own regulations in place.

This means that the high seas are actually a place of positive freedom, which is the ability to actively pursue your own goals and make choices, by possessing the resources and opportunities to do so.[4] While negative freedom is about not *stopping* people from being free, positive freedom is about *helping* people to be free.

To put it in more practical terms, negative freedom would be saying people can fish wherever they want but offering no tools or guidance, so those without fishing rods can't participate while others overfish. Positive freedom, on the other hand, is providing fishing rods for everyone, teaching people where and how to fish sustainably, and ensuring everyone benefits without exhausting the resources. UNCLOS gives countries both the rights and the framework to responsibly manage ocean resources, with the aim of ensuring long-term economic and environmental sustainability for all.

No matter how it feels psychologically, the oceans aren't actually lawless.

But, as the crew of the *Bob Barker* knew when they followed the *Thunder* into the seas of Antarctica, there are enforcement deserts that are being exploited. Where ships are not being watched and people aren't appropriately using their internal conceptual tribunal to make ethical choices. But before we get back to the pursuit of the *Thunder*, let's look at why we should care about criminal fishing in the first place.

FISH CRIME

If you eat fish, you have almost certainly eaten fish that has come from what's collectively referred to as illegal, unreported and unregulated fishing, or IUU. It has been estimated that, out of every five fish that are caught, at least one is netted and traded illegally.[5]

Fishing is illegal when people extract fish that are endangered, fish in a location they aren't supposed to, catch more than they should, pretend they didn't catch as much as they did, don't have a permit, or use methods known to severely harm ecosystems.

Methods of illegal fishing can be intense. Like using electrocution or explosives to kill or stun all the wildlife in a certain area and scoop it up. Or cyanide fishing, which involves diving into coral reefs and squirting cyanide at fish as you encounter them. This incapacitates the fish without killing them, making them easy to catch. Cyanide fishing is used particularly by those who cater to the live fish market, such as those catching exotic fish for aquariums. While the cyanide may not kill the fish, it kills the reef at a rate of one square metre for each live fish that is caught.[6]

In the case of the *Thunder*, the crew were using set gillnets to catch patagonian toothfish. A gillnet is like an invisible curtain. It can be free-floating, or anchored to the seabed. This is a passive way of catching a lot of fish. But because it catches everything indiscriminately including fish, seals, sharks, and other marine animals, it is illegal to use them in Antarctica.

Showing up to a dock with gillnets would be obvious evidence of illegal fishing, so crews dump the nets at sea.

These dumped nets become another ecosystem nightmare: ghost nets. Drifting for months or years, these bunched nets entangle anything that swims into them. And they continue to do so until they are finally hauled out of the water by an organisation like Sea Shepherd, or are washed ashore on a beach somewhere.

The *Thunder* went on three expeditions annually, each time leaving port with about 600 kilometres (373 miles) of gillnets. These nets would be recovered every few days, pulled out and then reset in the sea to catch more fish. That means in just one year, they would be dropping thousands of kilometres of fishing nets. Even to those who are used to fish crime, this is, in Captain Hammarstedt's words, 'just a crazy amount'. He then elaborated, shaking his head: 'I mean, we talk about people saying no to plastic straws at restaurants. Because they understand the plastic pollution problem. Here's 1,800 kilometres of fishing net dumped overboard by one ship every year.'

There are many reasons we need to care about illegal fishing. You might think that killing off one species of fish wouldn't be the end of the world. But you're not just killing off one species, you're potentially killing off a whole food web. When you remove a predator from an ecosystem, it can lead to something called trophic cascade. Toothfish, for example, are predators in Antarctica. That means they kill other fish. If you kill all the big fish who normally eat the smaller fish, you will get an increase of the smaller fish. Smaller fish tend to live off plankton and algae, so a population boom can lead to a collapse of these ocean organisms and the small fish eventually starve because they ate all their food too quickly.

If you start to kill the small fish at scale, for example by pulling them up as by-catch, this can cause problems related to the food they eat. Small fish eat algae, and if there are far fewer small fish to do this, then the algae will grow unchecked. This blocks sunlight from reaching underwater life, killing off seagrasses and coral reefs. Algal blooms can also use up all the oxygen in the water, creating dead zones where marine life can't survive. And this can kill the plankton.

Killing the tiniest organisms in the sea is what will land us in the biggest existential trouble.

Plankton are the tiny, translucent plant and animal organisms that float in our oceans. Like snowflakes, they come in many delicate and intricate shapes. Plankton create about 50–80 per cent of the world's oxygen.[7] And life in the ocean has absorbed about 25 per cent of the total man-made CO_2 emissions from the early 1960s to today,[8] although there are concerns that the warming of the oceans is already making parts of this crucial carbon sink far less effective.[9] In other words, we literally need them to breathe.

By killing too many fish, we risk throwing the entire underwater web of life out of balance. If you found it unfathomable that twenty-six people would agree to stay on a ship in the freezing Antarctic to catch fish criminals, perhaps now it makes more sense. They were fighting for all of our our lives.

Fish crime is a particularly urgent problem because it makes it impossible for us to keep our seas sustainable. It's like a leaky bucket. As long as there's that hole in the bottom created by fish crime, our resources are being drained faster than they can replenish.

Would it be easier to just shut down the whole fishing

industry? Well, it's not that simple. About 90 million tons of fish are pulled out of wild waters each year,[10] which is half of our global fish supply. The other half comes from aquaculture, better known as fish farms. Halving the number of fish we have to eat would lead to widespread starvation.

Fish are an important part of the daily diet of approximately 3.3 billion people, disproportionately feeding people in lower- and middle-income countries. They are also important for food security in a way that cannot easily be replaced with land-based alternatives. Turning more land into farmland to replace that protein would come with its own problems, like deforestation to make space for crops or other animals.

To understand the realities of illegal fishing, I spoke with a prize-winning investigative journalist who is near-obsessed with exposing crimes at sea, sometimes called 'blue crimes'. Ian Urbina is the founder of the Outlaw Ocean Project, a non-profit journalism organisation that produces investigative stories about human rights and environmental abuses at sea.[11] Urbina and his colleagues only cover stories that they can report 'in theatre'. That means they climb aboard ships to get their interviews, footage and stories, both at sea or on the docks.

With his high energy and bright eyes, Urbina tells thrilling tales of his adventures. His work straddles, in his words, the 'electric fence' between journalism and advocacy. 'Fishing is a thin-margins business,' he explained, and one way to increase your profitability as a company is to 'tell the captain he's got a quota, and make it clear that you don't care how he does it'.

One of the biggest investigations Urbina and the Ocean Outlaw Project conducted was into fishing vessels going 'dark'. Fishing vessels are supposed to have something called an automatic identification system on board, which provides real-time tracking information about where the vessel is. The International Maritime Organization, a specialised agency of the UN, requires vessels to keep their automatic identification systems on. Although, it is not always the case with fishing vessels, where whether they need to be visible at all times depends on the flag state. This means that sometimes fishing vessels will keep their system off, so the competition doesn't get wind of where they are fishing. But it can also be a sign of illegal fishing. Urbina looked into which vessels were going dark, and where they were from. He wrote up his findings in a report that was published in 2023. 'We documented hundreds upon hundreds of vessels that were going dark for over a week,' Urbina told me. 'They're not allowed to go dark for over an hour.'

And where were these 'dark ships' registered? China, mostly. 'A third of the entire Chinese fishing fleet was going dark for longer than a week,' said Urbina. Which is really bad news, because almost all the fishing vessels on the high seas are part of the Chinese fleet. About a third of global fish comes through China, making it the world's biggest producer.

In 2023, China had about 6,500 distant-water fishing ships. For reference, the whole of Europe only had about 300, as did the US. According to the Ocean Outlaw Project report, China's enormous fleet 'is the worst perpetrator of illegal fishing in the world, helping drive species to the brink of extinction. Its ships are also rife with labour trafficking, debt bondage, violence, criminal neglect, and death.'[12] This finding is backed up by the IUU Fishing Risk Index, which is an excellent resource to check how much countries are perpetrating fish crimes. China is the country that comes out the worst, by far.[13]

While a lot of the catch from their fleet is used to feed China's increasingly large domestic market, a huge chunk of it gets exported to western countries at minimal cost. And much of this fish comes from questionable sources or problematic ways of fishing. 'It's a globalisation luxury that we don't really need to know all the nitty-gritty details of where that stuff is coming from,' said Urbina. 'If we are honest about globalisation, what it does is allow plausible deniability of the end consumer, you and me. And of the companies that sell to you and me.'

If we really examine how fish products are getting to us so cheap and fast, the answer lies in the shady mechanisms of the fishing industry. One of the problems is unrelated to the fish themselves, or even the wider environmental effects of overfishing, but rather the human rights abuses that occur at sea. Urbina estimated that about 50 million people are on fishing vessels. When he was boarding ships as part of his investigations, he was finding dire conditions.

'We're climbing on board the vessels and the guys are saying: I've been beaten. My passport was taken. Could you rescue us? I'm being held against my will. I haven't eaten anything but rice and pasta for a month and a half, and I'm getting very dirty,' Urbina stressed with intensity. Human rights violations are known problems of the fishing industry, and abuse can go on for years. This is because of the island-like self-sufficiency of many of these deep-sea trawlers. If the ship doesn't dock, then people can't escape.

Ships can be traps. Which takes us back to the *Thunder*.

A PERFECT DAY TO SINK

After weeks of drifting with the *Thunder* in Antarctic waters, the crew of the *Bob Barker* had found themselves in the warmer waters of the Gulf of Guinea. The Sea Shepherd team noticed something strange. In the middle of the night, the crew of the *Thunder* were seen burning things in oil drums, and at first light, it became clear that there were fewer buoys on deck, and less fishing gear. This went on for a couple of days. It seemed like the crew was preparing for something.

Then the *Thunder* changed course, heading towards the tiny island nation of São Tomé and Príncipe, which is near the equator, about 150 miles off the coast of Central Africa. A small population of about 225,000 people live on the two main islands. It seemed the chase was finally coming to an end. That they were heading to shore. The crew was hopeful.

What they didn't expect was that, at 6.30 a.m. on 6 April 2015, the crew of the *Thunder* would suddenly be standing on deck in lifejackets, throwing life rafts overboard.

The *Thunder*'s captain put out a distress call, asking for immediate rescue. Under international maritime law, any nearby vessel was required to assist. And who was right there, just 500 metres away? The *Bob Barker*.

On the radio, the captain of the *Thunder* demanded that they bring his crew onto their ship. It was surreal. And suspicious. The sea was calm, with barely half a metre of swell and no wind. Captain Hammarstedt told me, 'If you wanted the perfect day to sink, this was it. Nothing is going to go wrong. You're going to get rescued.' He radioed Captain Watson, who was monitoring the ships from shore, and made it clear that they had to be prepared to accept the crew. Watson also made it clear, that the whole ordeal would be for nothing if they didn't secure the evidence on board the *Thunder* before it disappeared into the sea.

Now Hammarstedt had to make a decision. How could he safely bring this enemy crew aboard? They couldn't just bring forty people onto their ship from a potentially criminal enterprise without being relatively certain that they could ensure their own safety. The crew of the *Thunder* outnumbered them; their intentions were unclear. It was too dangerous. They needed backup.

So, they called their sister ship to help. It took the *Sam Simon* over four hours to get there, but that gave them time to put in place the necessary security measures to contain the enemy crew. The crew of the *Sam Simon* installed internal locks, and used an angle grinder to slice off the ladders on the back of the ship. They created a floating citadel.

By the time they arrived, the Nigerian Air Force was circling overhead, filming the rescue. One by one, the crew from the *Thunder* were brought on board the *Sam Simon*. They were searched and led to safety.

Meanwhile, red and orange rescue gear was piling up everywhere. It was impossible not to notice that the name on the hull of the ship was different from the name painted on the life rafts, which was different again from the name stencilled onto the lifejackets. It was a visual history of the ship's various pseudonyms, its conspicuously criminal history.

Rescued from the *Thunder* were thirty Indonesian fishermen. These were the workers. Exhausted men, who went placidly. The other ten were Spanish, Chilean and Portuguese men who were in charge of the vessel itself. They were more aggressive, uncooperative. When everyone was safely on board the *Sam Simon*, the crew radioed Captain Hammarstedt.

They had spent 110 days chasing this ship, and hundreds of hours retrieving the nets, and it became clear that the evidence would just sink in front of them. They knew that because the ship was going down and it had been abandoned, international salvage laws applied. They were legally allowed to go onto the ship and bring back the things they found.

An engineer from the crew proposed going on board the sinking ship to save the evidence, to which Captain Hammarstedt replied, 'If you do it, it's your responsibility. It would be an incredible thing, but I can't order you to do it.'

The engineer and two other volunteers decided to jump into one of the rescue boats, sail it over to the sinking *Thunder*, and climb aboard using the rope ladder. Which is where this chapter began. After thirty-seven terrifying minutes on board, they returned triumphantly. With bags of hard drives and documents and, of course, the huge frozen Patagonian toothfish.

Back on the *Sam Simon*, a strange, rescued crew awaited them. Who amongst them was to blame for these fish crimes?

LAWLESSNESS PREVAILS

The fishermen on the *Thunder* would probably have known that using gillnets wasn't allowed and was bad for the sea. That tossing those nets overboard, and thereby illegally polluting the water and creating ghost nets, was illegal. And they definitely would have known that burning evidence in oil drums was, at the very least, highly unusual. But, according to Hammarstedt, they weren't really criminals. They were poor, exploited men. 'Did they know what they were signing up for? Most likely, no,' Hammarstedt told me. 'They're making $350 a month and have no control over where the ship is going.' And by the time they realised this was an illegal fishing vessel, even if they didn't want to be there, they couldn't opt out. They were stuck on the ship, where they couldn't resist or refuse the work. Even if it was clearly illegal.

The officers, however, had a choice. Including the captain, the fishing master in charge of the fishermen, and a few other senior officers. 'The captain was making about €10,000 a month. And the fishing master was making about €12,000 a month. So, these were not poor fishermen,' Hammarstedt explained. This was supported by the ship's falsified paperwork, which had been forged either by the officers or the owners, creating two sets of identifying documents to rotate between. The men in charge had to have known that they were not legally registered to fish in Antarctica, and that gillnets were banned. Yet they commanded the men to do this work.

This means that if we want to stop fish crime, we need to understand the minds of the officers rather than the fishermen. For them, it seems clear that greed and impunity played a role. Until the Sea Shepherd ships came along, the *Thunder* had already been suspected of fishing illegally for a decade. By the time it was wanted, it had made an estimated 50 million euros in profit. But greed and impunity are never the complete answer. There are many things people can do to make a lot of money that don't involve green crimes.

'I think to understand these guys, you have to understand Galicia,' Hammarstedt explained, referring to the men's place of origin in Spain. 'Their fathers are fishermen, and their grandfathers are fishermen. There was a period when these guys ran the place. It was largely lawless. I think that lawlessness still prevails.'

It's also something Maria Alcaide, the Interpol officer who worked the case, touched on when we talked. There was something in the community these men grew up in that was relevant to their mindset. Something that helps to explain other hotspots of green crime around the world.

But to find that secret ingredient of their criminality, Alcaide first had to undo some of the remaining knots in this twisted story. And, ideally, get a confession.

IT'S ONLY PENGUINS

Mario Alcaide's world is one of investigations, forensic evidence and chains of custody. For ten years he worked as a criminal intelligence officer at Interpol, and one of his first assignments was the *Thunder* case.

When I spoke to Alcaide, he was at sea, heading out to inspect fishing vessels. The camera showed that he was in the white cabin of a ship, luggage on one side, windows on the other. The coastless ocean visible through the porthole behind him came in and out of view with the motion of the waves. Alcaide was wearing his navy polo work shirt with the letters EFCA printed on it in bright white letters. He had recently changed jobs, moving from Interpol to the European Fisheries Control Agency.

At Interpol, he had found it frustrating when people thought that intelligence officers like him would go around arresting people. Interpol helps police forces from 195 countries work together to tackle international crime. While it doesn't have its own police officers, it does provide a secure network for sharing data about criminals and supports investigations across borders. This makes it crucial in the global fight against green crime.

Alcaide was in the Interpol office in Lyon, France on the riverbank of the Rhône, when news arrived via email that the *Thunder* had been located. 'We got excited, went to the meeting room to discuss the next steps,' he recalled. 'We have these paper notebooks for each case, and we cracked open a brand new one because we knew that this was going to be important.' One of the things Alcaide was responsible for was making sure there were local police waiting when the ships arrived at the nearest port, to help get the crew from the *Thunder* off the rescue ship.

He was also responsible for some of the forensic analysis. Alcaide examined the nets that had been pulled up for clues to connect the abandoned gear with evidence found on the *Thunder*. He explained that knots, and the way nets are built, are like signatures. 'Everyone has their own way of doing knots and setting up nets. You can look at the number of threads they use. Is it three? Is it two? Every fisherman does it differently.' He also examined the buoys that were retrieved and traced them back to a company in Spain.

Then, he found himself on the other side of the world, in São Tomé and Príncipe, the country which had agreed to take on the responsibility of prosecuting the *Thunder*'s captain and senior officers. The investigation, however, remained an international affair. Before he could continue with the case, he needed to head to the cobblestoned German city of Bremen.

Germany had accepted the *Bob Barker* to head into port. Interpol policy required that the investigation had to be handled by the local police, so the burden fell on the Bremen police. They had to ensure the chain of custody for the evidence so it could later be used in court. This meant the crew of the *Bob Barker* had to give their official statements to the Bremen police, through a mandatory translator who happened to speak worse English than the interviewing police officer himself.

The police in Bremen also faced the bizarre task of having to figure out what do to with this huge frozen toothfish. Luckily, they wouldn't need to store it for long, because a delegation from São Tomé and Príncipe, including two prosecutors, had flown all the way out there to pick it up in order to avoid breaking the chain of custody. They didn't want this fish to be left unattended, lest someone contaminate the evidence. Eventually, the police collected and analysed a tissue sample from the fish, and the authorities used the results as evidence in the case.

Back in São Tomé and Príncipe, Alcaide conducted interviews with the two main officers from the *Thunder*. The fishing master, who'd been in charge of the fishermen, and the captain, who ran the ship. Every night in his hotel, he would draft forty questions. And every day, during the interviews, the officers would dodge them. But he was patient. 'It's a psychological game, you see . . . like a dog in a chase,' he told me.

It was interesting to hear Alcaide talk about interviewing in this context. In my own work, I educate lawyers and police on how not to mess up interviews. I wondered if it was easier or harder to get someone to disclose information they would rather conceal when it was about environmental harm rather than direct harm to people.

I certainly recognised one strategy that Alcaide used. Minimisation is when you downplay the ethical or criminal aspects of an act, to encourage people to admit that they did it. In this case, Alcaide downplayed the fact that Patagonian toothfish were an endangered species. 'I'm very proud that I managed to get the fishing master to confess,' he said. Alcaide got him to sign a statement declaring that he was poaching toothfish.

Research shows that being nice to people you want information from is far more effective than being mean to them. People like sharing information with others they believe are on their side, much more than they do with someone trying to pressure them.

Alcaide's downplaying the nature of the fish crime in the investigative interview makes even more sense when you look at the psychological context in which the criminals were operating. It wasn't just that the criminals had long been evading legal consequences. They had also avoided social repercussions. 'It's not like if you are a drug smuggler,' Alcaide explained. 'They're just fishermen. It's less socially criticised.' Going home and telling their families and friends about what they had been up to didn't come with the same social condemnation as other kinds of crime.

While people tend to think of those that commit more stereotypical kinds of crime as dangerous and likely to end up in prison, fish crime comes with little baggage. 'If you go to Galicia, you would see that the locals, they do not retreat. They do not have bad words about these guys. They say they're not harming anyone.' In the court of public opinion – the second part of Grotius's conceptual tribunal – what they were doing was ethically permissible. Besides, as Alcaide put it, they thought: 'It's Antarctica. It's only penguins.'

Let's explore where that attitude comes from.

BIOSPHERIC VALUES

Most of us want to act in line with the values of the social groups we are part of, and not stick out too much. In doing so, we try to align ourselves with the norms of our peers. Social psychologists have long found that two norms in particular influence how we behave.

Injunctive norms are what we believe others think we should do. When your friends frequently criticise petrol-guzzling SUVs as 'planet-killers', they're signalling that big cars are frowned upon in your group. This unspoken expectation might make you hesitate before buying one, knowing it would likely lead to their disapproval.

Descriptive norms, on the other hand, are based on what people actually do. If you see these same friends regularly arriving by bike or in electric cars, their choices demonstrate a preference for sustainable options. Without needing to say a word, they are communicating that eco-friendly choices are the norm in the group. They are leading by example.

The influence of social norms and values has been the research focus of Linda Steg, professor of environmental psychology at the University of Groningen. In her research, Steg has found that people are generally motivated to act sustainably. The big question she has is: so why don't we act accordingly? Why do any of us do things that we know will harm the planet? In 2023, Steg published a review of the psychology of climate change. She found that people tend to try to copy those around them, but that this also leads to curious misalignments.

One such misalignment that surprised me the most was that people tend to assume that others care less about the environment than they do. I often think about this when I plan dinner parties. If I make it vegan, for a group of non-vegans, will they judge me? My belief is that I care more about limiting my animal products than they do. But this isn't necessarily true; it's just my assumption. If I surveyed all of my friends and asked how much different types of sustainability mattered to them, they would probably surprise me. But because I am not going to be the psychologist handing out surveys at dinner parties, I'll never actually know. I'm just going to continue being relieved to be able to set aside the burden of public opinion every time a vegan guest joins and we default to a plant-based meal.

Thinking that we are more planet-conscious than others can undermine our motivation to act. We fear that our friends will judge what we do, think of us as ethically performative or make fun of us. This is amplified in parts of the world, like the US, where the climate change debate is tied in with political beliefs. But according to Steg's summary when people around the world in various life circumstances were asked about their beliefs, most said they believe strongly in the reality, human origins and negative consequences of climate change.

To counteract the misalignment between our pro-planet beliefs and our behaviour, we want to encourage what Steg calls 'biospheric values'. Having biospheric values means that nature is important to you, and you want it to be protected from harm. Because of how norms spread through groups, biospheric values can proliferate in communities. This is excellent news. It means that, as individuals, we have the power to change what those around us do. But it only works if others assume, or know, that we are behaving sustainably.

Think of it as sustainability influencing.

The key is to make pro-environmental behaviour a status symbol. Something that people will see as a way to gain approval from their peers. A great example of this from recent years is the increased cool-factor of vintage clothing. Steg also found in her research that symbolic factors are particularly important in the early adoption phases of sustainable behaviours.

For example, when the first mainstream electric cars came out, Tesla gave their early cars impressive sci-fi features like winged doors. This made the cars look cool and futuristic. Praise from our peers can help new technologies take root, particularly if there are potential downsides to overcome, like concerns about having to plug in cars to charge.

Unfortunately, sometimes a company can do many things that foster sustainable solutions, but this positive change isn't inherently permanent. As we have seen with the shift in the opinion of Tesla, things unrelated to sustainability can also destroy the desirability of a green product.

By fostering and reinforcing biospheric values through both injunctive and descriptive norms, we can promote consistent pro-environmental behaviours. This is not just about individual awareness. It's about creating a culture where environmental action is both expected and observed.

And this is precisely what was lacking in Galicia, where the officers of the *Thunder* came from. They managed to divorce the issue of climate change from their own actions at sea. And when they got home, they were praised for their hard work, even when people knew exactly where and what they had been fishing.

After the sinking of the *Thunder* on that perfect day in April, however, the men did not get to go home. They were arrested and sent to trial.

ISLAND TRIAL

The court was a relic. It was once a governor's residence, now the Supreme Court of São Tomé and Príncipe. Light pink paint flaked off the walls, and an old iron sign hung above the entrance looking as though it was melting over the colonial door. Along the shore the palm trees stood guard.

Captain Peter Hammarstedt walked inside the building

with the prosecutor, sweat already trickling down their necks from the oppressive heat. In the small white box of the court, lush red curtains hung over the narrow windows, and a standing fan in the back wheezed helplessly. Two heavy wooden benches were at the front of the gallery: pews taken from a church, giving the proceedings an air of divine justice. A stenographer was ready to go, dwarfed by the towering pile of yellow legal pads next to a box of blue pens.

Hammarstedt was one of the first people to arrive, so he sat down to wait next to a photographer. After a few moments, he looked up to see the captain of the *Thunder*, Captain Luis Alfonso Rubio Cataldo, whose expression was livid. Cataldo locked eyes with the photographer next to Hammarstedt and, as if ignited by a shock of electricity, lunged towards him.

'No, no, no! Don't, don't, don't!' his defence attorney yelled at him, pulling Cataldo back just before it could come to blows. At least that is how Captain Hammarstedt recounted the moment to me.

Then Cataldo turned, eyes blazing, and pointed at Hammarstedt. During their months at sea, the two captains had been in touch almost every day, at times exchanging furious insults. 'It was always late at night,' Hammarstedt recalled. 'He always seemed inebriated. I don't speak Spanish fluently but understood enough to know that he was disparaging my mother.' These insults had, however, always been behind 500 tons of steel. And Hammarstedt had never even seen Cataldo without a balaclava. In person, in this small courtroom, all Hammarstedt could do to diffuse the situation was put his hands up as Cataldo shouted at him in Spanish, until his lawyer managed to calm him down.

As the proceedings officially began, the local police marched into the court. They were kitted out in tactical gear, with semi-automatic weapons slung across their chests and wraparound sunglasses hiding their eyes. They stood imposingly by the accused. In the dock, next to Captain Cataldo sat Chief Engineer Agustin Dosil Rey and Second Mechanic Luis Miguel Perez Fernandez. The judge read out the charges against them. Forgery. Pollution and damages to the environment. Recklessness. All related to the illegal registration of the ship itself, and the deliberate creation of a shipwreck.

Why prosecute them for creating a shipwreck, rather than illegal fishing?

Countries often treat illegal fishing like a game of hot potato – tossing around the responsibility for prosecution until the case lands with a dull thud in no man's land and rolls into impunity. As former Interpol officer Mario Alcaide explained, most countries and their courts didn't want to have to deal with this case. 'When they [the crew of the *Thunder*] were discovered and scuttled the boat in São Tomé's waters, at first, everyone was saying, "Listen, this vessel doesn't belong to us. The crew isn't ours. The company isn't from São Tomé."

So, countries where the case could have been tried were basically saying, "Not our problem. They haven't committed any crimes here."' Technically, São Tomé and Príncipe could have said the same thing, since the fishing crimes were all committed out in Antarctica, beyond the local jurisdiction. But they chose to take the case. That's why in cases like this, Alcaide said, 'You throw all the books on the shelf at them, followed by the shelf itself if necessary.'

The problem was that people in the other countries 'were

only seeing it through the fisheries' lens. They weren't seeing the bigger picture,' Alcaide explained. This is an issue that those who want to help prosecute fish crimes constantly face. Illegal fishing is treated as an administrative problem, a question of fishing licences and permits. 'They don't think about the criminal side,' Alcaide continued. 'We're talking about food security, right? It's not just a fisheries issue. It's a serious crime. It's theft.' And it was up to Alcaide and the prosecutors to find charges that would actually stick.

Ships are required to follow strict rules about pollution, garbage disposal and oil discharges, regardless of where they operate. The International Convention for the Prevention of Pollution from Ships, more commonly known as MARPOL, is the treaty that regulates this. When a ship docks at a port for fuel, supplies or to offload its catch, the port state has the authority to inspect it for environmental compliance. If violations of MARPOL are found, the ship can be detained or fined. This makes MARPOL one of the most important tools in the fight to save our seas.

In São Tomé, Alcaide helped the local police apply MARPOL, UNCLOS and other international convention regulations, framed by national penal code. It was a huge help that the prosecutor was a young and very committed public official, who was tirelessly committed to seeking justice in this case.

In court, the defence stated that the ship hadn't been scuttled. Scuttling a ship is the maritime term for sinking on purpose. Those in charge on the *Thunder* claimed that the ship had hit something. But this argument was undermined by the rather farcical fact that, before the ship began to sink, plane tickets had been bought for the whole crew.

These tickets just happened to be leaving from São Tomé, and the plan had initially gone pretty well. After the *Thunder*'s crew had arrived on the island, shipped in by the *Sam Simon* from their emergency evacuation, they were not initially held in custody. It was a mayday, after all. In fact, the perpetrators made it all the way to the airport, and were about to fly out when they were finally arrested.

In court, according to Hammarstedt, there was also an attempt to flip the accusation around. They claimed that the *Bob Barker* had harassed them. That they had been scared for their lives by this ship painted like a shark with a skull and crossbones flag, chasing them into the icy waters. But this argument also fell apart quickly. If they were so scared, then why not go into port earlier? Why not contact the authorities?

To this, Cataldo simply replied, 'I had my orders', according to Hammarstedt.

Evidence the crew had collected during those tense thirty-seven minutes they were on board the sinking ship, including video footage of doors tied open, was crucial to proving that this was a deliberate shipwreck. The trial ended with a landmark decision from the Supreme Court of São Tomé and Príncipe. The three men were each sentenced to between thirty-two and thirty-six months in prison for forgery of the ship's documents and recklessness towards the crew. The men were also fined 15 million euros for the pollution and damage to the environment caused by the intentional sinking of their vessel.[14]

There was still the fishing master, who had confessed to Alcaide that he had been illegally fishing toothfish. Because he was Galician, he was supposed to be tried by the Spanish courts. But Spain decided they didn't have jurisdiction, and dropped the criminal case.

Still, it was a major win. Proof that willpower and a creative application of the law can hold environmental criminals accountable even in the most seemingly lawless parts of the world. But someone in the chain of command was missing. Who had given the orders to the captain?

Before I get to that, let's examine the best way to stop ocean crimes.

DETERRENCE THEORY

In January 1923, the president of Columbia University stood up in a room full of American lawyers and 'men of affairs' – important people – and spoke about what he perceived as a rise in lawlessness in the United States. 'Disregard of law, disobedience to law, and contempt for law have greatly increased,' Nicholas Butler lamented. That was more than 100 years ago, and today some people still feel, probably incorrectly, that lawlessness is on the rise. This can become a self-fulfilling prophecy. Contempt for the law fosters more contempt for the law. It's a spiral of disillusionment. Or, in the case of green crime, a race towards our own demise.

It surprised me to learn that even a century ago, in his speech to these men of affairs, Butler didn't advocate for harsher prison sentences. Instead, as he put it, 'Human experience has long since exploded the doctrine that a severe punishment will deter from the commission of crime. The fear of detection will so deter, but the fear of punishment will not.'[15] In other words, he was arguing that threatening people with long and harsh sentences for crimes is far less effective than people knowing that they will be caught in the act.

The most obvious way to create the fear of detection is by introducing what criminologists call a capable guardian. In the case of the *Thunder*, the capable guardians were most notably Captain Hammarstedt and the rest of the *Bob Barker* crew. They were prepared to enter the most remote waters in the world in order to get eyes on the enemy. And they refused to let the ship out of their sight for 110 days. During that period, as they had predicted, the *Thunder* did not fish illegally. With the ships so close together, the fear of detection deterred them from committing this crime as they knew they would almost definitely suffer consequences.

Criminologists call this deterrence theory. It's the idea that by increasing the risk of being caught, and thereby making undesirable consequences very likely, people are less likely to commit crimes and therefore crime levels decrease. These consequences don't need to be huge; they just need to be likely. That's why even the best-laid criminal plans are often derailed if a police officer happens to show up. The risk-reward ratio tilts quickly.

A 2021 review of research on the general impact of police presence on crime found that it significantly prevented crime.[16] This was particularly the case when police focused on specific types of crime, were visible at peak times that crimes were being committed, and were located in the hotspots where crime was being reported. Basically, targeted policing was far more effective than just throwing a police officer on every corner of a city. The review also found that it was more effective for police to stick around the same area for a longer period of time, rather than making lots of short visits.

In cities, there is a risk of using this finding to justify overpolicing neighbourhoods with a high proportion of minority or immigrant backgrounds. It's important to consult with the people who actually live in an area to make sure the policing isn't just *of* a neighbourhood, but *for* it. In the ocean, the closest equivalent to this community-oriented policing is to consult with legal fishermen on how policing the high seas should be carried out.

The Sea Shepherd team took an approach in line with what seems to work in policing. They focused on a specific crime: the poaching of Patagonian toothfish. They concentrated on the months when this was common, between December and April, in the location where they knew this kind of crime was common, the remote waters of Antarctica. Then they spent months out there, watching.

The idea of the targeted policing of fish crime perpetrators makes particular sense because it is a few vessels that are committing a disproportionate number of crimes. One study analysed global fisheries-related crimes between 2000 to 2020 and found that about 33 per cent of these offences were tied to just 450 industrial vessels and 20 companies. They were mainly based in China, the EU, and several tax havens.[17] Stopping these repeat offenders should be the first priority. But we also need to make sure that justice is served to the right people.

We don't want more policing of the seas to lead to crew criminalisation, where small fines and sentences are issued to the people who happen to be on the boat when a crime is committed. Sweeping sanctions that criminalise illegal, unreported and unregulated fishing can also unjustly hurt artisanal, small-scale fishers. These are the people out on small boats, catching a few fish without a permit. Enforcement efforts should instead focus on industrial fishing vessels, and punishments should include companies having their ships seized and their owners facing legal and financial consequences.

Speaking of owners. Did they ever find the elusive owner of the *Thunder*? Investigators had to peep carefully through the many loopholes that had been used along the way and every fake flag he used to cover his tracks.

TYCOON

Every ship on the sea needs to be flagged. Flagging a ship means registering it under the laws of a specific country. This is known as the flag state, which is responsible for defining and enforcing the laws on that vessel, including safety standards, labour laws and environmental regulations.

You might think that, say, a German-owned ship would have to be flagged in Germany. However, largely because of the principle of freedom of navigation, under UNCLOS, shipowners can choose their flag state. And some countries cater to this, with open registries that allow foreign-owned vessels to fly their flag. This creates an issue of 'flags of convenience', a loophole that companies take advantage of. Countries like Panama, Liberia and the Marshall Islands are particularly known for this. These countries are trying to attract the money associated with flagging ships, because each ship needs to pay to use their flag.

If you have a flag from a country that doesn't care about fish crime, they are unlikely to put much effort into checking for wrongdoings, or enforcing international laws. This makes it easier for owners to engage in activities like illegal fishing or environmental degradation.

In addition to flags of convenience, there's also the illegal practice of using false flags and false identifiers. This is when a ship flies the flag of a country it is not registered with, or goes by a fake name, often to disguise its true identity or activities.

When the Interpol Purple Notice first went out for the *Thunder*, it had already been operating under a series of names and flags. In July 2012, it was registered in the land-locked country of Mongolia under the name *Wuhan 4*. The following month, it was seen in the North Indian Ocean, now under the name *Kuko*, and it wasn't clear what flag it was under. In October of that year, it was seen in a Singapore shipyard under the slightly modified name *Wuhan N 4*, now back under a Mongolian flag. Six months later, in April 2013, it docked in Malaysia under *Wuhan 4*, but when inspected a few days later in Indonesia, it went by *Thunder* and was flying the Nigerian flag.

This would turn out to be a mix of true and false flags. Interpol knew the ship was owned by a Nigerian company, and that company was owned by a Panamanian company. But initially that was as far as they could trace it. It took spectacular international cooperation to track down the rest of the information that was needed. Spain, Portugal, Indonesia and Chile all shared what they knew about the ship and crew. Panama provided data from their company registry. Nigeria had information about the flag the ship was sailing under. And São Tomé and Príncipe had to combine this with their own evidence. Each country had a different piece of the investigative puzzle, deciphered by the Interpol environmental crime programme.

There was also a baffling and lucky twist of fate.

About a month and a half after the *Thunder* sank, 'I got a phone call from an insurance investigator in Spain,' Captain Hammarstedt told me. The insurance company had allegedly received a claim from the apparent owner of the *Thunder* for 1.7 million euros for the total loss of his vessel, including thirty-three tons of toothfish. The man making the claim, Florindo González Corral, was Spanish, and from Galicia. The press would later refer to him as 'the tycoon' because he had previously owned multiple fishing vessels and companies.

Hammarstedt couldn't believe it. 'It's featured in the *New York Times*. The most known fishing boat in the world. And he's like, yeah, I'm going to claim insurance on it. It just goes to show how brazen these guys are.'

Interpol and twenty-six different countries had been involved in catching the *Thunder* and building the case. Everyone wanted to see the owner held to account. The Spanish national police raided Corral's office, and then his home.

'The fact that companies insure vessels that are on an international blacklist is insane,' Hammarstedt said. And the *Thunder* wasn't even the only one of the Bandit Six that had insurance. 'Two of them with international Purple Notices, and all of them were on at least one illegal fishing blacklist. But some insurance company was like, yeah, I'll insure that.'

This points to the role of insurance companies in green

crime. In economic terms, they are able to create moral hazards, which is when someone is willing to take on more risk than they should because someone else will suffer the consequences. It seems less likely that the owner of the *Thunder* would have been willing to sink the boat, or even send it to Antarctica, if it had been uninsured. It certainly would have changed his cost-benefit calculation.

Insurance companies are the gatekeepers of risk. In addition to reducing the risk of illegal projects such as the *Thunder*, there are a lot of legal projects that can't, or won't, go ahead without insurance. Like oil rigs, dams or wind farms.

Divesting from harmful practices to sustainable ones is part of the global conversation on corporate practices called environmental sustainability, social responsibility and transparent governance, or ESG. It's an important shift, and it can't come quickly enough.

A criminal investigation into the owner of the *Thunder* for money laundering and other criminal acts was initiated, and charges were brought. But, as with the fishing master, the Spanish Supreme Court dropped the criminal charges, with one judge ruling that they did not have jurisdiction. Corral was not, however, able to get out of the civil case. In 2018, almost exactly three years after the *Thunder* sank, he was fined 8.2 million euros by the Spanish government.[18] Spain was making it clear that it would no longer tolerate being a haven for pirate fishermen.

THE SIX PILLARS OF ILLEGAL FISHING

The pursuit of the *Thunder* demonstrates how all six pillars of green crime can fuel illegal fishing.

Ease was inherent in their methods. Using hundreds of miles of gillnets allowed them to catch as many expensive fish as possible with minimal effort. At sea, crimes were easy to conceal because the evidence could simply be thrown overboard.

Impunity allowed the *Thunder* to fish illegally for over a decade. By changing flags and names, they evaded consequences until the *Bob Barker* intervened.

Greed drove the *Thunder*'s owner, captain and senior officers. As former Interpol officer Mario Alcaide put it, 'To them, fish are money swimming in the sea.' Illegal fishing brought them an estimated 50 million euros in profits over ten years.

Rationalisation flourished in the idea of 'negative freedom', the absence of laws. By viewing the seas as lawless and fish as everyone's property, the crew minimised their actions. After all, how can you steal something that already belongs to you?

Conformity was evident in Galicia's norms. Illegal fishermen there were celebrated, not condemned, for their actions. Their justification was that it was not a real crime because it's 'just penguins' out there in the remote waters of Antarctica.

Desperation shaped the lives of the Indonesian fishermen. These underpaid labourers, unable to leave the ship, likely felt they had no choice but to comply with the illegal orders.

The chase of the *Thunder* shows that it is possible to hold environmental criminals accountable even if they commit crimes in incredibly remote areas. But it also illustrates a concerning lack of enforcement. It can't rest on the shoulders of volunteers to keep our global fish stocks safe from criminals. To stop fish crimes, we need nations to actively invest in and tackle this problem.

OCEAN POLICE

Sea Shepherd is not a police force. And there are serious questions we should be asking about rogue organisations taking justice into their own hands. Vigilantes in ships painted like sharks with faux pirate flags on deck are not a sign of a functioning system. They are a sign of an enforcement vacuum. For a long time, Sea Shepherd as an organisation was angry at police and other government agencies for not enforcing regulations. Its members saw these institutions as the enemy, because they were clearly letting those committing fish crimes off the hook.

'They used to throw rocks at government boats and officials,' Mario Alcaide explained, speaking figuratively about the tensions between the two. But the case of the *Thunder* was a turning point. 'They pivoted their activity and started working alongside governments, providing assistance in areas where governments lack them. Particularly long-range patrol boats. So that's what they are doing today.'

In fact, the point of pursuing the famously blacklisted *Thunder* was all about making people realise that the world needed eyes on the seas. As Captain Hammarstedt told me, 'The amazing thing about the *Thunder* chase was, we set off to show what the world's governments should be doing. I was hoping the media would start reporting. Asking, why is an NGO doing it? Shouldn't this be the work of governments?'

One by one, all five of the rest of the Bandit Six were

found and the people running them arrested. They were located by various authorities from around the world, with the help of Interpol. One was intercepted and sunk by the Indonesian Navy in 2016, as part of Indonesia's crackdown on illegal fishing. Another was detained in Thailand, and two were seized in the Atlantic Ocean by authorities in Cabo Verde. In several cases, the officers and owners faced fines, the forfeiture of their illegal catches, and charges related to fishery violations. 'Since then, as far as we know, there's been no illegal fishing down in the Antarctic,' Hammarstedt told me proudly. It's a testament to what can happen when capable guardians patrol wild spaces and work together.

After the successful capture of the *Thunder*, the Sea Shepherd team started partnering with governments around the world. For example, in Gabon, Central Africa, they patrolled alongside the authorities in order to arrest illegal fishing boats. By 2024, they had helped to arrest thirteen illegal fishing boats just in the waters off Gabon.

Sea Shepherd isn't the only organisation actively engaging in this fight. The United Nations Office on Drugs and Crime has led a series of initiatives to help fight crime in the fisheries sector. These include the Global Maritime Crime Programme, which trains prosecutors on fish crimes and helps countries to put in place appropriate laws and regulations.[19] Since 2020, they have also held Maritime Domain Awareness courses, which focus on the various ways of detecting illegal fishing vessels.[20] And then there is the Blue Justice Ocean Surveillance Programme, in collaboration with the Norwegian Space Agency, which uses satellites to help catch illegal fishing vessels from space.[21]

'There are these leaps and bounds in terms of satellite

monitoring,' Hammarstedt told me, referring to the new surveillance tech. 'But I think that can sometimes give the false impression that the illegal fishing problem is taken care of. At the end of the day, the police still need to get boots on the ground to arrest operators. And nobody is equipping the police on the ground with the tools they need to get the job done.'

The oceans aren't lawless, but the ocean laws don't matter if no one is enforcing them. This is something that can, and that must, be fixed.

In the meantime, Sea Shepherd, and others like them, are still out there every day.

The eyes on our oceans remain vigilant.

5

THE THIEVES

Justice wasn't soft, and neither was she.

Her police-issued boots crunched through the white rocks, sending up orange dust from the dirt below. She approached the entrance to the Stilfontein gold mine, peering down, her blue cap shielding her eyes from the bright sun. Below her, the mineshaft burrowed straight into the earth. The walls of it were smooth, unclimbable, reinforced rock. She had a desire to shout into the void, and felt that she would hear no echo from the darkness. There were allegedly thousands of people somewhere down that hole, up to two kilometres below her feet.

To her, this was a nest of criminals.

She was one of the officers sent here to 'smoke out' the illegal miners, known as zama zamas. As President Cyril Ramaphosa had said in his statement to the nation: 'The Stilfontein mine is a crime scene'.[1] This illegal gold mining site needed to be shut down. As was standard police practice, they had secured the scene and blocked off the escape routes. The only way in or out was the perilous white rope attached by a shaky carabiner above the centre of the void.

For weeks, food and water had been cut off. As government minister Khumbudzo Ntshavheni stated, 'We are not sending help to criminals.'[2] But this decision had been ruled unlawful by a court and hundreds of people had gathered around them. Some of the people had cardboard signs. Others shouted for the return of their husbands, brothers, sons. The protestors called for the police to show mercy and send down supplies so the miners wouldn't die. But to her that was out of the question. These men had made their choice. She was just here to hold them accountable.

Thirst and starvation would drive them up. More would be arrested. And once these men were convicted and detained, or shipped back to wherever they came from, their fate would send a message to all the other criminals out there. Many of them, she had been told, weren't even supposed to be in the country. They had crossed into South Africa illegally just to infiltrate the abandoned mines.

These zama zamas weren't just siphoning off South Africa's veins of gold. This was an assault on the land itself. She had seen the reports. Arsenic contaminated the water, mercury poisoned the soil, and in these scarred landscapes nothing more could grow.

And then there was the violence. Zama zamas were armed and dangerous, implicated in brutal crimes. She had heard stories of extortion, gang rapes, murders. Their presence was a constant threat to good citizens.

She watched with hard eyes as a zama zama was pulled to the surface. He was dirty, pale and weak. Her colleagues searched him, then he was handcuffed and taken away.

This chapter looks at how we can deter environmental criminals, and what happens when the fight goes too far. It tells the story of South Africa's self-declared war on zama zamas.

The opening scene of this chapter is based on news coverage of the controversial Operation Vala Umgodi (or 'Close the Hole'). It was a shocking crackdown on illegal mining that started when I briefly lived in South Africa. I arrived in October 2023, just a week after the president had announced the initiative.[3] Illegal mining was one of the major issues preoccupying the country, and it became a focus of the 2024 election campaign. I could barely turn on the radio or see a newspaper without zama zamas being headline news. This got me thinking about the practical and ethical implications of this kind of ultra-tough-on-crime approach to green crime.

It also made me wonder what kind of person goes into these abandoned mines, doing what I consider to be one of the most terrifying jobs in the world. Entering claustrophobic, underground tunnels where air is scarce and miners know they can get crushed to death at any moment. I spoke with clinical sociologist Vidette Bester, who has worked with zama zamas to understand what drives illegal miners into these perilous conditions. Her research counteracts the caricature of environmental criminals that infiltrates our feeds.

This chapter also explores the role of corruption in green crime, and what interventions can make people more, or less, corruptible. And it asks how we can help dirty informal industries turn to cleaner alternatives.

The war on zama zamas is the story of a tragic incident leading to a harrowing response. It involves secret informants, shady police, and private guards willing to look the other way. But most of all, this is a story about stories. About who controls the narrative of the heroes and villains in the fight for our future.

And the perilous path into this underground world begins with the testimony of a man called Mr X.

INSIDE MAN

Mr X was once a legal miner, part of South Africa's vast gold mining workforce. But when he lost his job, he found himself desperately in need of work. Like everyone else in South Africa, he had heard of the zama zamas. Their illegal work would be far more dangerous than his previous job. He would be crawling through abandoned mineshafts, some barely wide enough for a person to fit through. And he would only be earning half the pay. But he needed the money.

Mr X soon found himself trespassing on the sites of poorly closed gold mines. He was used to wearing protective gear, but in the world of the zama zamas, all he had were his regular clothes. Jeans and a T-shirt were his new uniform. And instead of going home at night, he was now forced to stay in the mines for weeks, or even months. It was gruelling work, and he knew he could get arrested. But still he went down into the muddy, dirty mines.

It is unclear for exactly how long Mr X was a zama zama, but what we do know is that, in 2009, he was caught and arrested. He was told in no uncertain terms that he was a thief and a criminal, and they threatened him with the only thing worse than the mines. He couldn't bear the thought of prison.

That's when he was presented with a choice. Using everything he had learned, all the connections he forged, would he help the authorities take down the zama zamas? Would he agree to work as their man on the inside? It would mean snitching on his friends and colleagues. The men who had taken him in, when losing his legal employment had left him destitute.

But it was still better than prison.

He chose to trade information for his freedom, and from that moment, Mr X lived a secret life. He became a registered informant with the Hawks, a unit of the South African Police Service that targets organised and serious crimes. As part of his cover, by 2014 Mr X was legally employed at the Lily mine, a gold mine in the northeastern bit of the country. His 'handler' was a man called Dirk van den Berg, a security specialist who was part of the Fidelity Group, South Africa's largest private security company. Mr X had been sent to the Lily mine on a specific mission. He was told to find the source of the explosives that had been used in a series of cash-in-transit (CIT) heists.

CIT heists are as brutal as they are precise. Armoured vehicles are ambushed, forced to a stop, and blown open. The guards, armed and protected by bulletproof vests, are often outnumbered by attackers wielding semi-automatic weapons. Some guards are gunned down, others are left to burn alive inside their vehicles. Then, any remaining guns are grabbed, the money is stolen, and the robbers do their best to outsmart and outrun the police. Gory images of these attacks, with blood and bullets and burned-out cars, have been a mainstay of South African news for decades.

The heists are a persistent source of anger and contribute to a widespread fear of crime. In 2014, there was a cash-in-transit incident every other day.[4] The CEO of Fidelity has said that 'CIT robbers are probably the most dangerous people in the South African criminal underworld'.[5] One of the groups organising these brutal attacks in 2014 was thought to be stealing the explosives they were using in the heists from the Lily mine.

With his access to the mine through his legal job, and his previous experience as an illegal miner, Mr X was able to quickly gain the trust of the zama zamas who were a known problem around the mine. And he quickly learned that, as his handler had worried, they were indeed stealing the explosives. They did this by sneaking into the mine and breaking into the storage boxes when the staff weren't paying attention.

But, unlike what his handler had suspected, the explosives weren't intended for CIT attacks. In fact, the explosives never even left the mine. The zama zamas had infiltrated parts of the huge underground network of tunnels that were no longer being worked on by legal miners, using the stolen explosives to blast out the leftover gold.

This is possible because commercial gold mining does not extract all of the gold ore out of a mine. It's expensive to extract gold, so there needs to be a high density of it in an area of rock for the process to be financially worthwhile so quite a lot of little gold nuggets are left behind. The zama zamas were after this leftover gold.

They were most interested in the crown pillar, which was effectively the roof of the mine. This was a slab of solid natural rock, intentionally left to separate the loose rock that filled the former old open-pit mine above ground, and the newer mining tunnels below. Without the crown pillar, the rocks would roll down and fill the tunnels, collapsing the mine. Because of its structural importance, the crown pillar couldn't be mined by the company and it glittered with substantial quantities of visible gold.

This was like a shining beacon for the zama zamas, who were used to working with the dregs of the goldmining process. It was an opportunity they couldn't ignore.

In his undercover role, Mr X saw that the zama zamas had managed to construct scaffolding around parts of the crown pillar. He could see that they were tunnelling horizontally through the rock, following the visible 'band of gold' and drilling 35–40mm holes to cut out the bits of rock that glittered.

There were also bigger holes, called stopes, blasted into the rockface. Each of them was large enough to hold seven or eight people, and provided a temporary refuge during the explosions that made the gold more accessible as they worked their way along the crown pillar. All the equipment they were using had been smuggled in, and it was powered by generators or plugged into the mine's electricity supply through incredibly long extension cables. The tangle of wires, maze of scaffolds, and carefully calibrated holes was an impressive sight.

To make themselves as invisible as possible to guards and police, they would enter or leave the mine only rarely and usually at night, and to ensure that these explosions wouldn't be noticed, they synchronised them with the mine's scheduled blasting. Geologists later testified that the zama zamas' excavations had fundamentally weakened the structure. With every blast, vertical forces pressed down harder on the crown pillar.

After seeing the zama zamas' operation for himself, Mr X confirmed that a thriving criminal network was active in the Lily mine. This was troubling news.

Van den Berg was at constant war with the enemy miners. Illegal mining was, in his words, a 'cancer'. Cancer happens when your own cells turn against you. And Van den Berg would learn that the biggest threat wasn't the people outside his mine, but those already within it. The people he had trusted to keep it safe.

But before we get to the disaster that struck the Lily mine, and how the testimony of Mr X would change the outcome of the trials that followed, it's important to understand the harm that is caused by illegal mining. As the magistrate wrote in the inquest judgement, the illegal miners were 'creating an environment harmful to the health and well-being of a community at large, through the causing of ecological degradation'.[6]

But what harm were they causing, exactly?

DANCING CAT FEVER

'The topic that has probably received the most attention when we talk about environmental damage is the use of mercury in artisanal gold mining,' Vidette Bester told me.

Bester is a clinical sociologist who studies illegal mining in Africa. Her introduction to this world was in 2011, when she was involved in a research project that took her to the Democratic Republic of Congo (DRC). While she was there, she found herself frequently interacting with artisanal miners, and was profoundly impacted by the immense poverty and desperation they faced.

The term artisanal and small-scale mining, shortened to ASM, covers a wide range of mining activities that are both legal and illegal. It includes everything from panning for gold, to digging for gemstones along riverbanks, to using excavators and drills.[7] It is different from large-scale or industrial mining because it has less capital investment, rarely uses heavy machinery or sophisticated tech, and requires more intense manual labour.

As Bester told me, 'There is no universally agreed definition. But, typically, artisanal mining involves hand tools or rudimentary tools with no to minimum level of mechanisation.' ASM also often happens in areas where there are only small amounts left of the metal or mineral being mined. It's too little to be worth it for bigger companies. Like in abandoned mines.

In 2020, the World Bank estimated that at least 44.75 million people across eighty countries were working in artisanal and small-scale mining.[8] That number had more than tripled over the previous two decades. These workers are essential to global supply chains, contributing 80 per cent of the world's sapphires, 25 per cent of global diamonds, 20 per cent of the world's gold, and 18–30 per cent of the world's cobalt. But despite this enormous contribution to industries such as technology, clean energy and luxury goods, their work is largely ignored.

Most artisanal and small-scale mining occurs 'extra-legally', which means it takes place outside of legal economies. This is usually because the miners don't have the licences they need. And sometimes, like in the case of the Lily mine, people are committing crimes by breaking into mine shafts and stealing the gold.

As a sociologist, Bester wanted to know more about the people who were part of this underground world. So she decided to pursue a PhD in sociology at the University of

Johannesburg, and spent years interviewing illegal miners in South Africa. In 2025, she published a book called *The Untold Story of Zama Zama Miners in South Africa: Unearthing Hope*. She explained to me that the mercury use in artisanal mining is a huge problem for humans and nature. 'The release of mercury causes ecological devastation. It goes into water bodies, surface water, and groundwater.'

And the circumstances that led to the discovery that mercury is harmful to our health were both tragic and bizarre.

In the early 1950s, people around Minamata Bay noticed that cats were 'dancing' around the neighbourhood for days, then keeling over and dying on the street. One cat after another danced itself into an early grave. The birds too began behaving in a troubling way, convulsing and falling from the sky.[9] Then, in 1956, a local doctor, Kaneyoshi Noda, reported 'a high incidence of central nervous system disease of unknown etiology' to the department of health.[10]

The loved ones of those affected by the disease later reported that the unexplained illness would worsen day by day, manifesting in convulsions and drooling, and struggling to walk and speak.[11] Some passed away within months, in the isolation of a university-run infectious disease ward. Others who developed the disease, particularly children, were left with lifelong cognitive issues and other impairments. Babies were born with unexplained disabilities. They named the illness Minamata disease, but locally it was known as 'dancing cat fever'. After three years of research, scientists studying the disease stated that the most likely cause was mercury.

It might come as some surprise that we only started to understand the health consequences of mercury in the 1950s, given that in the UK the term 'mad as a hatter' had already been in use a century before, popularised by the tale of *Alice's Adventures in Wonderland*. People knew that hatmakers were more likely to mentally deteriorate, but they didn't understand why. Only because of the dancing cats did we realise that people had gone mad making hats because of the mercury used to make felt, the vapours of which poisoned the hatters.

After the Japanese researchers realised it might be mercury causing this dancing cat fever, they had to test whether their hypothesis was correct. So, one group of researchers went to collect and analyse the industrial runoff that the nearby Chisso petrochemical factory released into Minamata Bay. The scientists also found some stray cats that didn't display any signs of dancing cat fever, and fed them food sprinkled with the mercury-laden water. Then, in their strict experimental setting, they watched the cats to see what would happen.

One of the cats, given the ID No. 400, developed neurological symptoms that matched what had happened in humans. They developed convulsions, drooled, struggled to walk, and eventually died. But people who worked at the Chisso factory argued that this didn't prove anything. To the scientists it was, however, enough evidence to motivate them to keep going. They experimented on ten more cats. Within days, all but one developed severe symptoms, including chronic cramps, weird sprints and jumps, tremors, problems with balance, drooling and paralysis. The animals also lost a huge amount of weight. All of them died within a short period of being forced to develop dancing cat fever. To the researchers this was strong evidence that the mercury from the factory was poisoning the local water.

THE THIEVES

Unfortunately, it took until 1968 for Japanese government officials to finally accept that mercury was the cause of Minamata disease. And, it was only then that the Chisso factory stopped dumping mercury into the bay.

This was one of the most devastating incidents of industrial pollution in history. More than 900 people died and 2 million suffered health problems after eating fish from the bay that were contaminated with mercury. More still are thought to have been left with minor levels of mercury poisoning, which can lead to headaches, hearing loss and the inability to distinguish hot from cold.[12] There is no known cure for Minamata disease.

It would take another few decades for the world to sign the Minamata Convention[13], which came into effect in 2013. This was just a year before Mr X was deployed to the Lily mine. Countries from around the world came to a global agreement to protect human health and the environment by reducing mercury use and emissions, ensuring safe storage and phasing out mercury wherever possible. The agreement is named after Minamata Bay in Japan.

By this point, mercury had been phased out in many industries. But even in the 2024 version of the convention, the secretary-general of the UN, António Guterres, wrote: 'Too few understand that [mercury] is lethal, indestructible and present in everything from coal-fired power generation to certain mascaras and fluorescent lights . . . Like so many contaminants, mercury doesn't just damage individual victims. It damages entire communities. It fuels poverty, feeds conflict and pushes equality further out of reach. Take the example of a young mother working as an artisanal gold miner. While she is poisoned from handling mercury at work, countless others, including her children, are harmed by its impact on the environment'.[14]

The largest source of mercury emissions is artisanal and small-scale gold mining, which is responsible for about a third of the world's mercury emissions. For every kilogram of gold produced, about 1.32 kilograms of mercury is lost into the environment. About a third of this is burned into the air, and the rest seeps into soil and bodies of water.[15]

In the Lily mine, the zama zamas would mix the gold they blasted out of the rock with mercury, making it easier to carry out of the mine undetected. This gold-mercury mix would then be taken to local townships, where the mercury was burned off with a blowtorch and the gold was purified. In poorly ventilated mines or during the cooking-off process, mercury's odourless vapor would be inhaled by the miners, often without them realising the risk.

Because of the harm caused by mercury, countries are expected to have a national action plan to reduce and, where feasible, eliminate its use in artisanal and small-scale gold mining.[16] One way to do this, arguably, is to go to war on the illegal miners.

But it's not just mercury that is a problem. As Vidette Bester told me, 'Across South Africa there are around six thousand abandoned or derelict mines that did not close properly, let alone be rehabilitated to legislation standards. What's going to happen if you don't close them properly?' she asked rhetorically.

One consequence of poor mine closure is tailings mismanagement. 'In Johannesburg alone, there are an estimated 270 tailing dams that are not monitored properly,' Bester elaborated. Tailings are the mineral leftovers from the mining process. In Soweto, a township near Johannesburg that has a long history of gold mining, tailings are piled up all around the low-income neighbourhood. Flat-topped hills loom at the edges of the town. At times, these hills have filled the air and blanketed local communities with a fine dust that has led to widespread complaints of asthma and breathing difficulties.

Other tailings are wet, stored in pools of slurry. Mismanagement of this waste can lead to acid mine drainage. Acid mine drainage is a process in which heavy metals from the mine contaminate nearby lakes, rivers, and underground water sources with arsenic, cyanide and heavy metals, including mercury. Sometimes the waste even contains uranium, which is radioactive. Acid mine drainage and the resulting high concentrations of toxic elements can persist for more than seventy years after a mine has been abandoned.[17]

This has broad health impacts on the humans who live near the mines. People in areas with acid mine drainage can indirectly ingest these toxic chemicals by drinking water irrigated with the polluted water, eating fish that live in the contaminated water, and eating meat from cattle and other animals that drink from the toxic rivers.[18]

Tailings mismanagement can also directly lead to death. In 2022, a mine called the Jagersfontein mine dam burst, with the slurry exploding out and flooding the nearby area. Two people died and one person was never found. Nearly 200 nearby houses and a huge area of agricultural land were damaged in the disaster.[19]

While there can be major issues with mines not disposing properly of their tailings, many legal mines do take precautions to minimise the environmental impact of their operations. However, in the context of small-scale illegal mining, people often have neither adequate skills nor the proper equipment to safely dispose of the toxic substances. When they go into improperly closed sites to mine, they can release some of the tailings, or create more. And the consequences can be catastrophic.

Given how damaging these consequences can be, both for the environment and individuals, why do people risk it?

DON'T OVERTHINK IT

Even though illegal miners know that they need to hide from the police, smuggle in food under the cover of night, and sell their goods to shady people, many don't think of themselves as criminals. As Bester told me, 'The moment that you start probing and having discussions with the zama zamas and you ask them "So why are you doing this?", they will say to you, rather ironically, "Because we don't want to turn to a life of crime."'

To them, stealing gold from an abandoned mine shaft is different from stealing gold from a jeweller. Cooking off mercury is different to making drugs. And a shootout in a mining area is different to a shootout in a township. There is constant rationalisation and minimisation that allow illegal miners to justify their actions. One reason for this is that they understand the consequences of more stereotypical kinds of crime on humans. But they do not recognise the consequences of their own green crimes.

This pattern of rationalising illegal mining is not unique to South Africa. Similar attitudes have been found all over the world.

In a 2022 study conducted in Ghana by researcher Lydia Osei and her colleagues, small-scale gold miners said that there was little or no environmental harm caused by their actions.[20] Some accepted that washing gold could be bad for the local water. But they minimised their own role in this, saying it was other miners who were contaminating the water more than they were. Other miners preferred not to think about it at all. As one of the men said, 'If I overthink about how Galamsey [the illegal mining area] is polluting the water, I can't do this work.'

In cases where there was a lack of knowledge, this meant they were also putting themselves in danger. They were using the water for bathing, drinking and cooking. As some of the miners told the researchers, why would they pollute something they themselves relied on? But scientific illiteracy comes with consequences. The men were effectively unknowingly poisoning themselves, and many miners reported suffering from skin diseases and bowel disorders. These are known consequences of exposure to contaminated water.

The miners were also baffled by the suggestion of the researchers that the soil around the mines was degrading because of their actions. After all, they were not mining on farmland. These were bushy and barren areas where food couldn't grow, and it had been that way long before they got there. They didn't realise that one of the reasons the land stayed infertile was because they kept poisoning it.

One solution to environmental harm is to teach people on the ground about what they are doing, and to propose safer and less harmful alternatives. This is why education, outreach and skills-building to help reduce the use of mercury in small-scale mining is written into the Minamata

Convention on Mercury. Without it, illegal miners will continue to blindly harm themselves and the communities they work in. 'This was said to me by the zama zamas themselves,' Vidette Bester explained, 'and I found it in my fieldwork too. They are completely oblivious to the harms and dangers.'

But education alone is insufficient.

A review of the attempts to curb mercury use in artisanal gold mining found that demonstrating cleaner techniques to local miners didn't work. They didn't suddenly start using them. What did work, however, was when artisanal miners were able to collaborate with gold processing companies and use their facilities.[21] 'This has happened in several African countries,' Bester said. 'Through collaborative efforts involving large gold mining companies, governmental entities, civil society, and the artisanal miners themselves, initiatives are being undertaken to reduce the use of mercury. In some initiatives, artisanal miners are allowed to access facilities to process their ore. In many such instances smelters and processing facilities have been put in place for these illegal miners.' In some cases, workers are then able to sell the gold to the companies. This allows small-scale miners to use cleaner techniques, and it makes them more money than they would get in black market deals.

This financial benefit is important. Many artisanal miners are in this situation in the first place because they are poor, and poverty is a root cause of green crime.[22]

As Bester explained, zama zamas go into illegal mining 'most often absolutely out of desperation. A lot of them will say that they don't like it. If something else comes along, then many will grab an alternative opportunity.' South Africa, she stressed, 'has an unemployment rate of nearly 40 per cent, as estimated in 2024'.

'Of course, not all zama zamas act with the purest intent, and there is a criminal element in the sector that cannot – and should not – be ignored,' she continued. 'But to label and treat every zama zama as a criminal without an interrogation of the drivers of this sector is wrong.'

Bester also told me that there is a misconception that only men are zama zamas and go into the mines. 'The literature confirms that women are most often involved in the crushing of ore and other supportive work. This is correct. However, when I had my discussions, some women do go underground,' she told me. The miners she spoke to explained that the gender division of labour is site-specific. The work at some zama zama sites is more gender-integrated than others.

Like men, women are also in this work to make ends meet. But, unlike men, 'When I had my discussions with the women artisanal miners, they viewed it as a way to get away from exploitive domestic work.' In South Africa a lot of women get paid very little to be 'domestics'. 'So for them,' explained Bester, 'it was a way to earn a better living and, for example, pay for schooling for their children or to look after their elderly parents and the wider family.'

This is one of the reasons Bester was first drawn to studying illegal mining. 'The levels of poverty and desperation just struck me, and also the power imbalance between governments and cooperatives on the one hand, and the impoverished on the other. It's also dangerous. I remember once having a discussion with a zama zama, and his friend had passed away the previous week because of a rockfall underground. He told me that since then he is scared every day to go into the mines.' The miners sometimes get crushed when the overworked tunnels collapse, or they can suffocate from lack of air.

Despite the demonstrated positive impacts of collaborations between artisanal miners and gold companies, South Africa has chosen to go to war against the zama zamas. And, illegal miners are treated as hardened criminals.

This takes us back to the Lily mine, where Mr X found the integrity of the crown pillar was being gradually eroded with stolen dynamite. What was unusual about this situation was that the mine was still active. It was filled with dozens of employed legal miners, who were going in and out of the mine every single day. How did no one notice that stuff was going missing?

As it turned out, staff had noticed.

CRIMINAL CHAMELEONS

Dirk van den Berg, the security expert and handler of Mr X, had a theory. There were two types of criminals infiltrating the mines. The 'illegal miners' were people from abroad, often from Mozambique, Zimbabwe or Swaziland, who mined on their own and were part of a criminal syndicate. But it was the second group they really had to watch out for. He explained that the 'criminal miners' employed by the mine were stealing from their employers and facilitating the illegal mining.

Finding illegal miners was easy, but criminal miners? They were chameleons.

Mr X knew this more than most, after retracing the movements of the zama zamas in the Lily mine. They got into the mine either by paying bribes or by dressing up as legal mine workers. And those who didn't want to go in through the expensive front door found other ways. 'There were many ways of accessing Lily Mine, including through ventilation shafts,' Mr X later said in court. 'We also used holes that led us deep into the mine.'[23]

They would bring expensive drills and generators with them, paid for by the gold buyers on the surface. And corrupt mine employees would give the zama zamas other things they needed, including lamps and drills. Because the zama zamas would spend weeks, or even months, underground, a gold-for-food bartering system emerged. The corrupt mine employees would bring the zama zamas chicken, tins of food, and bottled drinks. They even helped the zama zamas get access to some of the explosives.

According to Mr X, one of those complicit went by the nickname Yster. Yster is an Afrikaans word that means 'iron'. He was the head of mine security. And, according to witnesses who would later testify, not only was he involved, his family were too, as were the employees at the mine who worked for him.

When mine employees were asked about the situation at the Lily mine, many denied ever seeing the zama zamas. But some, including the general manager of the mine, Mr Potas, told frightening stories. In 2009 he was involved in the investigation of a hostage situation where the police were called. The police did a sweep of the level known to be popular amongst the zama zamas, and they found drills and generators. Mr Potas had also seen them on CCTV, sneaking around and using the mine equipment.

Those who did speak of the zama zamas were also afraid of them.

Not only were the hallways of the Lily mine deep underground, they mostly consisted of long, straight corridors, with access between the levels only at select points. Mining only ever took place in a few sections, so much of it was empty. The employed miners who admitted learning about the problem, stayed away from the areas known to be illegally mined. They feared that if one of the zama zamas pulled a weapon, there would be nowhere to run.

When the terrified staff at the Lily mine did turn to the police for help, they were of little assistance. The police would confiscate equipment from the zama zamas, only to later return it to them.

Vidette Bester also came across this in her interviews with the illegal miners. 'Most often, the police will come and confiscate their tools, the few tools they have, and basically tell them "if you don't give us X amount of money, you won't get your tools back." They are asking for bribes.' Meanwhile, the women she talked to said that the only challenge they faced was abuse by the police. A report that came out in 2019 found that women working as zama zamas are often pressured into sexual favours to avoid arrest.[24]

In the Lily mine case, according to witnesses, police dockets on the miners would allegedly also get 'lost', meaning those who could have been prosecuted did not face legal consequences. Some of the police were themselves scared, others were allegedly actively complicit.

A family member of the head of mine security was also allegedly involved in the corruption, and he was a police constable.

Despite all this, it seems that the security situation wasn't even as bad as it was in other mines. As the mine manager later said in court 'Lily mine is a kindergarten.'[25]

Corruption is so fundamental to this case, and green crime in general, that it deserves deeper understanding. Only then can we truly understand what happened next to that crumbling crown pillar.

CORRUPTIBILITY

Corruption has been called the 'universal facilitator' of environmental crime.[26] Almost every interview I've done with environmental experts has made it clear that, without tackling corruption, all other efforts will be undermined.

Somewhat surprisingly, there is no universal definition of corruption. But, probably the most widely used definition comes from the anti-corruption organisation Transparency International, who define corruption as the abuse of entrusted power for private gain.[27]

While we can all be corruptors, we cannot all be corrupt. To be corrupt you need to have something to offer. Specifically, someone has to have entrusted you with power. And you need to then swap access to your power for something that benefits you. The most common context in which people talk about corruption is in the public sectors, including politics and law enforcement. That's because these jobs depend on ethically managing the power that society entrusts them with.

On the surface, corruption is simply someone asking *what's in it for me?* But the boundaries can be hazy. Where is the line between corruption and making conditions favourable for a business deal? Is the bro-rocracy of some public officials inherently a form of corruption, or is giving favourable treatment to people you know just an expected and acceptable facet of being human? Is taking the dean of a university out for an expensive dinner, hoping that it will encourage them to admit your child, corruption? What about a public official who pockets a good salary and decides to spend most of their week on the golf course instead of in the office?

Everyone has a corruption threshold. An ethical line that they will not cross to get something for themselves at the expense of society. This is why corruption has been called a 'thick' ethical concept with a lot of 'conceptual normativity'. In other words, what people believe to be corrupt behaviour depends on who they surround themselves with, and the culture they come from. Added to this, each of us constantly has to redraw our ethical line because it can fade surprisingly quickly when we aren't paying attention.

The UN has a number of categories of behaviours that count as corruption. Like bribery, which is exchanging something of value for influence, and embezzlement, which is stealing or misusing money that you have been trusted with. There is also the abuse of functions, which involves misusing a position of power to gain an unfair advantage or harm others. Money laundering is making illegally gained money or resources look like they were legally obtained, and illicit enrichment is when there is no way that the money someone has comes from legal sources.

Then there is what I think is the most interesting type of corruption – trading in influence, also called influence peddling. It often involves giving someone an advantage so they can, in turn, misuse their position to influence someone else; and laws regarding trading in influence aim to reach those who are in the 'neighbourhood of power'.[28]

An example of influence peddling would be a mining company CEO promising to bring jobs to an area, which would make a minister look good, as long as the minister puts in a 'good word' to the president so the company can get a mining licence. It's really hard to prove and can come awfully close to what lobbyists do, although lobbying isn't illegal.

Political scientists Kristina Weißmüller and Anna Zuber wanted to understand what makes public officials corruptible.[29] As they put it, 'Public sector corruption is one of the most pressing unresolved issues of our time.' They needed to figure out the psychological aspects that makes corruption more likely, and the context in which it normally happens. In 2023, they synthesized ninety-three studies from forty-three countries and found that corruptibility is not just about greed. It relies on a lot of rationalisation. That's how Weißmüller and Zuber came up with the micro-foundations of corruptibility. These are the psychological and contextual factors that together make it more likely for someone to engage in corruption. They set a public official's 'general benchmark of corruptibility'.

One of the micro-foundations is someone's basic access to information, which the researchers called 'corruption awareness'. An individual who doesn't understand what counts as corruption is, unsurprisingly, more likely to engage in it.

Other micro-foundations involve specific character traits related to corruptibility. They found that people who are more selfish, lie often and take more risks are more likely to be corrupt. This is partly because they tend to morally justify their behaviour in a self-serving way. This relationship between personality and corruption is amplified when the person thinks that everyone is like them. That everyone is engaging in corruption, which normalises it. Or, when people convince themselves that there is too much 'red tape'. The red tape argument can be a convenient story that some people use to justify why they should break the rules and get a little something extra on the side.

To Weißmüller and Zuber there is also a central inner conflict that is hardly discussed but is crucial for understanding corruption, which affects what they call the 'moral locus of accountability'. This happens when people have to choose between serving society and helping individuals that they have personal relationships with.

For example, in the case of the Lily mine, allegedly the brother of a police officer asked him to ignore the illegal miners. The police officer then had to decide whether to help his brother, or whether he should uphold the ethical code of his job. If he chose to help his brother, this would be a shift in his moral locus of accountability. He would shift from feeling morally accountable to society, which you can picture as a huge circle of people, to being accountable to an individual, or a tiny circle.

This is how corruption can deceptively feel like altruism. Because it isn't always a selfish decision; at least not inherently. It is a shift in focus. In fact, it can feel very much like selflessness, because the person might be risking their job in order to help someone in their inner circle. But what the person has decided is that their inner circle is more important than society as a whole. Which is, at its core, selfish and entitled. Why should individuals in their inner circle be allowed to bend the rules, just because they know someone with power?

The opposite of this kind of belief is something called public service motivation. People who really want to serve the public interest are less likely to engage in corruption. Public service motivation is on a scale, and it depends on how important work is to someone, why they went into the job in the first place, and how rewarding they find their work.

What also matters is whether people feel like they are being adequately compensated for their work. That's why researchers have studied whether people who make less money are more corruptible. And the answer they have found is somewhat counterintuitive.

First of all, what matters isn't necessarily a person's actual salary, but their salary satisfaction. This is often related to the actual number, but not always. If someone is unhappy about how much they are paid, they are more likely to be corruptible, because they will look around at their colleagues and friends and believe they aren't getting their fair share. This is called relative deprivation. And if someone thinks they are being treated unfairly, this can lead to resentment and a willingness to engage in corruption. These feelings are often related to actual deprivation, as those who get paid the least in an organisation are also often the least happy about how much they are earning. But there can also be a misperception. An unhappiness that grows based on how much more someone assumes their colleagues earn.

So, now we have looked at the psychological foundations of corruptibility, how can we stop it from happening?

THE PRICE OF HONESTY

You might think that paying those at the bottom levels more money could fix this, so they feel better about how much they earn. This is the premise of performance-related pay for civil servants, which involves offering them bonuses for ethical work.

But in an investigation into a performance-related pay programme in South Africa, political scientist Aksel Sundström found that bonuses can actually backfire.[30] The bonuses in the programme they studied were being co-opted by corrupt senior managers and used as additional rewards for junior colleagues in exchange for collusion. Instead of being used to promote ethical behaviour, this money was accidentally encouraging even more unethical behaviour.

That's because there is a U-shaped relationship between salary and corruption. Those who get paid the least and those who get paid the most are most likely to engage in it; the people in the middle are less likely. Why? Because those at the top can feel untouchable, and they often directly exploit the vulnerability of those paid the least. They are also the people with the most access to the things that people want. They have the ability to fast-track permits or give out licences, or make paperwork disappear.

For many environmental resources, licences are a good idea in principle. They are one way to check that a person or company who is going to extract resources is not going to take too much, or leave the environment broken. But this system can only work if licensing is actually feasible for the people it is trying to control, and if poorly managed it can open up corruption loopholes.

At the moment, for many ASM workers around the world, the barriers are way too high. Licences often cost money, as does buying the mining tools that are necessary in order to qualify for the licences in the first place. And given that these workers are often doing these 'dirty' jobs because they are poor, they often don't have the money to get their operation up to a legally compliant standard.

Applying for licences also requires a certain level of education and understanding to complete the often complicated paperwork. Most artisanal and small-scale miners come from rural areas and have very little access to education or the internet. Some miners, especially those who didn't start off in legal mining, don't even know they need a licence. Others, including migrant workers or people from marginalised communities, distrust the government and prefer to remain anonymous.[31] And in some places, even if you do all the right things, and have enough money, there are simply no licences available. It is in this kind of poorly applied system that corruption is particularly likely to flourish, because it is, or seems to be, impossible to do things legally.

Sundström also found that tackling corruption is not just about incentivising honesty, it's about reducing the cost of it.[32] Being honest can come with punishments. In one of his studies, he spoke with South African inspectors who enforce marine regulations in areas where gangs run illegal fishing operations. He didn't just interview current compliance inspectors but also former ones, who no longer faced the potential risks of speaking up.

The inspectors explained that bribes were so ingrained in the culture of these industries that their bosses would approach them and expect them to hand over a cut of the bribes. If they decided to go clean, this made their bosses upset and had negative consequences. They would be passed over when it came time for promotion. Even worse, some were intimidated or threatened with violence. This made the inspectors feel forced into taking the bribes, even if they didn't want to.

For their managers and bosses, this was partly because they wanted the extra cash. But there was also surely a fear that if someone stopped participating in the corruption, then they could become a liability. If, instead, they were all forced to participate in the crimes, who would be willing to speak up? It would be too risky, as it would mean incriminating themselves too. Thus, by forcing everyone to be an accomplice, it kept the corruption bubble safe from prickly police officers.

Perhaps we should turn the question of corruption around. Why does anyone stay honest? Especially for those at the top, what's the protective factor against corruption?

The Weißmüller and Zuber review found that those who are more able to resist the pull of the corrupt undertow keep at the front of their minds why their jobs are important to society. And they remember that they have the power to make their own decisions, even if sometimes they feel powerless. Keeping a sense of personal agency is crucial.

Corruption has long been studied by political scientists, but corruption related to the environment has only recently become a priority for anti-corruption experts. It is only since 2019 that the UN Convention against Corruption has explicitly included that states should engage in 'preventing and combating corruption as it relates to crimes that have an impact on the environment'.³³ This put anti-corruption clearly on the green crime map.

There are many examples of corruption in environmental settings. Some of these were listed in the first-ever UN report on the matter, published in 2023. They include trading in influence to steer environmental policies in a way that allows businesses to extract natural resources rather than protect them; the abuse of functions or the use of bribery to get export or import permits for protected species or toxic waste; and using bribes to prevent inspections in a protected area, like paying off police to not properly police a nature reserve.

These kinds of acts are hard to prove, because corruption is done in secret. Why would people in positions of power who are corrupt commission investigations into themselves? And even if they did, surely we couldn't trust the outcomes of these investigations? Such is the conundrum of corruption research.

One of the only investigations into environmental corruption was published by Interpol in 2016 as part of Project LEAF, and involved a global assessment of corruption in the forestry sector. The researchers found that this kind of 'green corruption' cost global economies around $29 billion in lost revenue and lost resources.

To learn more about how people are tackling corruption related to the environment, I spoke to Juhani Grossmann. He heads the Green Corruption division at the Basel Institute, an anti-corruption institution based in Switzerland.

'What we're trying to do with our programme is target the finances of natural resource crimes and corruption,' he told me. 'Our team of about twenty is split more or less half and half between prevention and enforcement. The enforcement staff typically have a background as ex-police officers or ex-prosecutors.'

His team write analytical and advisory reports for law enforcement to strengthen criminal cases related to the environment, focusing on financial elements. The idea is to help government agencies follow the money right to the corruption, and then ideally to root it out.

'The most common type of corruption in the natural resource space that we have observed is license-related corruption,' he explained. 'That typically involves bribery, but can also be more subtle than that. The permits can include those for drilling, logging or mining rights, as well as environmental impact assessments and other certifications.'

But catching perpetrators of environmental corruption takes time. Grossmann needs to convince financial donors, investigators and prosecutors to invest several years into a single case. This can be a hard sell, because of the focus on quick results. But when corruption has led to a lot of money or other assets being stolen, it can be worth it not just in terms of the environment but also for the governments and companies who want their money back.

Originally, the Basel started its Green Corruption programme with a focus on wildlife crime, but more recently they have shifted towards forestry cases. 'Lately, we have also seen a rise in other minerals, such as gold,' Grossmann said. His team's focus is on South America, another hub for legal and illegal gold mining.

Why gold? 'There are significant corruption risks and enforcement challenges in seizing illegally mined gold,' he explained, so authorities need support.

The chemical properties of gold are one such challenge.

'The physical attributes of gold make it perfect for laundering. Once it's refined, there's no way to tell where its origin was.' This is different from, say, trees, which can be more easily traced back to where they grew by the right experts.

Grossmann also told me that people's assumptions about corruption can be wrong. It's not just people in private corporations that do favours for politicians, police or licence-providers. State-run companies can also be culprits, and they often operate under much less scrutiny than the private sector because they are seen as an extension of the state. Collaborative deceit is also common between private companies and the police.

The cost of environmental corruption is huge. But there is what Grossman calls a 'green corruption paradox'. As he explained, 'There is significant corruption, significant illicit resources being extracted. But at the same time, the resources being allocated to tackle them remain very, very small.'

And, as security expert Dirk van den Berg said, corruption is a problem that can spread like cancer.

And, sometimes, cancer is deadly.

DARKNESS FALLS

On the morning of 5 February 2016, zama zamas waited in the Lily mine.

The miners were pleased that today it was their turn to access the famous band of gold. Their bosses rotated who got to go up into the holes, to make sure everyone got their bit of the treasure.

With each breath they inhaled the fine dust created by

their own drilling, and something sulphuric lingered in the air. They retreated to one of the many bigger holes that were visible throughout the crown pillar. There was room for seven, maybe eight, people.

The zama zamas knew from one of the legal miners that the morning blast was scheduled for 6.22 a.m. They had timed their own blast to perfectly coincide, hoping that this would make their comparatively small explosion undetectable. Right on time, they ignited the explosive.

Then they got to work extracting the ore.

At 8 a.m. that same morning, truck driver Aaron Sithole pulled up to the site for work. He crossed the surface of the main pit, a flat rocky area, drab and lifeless. The only structure of note was an unspectacular box-like building known as the lamp room. It was where staff checked in and grabbed basic things before heading into the mine.

Sithole saw some of his colleagues in the lamp room, gave them a friendly nod, and reported for work. Then he crawled into his heavy-duty truck to collect that day's gold-bearing ore from the depths. Slowly, the heavy tires pulled him towards the simple white sign with the name of the mine in hand-painted black letters.

He had just passed the entrance to the mine and turned on his headlights when suddenly there was a terrifying noise. The air filled with dust. It felt like he was suffocating. Suddenly, he was in a darkness so absolute that it felt like the world had disappeared.

He clambered out of his truck, struggling to find his way, confused by what was happening. His heart was exploding out of his chest. He knew he had to focus on just one thing. Direct all of his energy into one sense. He thought only of his hands, using them to see, to guide him, stumbling, to the back of the truck. When he turned around, light was making its way through the swirling dust.

The earth was giving way.

As if spared by an invisible energy, he found himself standing on a precipice. He watched as an avalanche of earth took down the lamp room behind him, and everything near it.

It only took twelve seconds for the crown pillar to give way and the mine to collapse.

The colleagues he had only just said good morning to had been swallowed whole.

After the shock subsided from the collapse, a rescue effort began. Employees of the mine were trapped underground with no ventilation. But how many, and who, were down there was difficult to know. The identity cards of those who had checked in were stored in the lamp room, and that had tumbled down multiple storeys into the sinkhole below.

Luckily, it didn't take long for the surface team to make contact with the crew underground, and seventy-six miners were brought to safety, including Aaron Sithole. But the three in the lamp room were trapped, and no one could figure out how to get to them. For weeks, excavations took place, with the loved ones of the trapped miners staying hopeful. But as the weeks turned to months and the lamp room remained inaccessible, it became clear to most people that not only were they probably dead, they might never be pulled out of this pit. Despite this, for years, the families of two of the miners desperately held on to hope that their children were still alive.[34]

Tragically, to this day, the bodies of Solomon Nyirenda, Yvonne Mnisi and Pretty Nambule remain entombed.

Mr X had known that the zama zamas were mining the crown pillar that day. But he couldn't stop them. And as he later told the court, we will never know whether any of the zama zamas died in the collapse. If they did, their secrets died with them.

The Lily mine inquest was launched to understand what went wrong and who was responsible. The hearings lasted more than a year, revealing compelling interviews with thirty witnesses, only some of whom were willing to open up about the situation in the mine.

After every witness had spoken, and the judge had time to interpret the submissions, on 19 October 2023, Magistrate Annamarie van der Merwe published the judgement. One of her key findings was 'the failure of the South African Police Services and the Department of Minerals and Energy, to assist the Lily mine management in their efforts to combat illegal mining and/or to effectively and constructively address the problem of illegal mining, thereby failing their Constitutional duties'.[35]

Three weeks later, on 9 November, the president of South Africa announced a drastic response. He authorised the military and the police to hire 3,300 people to 'conduct an intensified anti-criminality operation against illegal mining'.[36] The war on zama zamas was officially underway.

That decision would lead to the scene I described at the beginning of this chapter. The police barricading the Stilfontein mine, potentially trapping thousands of miners underground. Starving them to 'smoke them out'. But before we get back to them, I want to look more closely at this whole situation. On the surface, the war on zama zamas seems like a fight for our planet and the safety of communities. But is that really what this is about?

The press coverage of the war on zama zamas was fuelled by fear, and a wave of anxiety seemed to be building. Behind the rhetoric of public safety was a troubling element that I couldn't ignore. To the public, this was being presented as a fight between honest South Africans and dangerous illegal migrant 'thugs'. It's a story we've heard before.

A dangerous one.

Vidette Bester also mentioned this to me when we spoke, explaining that 'xenophobia is sadly embedded in the social landscape of South Africa'. You might think that given the long history of white colonialists' brutal treatment of Black Africans that the xenophobia would be directed at, say, the Dutch or the British. But in this case, it's actually directed at Black people from neighbouring African countries.

Bester told me that she was highly critical of the media and how they portrayed zama zamas. 'There are certain misconceptions that get recycled over and over,' she explained. 'It's not always criminal men and illegal immigrants who are involved in zama zama mining.' While many illegal miners come from neighbouring countries, some are legal migrants, and others were born in South Africa. The historic migrant labour system also cannot be ignored. Bester explained to me that, for years, migrants were lured to South Africa to work in the mines. The media also ignore the women involved in illegal mining.

The image of highly armed zama zamas was also misleading.

'While there are killings and turf wars related to illegal mining, these incidents of extreme violence are not wholly representative. But, Bester told me, 'The moment it happens, the media jumps in and they report it, disregarding the heterogenous nature of the zama zama sector.' This is how the idea of the dangerous illegal miner crystallises in the minds of the public into a terrifying menace that must be destroyed. In the world of environmental messaging, this kind of truth distortion is, unfortunately, quite common.

FALSE NARRATIVES

People are constantly massaging reality until it submits to their wishes. Spreading false information like seed bombs, hoping some will germinate in the minds of the masses. And it isn't just coming from the people you might expect it to. In the fight for the planet, people on all sides play dirty with the facts.

*Dis*information is when someone intentionally spreads false information in order to deceive people or for some goal. *Mis*information is spread by people who believe that what they are sharing is true, but what they share is inaccurate or misleading.

Research has found that people worry a lot about misinformation. But we tend to worry about how it affects other people, not ourselves. This is called the third-person effect, which is the belief that misinformation is a threat not because we are gullible, but because other people are. Particularly people who are 'distant' from us and we barely know.

Unfortunately, not realising our own vulnerability opens us up to being a spreader of misinformation, because we let our guard down. In 2024, one study found that as people in the US and UK became more worried about misinformation, they were also more willing to like and share 'alarmist narratives' about it. In other words, people were more likely to share misinformation . . . about misinformation.[37]

The same is true for environmental falsehoods. We all believe some things that aren't true, we just don't realise it. When we interact with the world around us, it can be easy to spot climate change deniers, but harder to identify those sharing alarmist, exaggerated or incorrect posts that seem to support our side of the argument. This can make us complicit in the spreading of misinformation.

Lobbyists, particularly those in contentious sectors like mining or fossil fuels, have long perfected the art of shaping narratives to suit their interests and lean into alarmism.

A popular corporate political strategy used by lobbyists is the policy dystopia model. This is when people focus on the potential economic losses of a proposed policy and instil fear that the green policy won't even be effective. This is disinformation, because it is an intentionally alarmist narrative that deliberately overstates the perceived risks of change in favour of maintaining the status quo.[38] The public is inundated with messages about job losses and economic collapse, to rally opposition to a green policy and reinforce the framing of environmental regulations as dangerous or unnecessary.

Environmental disinformation can also misdirect our time and energy towards environmental fights that are either insignificant or inefficient. One of the examples that I think of almost every day is the steady diet of misinformation and disinformation we have been fed about plastic waste.

Decades of campaigns have taught us to wash, sort and recycle our plastics. The message is allegedly one of empowerment. That by doing this, every single one of us is helping to save the planet, one rinsed yoghurt pot at a time. I remember, as a child in the 1990s, seeing awareness campaigns about recycling everywhere. Campaigns where plastic packaging was given little animated eyes, legs and bodies. Asking us to give it a 'new life' by recycling.

They managed to make plastic waste cute.

And I'm furious about it.

Plastic is a petroleum product. And 'big oil' has long promised that recycling, rather than plastic bans, is the best way forward.[39] But in the past few years it's come to light that while lobbyists and petroleum company press teams have told the world that the majority of plastic can, and will, be recycled, they have known this isn't true.[40] In the 1970s, industry leaders had already expressed serious doubt that plastic recycling would ever be economically feasible.[41]

It takes a lot of energy to clean, sort and melt plastic. And even when you do, it downgrades every time it is recycled, which means that the quality gets worse, so it can only really be reused a few times. That's why in most countries, a huge amount of recyclables are burned or buried, even when we think we're doing everything correctly. A 2024 investigation into the soft plastic recycling schemes in supermarkets in the UK found that 70 per cent of these plastics were burned rather than recycled.[42] And the plastics that aren't burned domestically are shipped from wealthy countries to poorer ones, where the plastic is often inappropriately dealt with and causes environmental harm.

On top of that, recycling is often so complicated that people give up and 'wishcycle' instead. That's when we put a container into the recycling and hope for the best, even if we don't know whether it can actually be recycled. Research has found that in 2024 basically everyone was doing it: governments, food producers, waste management companies, and individuals.[43]

There's a conflict here. The reason people sort their rubbish, and wishcycle, is because we care about what happens to the Earth and we trust that we have been told the truth. When investigations find that our trust has been betrayed, it can lead to anger and disengagement.

What we should be encouraged to do, is to avoid buying plastics and opt for things that can be easily recycled instead, like cardboard, glass and aluminium. Even better, try to avoid unnecessary packaging, and instead buy in bulk.

That's what the public service messaging should have focused on all along. Instead, plastics manufacturers have been allowed to put a dizzying burden of responsibility onto consumers.

Meanwhile, the necessary change in regulations that would actually reduce the amount of plastic in the world remains shockingly untouched.[44] There is some potential hope with the UN's 2022 global treaty to end plastic pollution. But even that has been slow, and well into 2025 no agreement had been reached.[45]

In the meantime, individuals are still drowning in plastic and being blamed for it. It's environmental gaslighting.

The disinformation was originally disseminated because selling the fantasy of recycling meant that people would buy more plastic.[46]

When something is repeated often enough, we are more likely to believe it. This is called the illusion of truth effect. It comes from our tendency to focus on cues that have nothing to do with the information itself, in order to determine whether we think something is true or not. These illusory truth effects can last for months after the first exposure to misinformation. And they are unrelated to how clever people are.[47] Even people who start off accurately knowing something, like that we should be reducing waste rather than focusing on recycling, can be pushed into overwriting these accurate beliefs with misinformation if they are repeatedly exposed to it.

Trying to undo the illusion of truth effect is also difficult. Researchers have found that, even when information has been debunked and people accept that it is wrong, misinformation is likely to have a lingering influence on reasoning.[48] The continued influence effect is that niggling feeling in the back of your mind that makes you subtly doubt facts that you know to be true. We accumulate compelling, fear-based narratives, and these undermine our confidence in the truth.

We can see this in the constructed menace of the illegal miner. Zama zamas are portrayed as greedy thugs from abroad who are endangering the lives and environment of the good people of South Africa. When really, most illegal miners are marginalised, desperately poor, exploited migrants who would rather be doing almost anything else rather than risking their lives underground.

Zama zamas are to environmental crime as plastic recycling is to the climate crisis. A misdirection.

Vidette Bester told me that 'a police clampdown is entirely putting the focus on the wrong issue'. As she explained, 'If the government is not creating jobs in the formal sector, nor stimulating the informal sector, and then you have these abandoned mine sites that are not closed properly and no rehabilitation has been done – so the land has not been restored and no one can use it, for example, for subsistence farming – what do you do?'

She continued, passionately: 'All of those things are driving this highly unsustainable sector, zama zama mining.'

When I asked her whether she thinks small-scale mining like this should be a crime, she said, 'Not at all. I think what needs to happen is that proper regulation should be put in place. The best way to address it is by formalising it.'

The fight for our planet cannot be a war on the poor.

If we mistake poverty for environmental malice, we will lose. People are going to keep pulling resources out of the ground. The key is to help make it as harmless and sustainable as possible, and to create jobs in sustainable industries that will help to absorb the shock of extractive industries moving or closing down.

THE SIX PILLARS OF ILLEGAL MINING

Illegal mining in South Africa illustrates how the six pillars of green crime create fertile ground for zama zamas to thrive.

Ease stemmed from poorly managed mine closures. Companies often abandon sites without restoring the land, leaving them accessible to illegal miners. Even active mines, like the Lily mine, are riddled with corruption, allowing easy entry for unlawful activity.

Impunity was uncovered by the Lily mine inquest. Witnesses described how employed miners and security staff facilitated zama zamas with an entire underground economy. Police often turned a blind eye, and were easily bribed.

Greed was evident in the corporations that abandoned the mines, presumably knowing the harm this could cause.

Rationalisation allowed zama zamas to downplay the environmental harm, or the fact that they were committing a crime at all, Others acknowledged it but chose not to 'overthink' it.

Conformity was seen in and around Lily Mine. While the manager of the mine allegedly demanded that others accept bribes to let the zama zamas in, police allegedly normalised allowing them to continue with only minor fines and temporary tool confiscations.

Desperation loomed largest. When mines close, they leave behind environmental decay and joblessness. Former miners return to work illegally, while high unemployment in South Africa and neighbouring countries like Mozambique and Zimbabwe drives others to join.

Together, the six pillars created the conditions for the tragedy of the mine collapse, and the overreaction that followed. It is easy for information about the environment to get out of hand, but it's important that we stop false narratives from dictating our reactions. So, how can we stop this kind of false information from spreading?

PREBUNKING

In a 2022 review of how to change false beliefs, Ullrich Ecker from the University of Western Australia and his colleagues found two methods of guarding ourselves against misinformation.[49]

Prebunking involves building resistance before we are exposed to false information. Just like vaccines introduce a weakened form of a virus to build immunity, prebunking introduces weakened persuasive tactics to bolster critical thinking. This involves two components: warning about the threat of misinformation, and highlighting the deceptive techniques commonly used.

For example, teaching people how companies can cherry-pick data to create misleading climate narratives, by only using information that supports a certain view rather than showing the whole picture. Or how to make sure that someone who is voicing an opinion on something actually has the relevant qualifications to make an informed statement about it. Or even how emotional, negative and fear-based language can override our better judgement. By recognizing the common tactics used in disinformation, people can better resist its tempting lure.

On the other side, there is debunking, which is when accurate information is presented after misinformation to try to undo the harm. This often requires someone else to point out that the information is untrue. If you have ever found that trying to debunk other people's misconceptions is really hard, that's because it is. But Ullrich and colleagues found that there are some things that make debunking more effective, such as providing detailed corrections that include alternative explanations to make the correction more memorable. Merely contradicting a claim without offering context is less effective.

The thing is, when people think about an issue, they tend to remember both the misinformation and the correction. And at a later date, your brain needs to choose which one to remember. It's like when you reach into the cupboard for a snack. You get to choose between the fresh, tasty, delicious snack, and the one that is thin, stale and out of date. You want the most delicious-looking memory fragment to be the correct information, so that your brain chooses it every time. To make the memory of the correct information more appealing, you want it to be filled with more examples and detail than your memory of the false information.

When it comes to tackling green crime, we need to share accurate information so that the strong grip of misinformation and disinformation on people's opinions can loosen. And, most importantly, every day we need to actively avoid letting our fear and outrage push us into sharing dystopian narratives that are untrue and alarmist. The same is important when it comes to news stories about social issues in our local communities, like the sensationalist coverage of zama zamas in South Africa.

Instead of declaring war on the poor, governments need to help mining companies to appropriately manage and close their operations, and hold the mines legally and financially accountable when they fail to do so.

At the moment, unfortunately, environmentalists, lawyers and regulators bear the brunt of proving that a company is not compliant with environmental laws. But it's hard to prove the negative, what companies haven't done. Their inaction and noncompliance. Instead, environmental lawyer Sophie Lemaître told me, the burden of proof should be on the companies. They should have to demonstrate that they have done everything they can according to environmental law.

But it can be hard for people, and governments, to change course. Even when the experts and the evidence all point in the same direction and change is called for to protect people and the planet. After the judgement in the Lily mine inquest was published, it wasn't a crackdown on corruption that was initiated. Instead, the government went on a rampage.

Which brings us back to our opening scene.

AN OVERWHELMING STENCH

By late 2024, the police and the military had been guarding the entrance to the Stilfontein mine for months. But as spring turned to summer, everything was getting more heated.

Each time a new emaciated miner emerged, the police swarmed towards them, handcuffed them, and took them away.

Most of the zama zamas emerging from the mine were foreign nationals from Mozambique and Zimbabwe. Some claimed they had been lured to South Africa to work legally in mining or construction. They explained that only when they arrived had they realised that they would be going into the mines illegally. Those who didn't approve of these new criminal instructions were forced to comply. This tracks, because offering fake jobs to people abroad is a well-documented recruitment tactic of zama zama bosses. But excuses are cheap, and it was hard to know exactly what to believe since the illegal miners were also trying to downplay their own crimes, especially after enduring such suffering while trapped underground.

Already, a couple of weeks into the barricade, the miners who had stayed underground were reportedly eating toothpaste mixed with toilet paper to try to keep their hunger pangs under control. Notes were sent up begging for HIV medication. Within a month, many were severely dehydrated and starving. Those who surrendered to the police said that the situation underground was dire.

People who wanted to exit the mine were being told not to by their bosses. Some of those who tried to leave, including teenagers, were beaten.

The day the first dead body was sent up was the day the public support for the mission really soured. On 16 November 2024, almost exactly a month after the mine was first barricaded, a court ordered that the crackdown on the mine was violating the constitution. The police were told that the mine 'shall be unblocked and may not be blocked by any person or institution whether government or private'. It was made very clear that any person in the mine should be allowed to exit.

But, the South African Police Force responded defensively saying that they weren't stopping anyone from leaving the mine, and that 'all those who resurface will continue to be assessed by emergency medical personnel on site, as has been the case'.[50] In the eyes of the police, these criminals just needed to be willing to face the consequences of their actions.

Against court orders, Operation Vala Umgodi did not slow down. Access to water and food at the Stilfontein mine continued to be blocked. Almost 1,500 zama zamas left the mine and were arrested.[51]

But eventually the flow of people turned into a trickle, sputtering out the last clusters of survivors. After a group of fifty miners emerged on 28 November, it was thought that only a hundred or so were left. That's when another note was sent up. It stated that the stench underground had become unbearable. Decomposing bodies lined the underground trenches in this war of attrition. Then, human rights lawyers and journalists watched with horror from the sidelines as the dead bodies were pulled up, one by one.

On Sunday 1 December, Pretoria High Court held a virtual sitting and ordered, again, that the tactics being used in Operation Vala Umgodi were unconstitutional. That people must be allowed to send food, water and medication to the trapped miners.[52] As South Africa's organisation Lawyers for Human Rights wrote, 'the state cannot use starvation and dehydration, internationally recognised elements of crimes against humanity, as a tool for purported law enforcement. This would be contrary to the right to life, human dignity, and the right not to be treated in an inhumane and degrading way.'[53]

But this again was disregarded by the police. Into early 2025, the Stilfontein mine remained barricaded, until everyone underground had either left or died. In February 2025, the South African police announced they were working to identify the ninety-three dead bodies of suspected illegal miners who had been pulled up.[54] Only three had been claimed by their families.[55] By then, some activists were calling it the Stilfontein massacre.[56]

Meanwhile, more gold mines were being barricaded. In the eyes of President Ramaphosa, the war on illegal miners had only just begun.

Operation Vala Umgodi is not the only time a misguided militarised approach has been has been used to tackle crimes related to the environment. As natural resources degrade and climate effects become more extreme, there will always be a new search for the culprit. This can be good, because it can lead us to pursue accountability and change for the better. But we must always be careful to choose our fights wisely.

Beware of those who are blind to the humanity of the poor and desperate. Beware of overconfident authorities who base their policies on fear rather than evidence, and tell simplified stories of who is to blame for environmental decay. And beware of the people co-opting serious environmental concerns for personal or political gain.

6

THE NEGLIGENT

SOMETHING WAS WRONG with the rig.

Steve Bertone was in the narrow bed of his cabin, in the harsh artificial light, his eyes on the first line of his book. An odd noise, faint at first, crept into his consciousness. The sound grew louder, rumbling like a freight train hurtling through his quarters. He could feel the rig itself begin to tremble in sync with the violent thumping. Faster and faster and faster, until it consumed everything and an explosion ripped through the air.

Then, darkness.

Ears ringing, Bertone toppled out of his bed and tore open the door. The white emergency lights in the hallway blinded him temporarily, and he looked back then lunged towards his clothes. The air was thick with the smell of fuel, biting at his throat, coating his tongue. Through the banging, a voice sounded from the overhead speakers: 'Fire! Fire! Fire!'

Before he could reach his clothes, a second explosion slammed him back across the tiny room. He scrambled to get up again, and this time he managed to yank on his coveralls, work boots and hard hat. He knew he needed to get out, so he stumbled into the bright hallway where four or five men already stood, stunned, their eyes wide from shock. 'Move!' he yelled. 'Emergency stations. Now!'

As the chief engineer of the Macondo oil rig, Bertone headed up to his station on the bridge. Once there, he found no power, no engines, no thrusters. He picked up the phone and tried to call the engine control room, but the line was dead. Terror rolled down his spine as he looked out the starboard window and saw the rig burning so hot that it might as well have been swallowed by the sun.

The alarm screeched again. 'This is not a drill. This is not a drill!'

Then, he could hear the crew running; some were crying out. A door to his left slammed open. Someone staggered through, forehead slashed, blood gushing from the wound. The man was so injured that he was unrecognisable, but he managed to stutter that the engine room, the pump room, it was all gone.

Bertone recognised who the man was by his voice. It was his colleague Mike Williams. Bertone rushed to the nearest bathroom to get some toilet paper, and when he came back he pressed it against Williams's forehead to stop the bleeding. Together, both now covered in blood, they stumbled out of the room, heading towards the upper deck in search of lifeboats.

Once outside, they were greeted by absolute chaos. Fire raged, thick smoke rose up into the sky, and thick black mud rained down on them, pulled up from the seabed and hurled into the sky by their own equipment. A seagull crashed onto the deck, blood pooling underneath. It felt like the rig was being tarred and feathered.

Bertone, Williams and the other 125 crewmembers rushed to the lifeboats. But the boats were being lowered precariously, unevenly, too fast. Desperate men were jumping onto them mid-descent. Some, in fear of further explosions, plunged right into the freezing sea below.

Eleven men died in this crime scene so big that it could be easily seen from space with the naked eye. And the first of more than 4 million barrels' worth of crude oil started gushing into the Gulf of Mexico. The 'well from hell' had kicked back furiously, sending a message to the world.

This chapter exposes the role of inaction in the crimes against our planet. It explores what happened during one of the biggest and most expensive green crimes in history, the Deepwater Horizon oil spill.

News coverage was widespread, with images of birds covered in oil being carefully washed by volunteers, beaches with washed up blobs of black goo and multiple public apology videos released by BP that did not go down well. People around the world grieved the environmental harm that was being caused, as the situation remained out of control for months.

What is notable about this particular green crime is the role of scientists in uncovering it. In particular, an oceanographer named Ian MacDonald. I spoke with MacDonald about how, in the days following the rig explosion, he figured out that something was very wrong with the information being disclosed to the public.

Exactly what happened on the rig and how we can

prevent such disasters in the future was largely uncovered by a US presidential commission called the National Commission on the BP Deepwater Horizon Oil Spill.[1] Importantly, this investigation was bipartisan. It was co-chaired by two commissioners – one Democrat, the other Republican. The commission should be a reminder of what can be achieved when, rather than fighting each other, people with different political beliefs come together and hold those who are destroying our planet accountable. The report provides many of the details I have relied on to understand the case, including the opening scene, which I recreated from Stephen Bertone's own testimony.[2]

Unfortunately, not all presidents or political influencers today are willing to listen to environmental scientists, and they are failing to prevent, or plan for, the climate risks we currently face. It is an existential imperative that facts still have a fighting chance against wishful thinking. That's why in this chapter I review the science of climate persuasion and how we can overcome people's reluctance to change their minds. Psychological research can help to explain why we are all vulnerable to getting our facts wrong, and how we can work to overcome our information biases.

This is the story of intelligent people convincing themselves of an impossible explanation. A man nicknamed 'Tiny Tony' who was desperate to get his life back. And how tragedy was overcome with one of the most successful environmental regeneration projects of all time.

And it all began deep below the ocean floor, when engineers hit liquid gold.

PAY ZONE

In September 2009, BP announced that they had made a giant discovery of oil in the Gulf of Mexico. In fact, as Ian MacDonald told me, it was such a big deal for the company that they were bragging about how high quality it was: 'They hit not only oil, but it was wonderful oil. Light, sweet, crude.'

Located about 40 miles off the coast of Louisiana, one of the spots where BP was going to drill for their new perfect oil was called the Macondo prospect. It was named after the fictional town in the hauntingly beautiful 1967 novel *One Hundred Years of Solitude* by Colombian author Gabriel García Márquez. In the book, Macondo is a town that is full of hope and good fortune until it is cursed by magic and modernisation. Eventually, it becomes 'a fearful whirlwind of dust and rubble'.[3]

At the Macondo well, the immediate problem for BP was that the newly discovered oilfield was 'ultra-deep'. 'The Macondo reservoir was some 4,500 metres [2.8 miles] below the seafloor, already at a water depth of about 1,500 metres [0.9 miles],' MacDonald explained to me.

Oil and natural gas are both fossil fuels, and they are often found together in nature. When you dig a deep hole and create an oil well, you'll find a pool of oil with a layer of gas on top of it. The gas is like a cloud, trapped from floating away by the rock above it. Natural gas is airborne, mostly made of methane, and is used for heating and electricity. The crude oil found below it is a liquid that is processed and made into things like diesel and petrol for cars and trucks, and asphalt for our roads. It's also used for a head-spinning array of other products, including soaps, paints and plastics.

But in this ultra-deep prospect the normal laws of matter did not apply. As MacDonald told me, 'The pressure and temperature in these conditions is otherworldly. Oil and gas exist not as conventional liquid and gas, but as a supercritical fluid that blends into a kind of superheated steam.' That's why these ultra-deep wells are approached by engineers with the utmost caution, because this state makes them incredibly dangerous.

In order to make an oil well, you need to drill a tiny hole and then tap it with a valve that is no more than an inch in diameter. And to be able to do that, you need to install an oil rig, which is a structure that goes over an oil well with special equipment for drilling and removing oil from the earth. Oil rigs are reusable and can be towed to new areas on big ships, and they are typically rented for specific projects.

The first rig that BP hired for the job at Macondo was the *Marianas*. It managed to drill about 1.7 miles into the seabed, but the work was interrupted when it was hit by a hurricane, having made it only about halfway to the 'pay zone'. The pay zone is the part of the reservoir from which oil can be profitably extracted. The crew needed to replace the rig with a new one to finish the job. That's when the Deepwater Horizon rig, owned by a company called Transocean, was sent to take over.

Ultra-deep rigs are always a challenge. But this particular prospect was so hard to drill that the Deepwater Horizon's equipment was struggling. Each layer of rock and sediment seemed to fight back.

The difficult drilling conditions also meant the release of

a number of 'kicks'. Kicks are exploding pockets of gas. By design, each time there was a kick, the impact of the explosion was caught by drilling mud. Drilling mud is liquid and can be pumped in and out of a well as needed. There are many varieties, but its basic feature is that it is heavier than water but won't break down in water. This is important, because it needs to sink to the ocean floor and act as a sort of weighted blanket to protect the rig from the explosive pressure being released from underground.

As the crew drilled deeper and deeper into the unrelenting rock, it wasn't just the pressure underground that started to mount. The project was running way over schedule, and every additional day was costing them a lot of money. This made the pressure on deck palpable.

And, the crew knew that even when they eventually hit the pay zone, they still had to spend time to plug the hole they had made so that the oil wouldn't escape into the ocean when the Deepwater Horizon rig left. Normally, when a team has finished drilling a well, it is filled with cement so heavy that gravity holds it down, forming a cement plug. The purpose of the plug is to seal the well until a new team, the extraction team, comes with their set-up. But pumping in enough heavy cement to form a plug takes considerable time and money. As does cracking it open when the next crew comes with the equipment to suck up the oil.

As the crew grew closer and closer to the pay zone, an idea was floated. What if they tried a different kind of cement plug? It was proposed that they could use cement foamed up with lots of tiny nitrogen bubbles to make it spread out. Like when you pour a beer and the bubbles expand and rush up to the top of the glass. Except with the liquid cement it would stick to the walls of the well and stay there, thereby sealing the hole. If it worked, it would require a lot less actual cement, which would save everyone a huge amount of time and money.

The problem was that this kind of foam cement plug had never actually been tried in this kind of scenario. A cement slurry must be tested before it is used in a cement job. Because the pressure and temperature at the bottom of a well can significantly alter the strength and curing rate of a given cement slurry, and because storing cement on a rig can alter its chemical composition over time.

According to the National Commission on the Deepwater Horizon oil spill, a Halliburton engineer asked lab personnel to run a series of 'pilot tests' on the cement blend stored on the Deepwater Horizon that they planned to use at Macondo. They tested the slurry and reported the results, which were sent to BP. To the trained eye, the test showed that the foam slurry design was unstable. Multiple additional tests came back with the same results: the cement foam was unstable. When nitrogen foam cement is unstable it can be because the small bubbles all cluster together into larger bubbles, making the hardened cement porous and unpredictable.

But wishful thinking, the dream of an easier solution to a hard and expensive problem, is often more powerful than fact.

Despite the bad results, the crew of the Deepwater Horizon went ahead with their idea and foam cement was pumped to the spot where the rig tapped the reservoir, at a depth of about 2.8 miles. To stop the oil from escaping while they made the cement plug, the well was backfilled with drilling mud. At first, everything seemed to go smoothly. At 5.45 a.m. on

20 April 2010, an email was sent by the cementing engineer on the Deepwater Horizon. 'We have completed the job and it went well . . . the Halliburton cement team . . . did a great job.'[4] Note that by this time the Deepwater Horizon project was six weeks behind schedule, and $58 million over budget.[5] Still, the crew patted themselves on the back.

But before the Deepwater Horison rig could leave, the team had to ensure the well was secure and that the foam cement would actually be able to hold on its own once the drilling mud on top of it was removed. They conducted a series of pressure tests to make sure. It quickly became clear that the pressure on the drill pipe wasn't right. It was way too high. The team tried to fix the problem by letting the pressure seep out, but once they were finished doing this the pressure would simply increase again.

If the well was leaking, which was the only plausible explanation for the increasing drill pipe pressure, they couldn't leave.

One of the crew members who had been on the rig since it was built said he had seen this kind of thing before. It was a 'bladder effect' – pressure caused by the drilling mud, some of which was, at this point, still sitting on the cement plug – rather than a leak from the well itself. He was highly respected as a man who understood the finer points of deepwater well control, and the explanation was accepted. This explanation was later called scientifically illogical.[6] A bladder effect couldn't have explained the pressure test results.

After a long discussion, they ran another pressure test on a different pipe, called the kill line, and they were successfully able to bring this one down to no pressure. The well was deemed stable enough to detach from the Deepwater Horizon, and the team began to pull up the drilling mud on top of the foam cement plug.

The muddy shield that had for months protected the Deepwater Horizon from dangerous kicks was being dismantled.

Around 9.40 p.m., still on 20 April, drilling mud began spewing onto the rig floor. The crew tried to stop it, but it was already hopeless. Then, just nine minutes later, a cloud of gas flowed into the rig and the engine rooms exploded. This was the explosion that would also throw Steve Bertone, who had been reading in his bed, across the room of his little cabin. The one that would send Bertone and the rest of the crew running for the upper decks, helping injured colleagues along the way. Eleven men died, and the rest escaped on the lifeboats and rescue boats that soon followed.

When the rig exploded, the pipes were still attached to the rig, which meant that as the rig sank to the bottom of the sea, the pipes became became kinked and broken. This tangle of metal pipes and rig parts was one reason why the site would become so hard to contain.

But who, exactly, was to blame?

Before I begin to answer that question, I want to rewind. To contextualise this case within the context of what is often simply called 'Big Oil'. An industry that has wilfully disregarded and obscured the existential risks of their trade for a very long time.

OIL MEN

Our love affair with petroleum really kicked off in 1859, when a man named Colonel Edwin Drake drilled the first commercial oil well. He was hoping that it would prove to be a cheaper and more efficient alternative fuel for lamps compared to other popular choices at the time, such as whale oil.

Drake had chosen a place in Pennsylvania that was called Oil Creek by the Indigenous peoples in the area, because of the rainbow sheen and pockets of oil that could be skimmed off the surface. He theorised that there must be some sort of underground reservoir from which this oil was coming. And, if that were the case, it could be lucrative to tap this resource. He was right, and he managed to refine the oil to kerosene and sell it to be used in lamps. Kerosene is still used today, for example as lighter fluid.

A report published by the New York Chamber of Commerce just over two years after Drake hit oil reported that New York State had exported 1.5 million gallons of petroleum just in the first quarter of 1862. This was from Drake's well and also others that emerged right after his discovery. As was written in the report: 'No article of commerce has in so short a period of time ever made such rapid strides into the first ranks of valuable earth products as this.'[7]

Hitting oil was like finding a fountain of money.

Unsurprisingly, new oil wells immediately popped up around the country, and the United States secured its place as the world's dominant oil producer. It was a new, exciting industry that was firmly aligned with the get-rich-quick American dream.

But not everyone was on board. One man, whose name is lost to history, was said to have argued with Drake, calling the extraction of oil immoral. The oil was needed by the devil underground, he said, to fuel the fires of hell. To withdraw it was to unjustly protect the wicked from their punishment. This ominous warning was laughed off.[8]

For the decades that followed, oil lit the bedrooms and streets and factories of much of the world. But the true Oil Age didn't start until the invention of oil-powered engines. First, the diesel engine, invented by Rudolf Diesel in the 1890s, replaced coal-powered steam engines. Then, in 1908, Henry Ford released the Model T, the first mass-produced car that ran on oil. It ran specifically on petrol. Oil was no longer just practical. It was sexy. It represented speed, technology and progress. It was the energy of the future.

This wild surge in demand led in 1954 to the first movable drilling platform being created and used off the coast of the Gulf of Mexico.[9] Mr Charlie, as it was called, could only operate in about thirty feet of water. But rig operators were encouraged to go deeper and deeper; and within just three years, dozens more were built that could drill in almost a hundred feet of water. Everyone was pushing for progress. For new tech to explore these exciting depths. As one oil executive said at the time, it was 'a billion-dollar adventure in applied science'.[10] The 'oil men', as they called themselves, were explorers, cracking and drilling their way into the Earth in search of treasure.

Oil also had amazing merch and branding. Plastics were a regular source of everyday dopamine for the modern family, coming in bright colours and previously impossible shapes. Then there was the space race, using oil to make the seemingly impossible dream of walking on the moon come true. Oil wasn't just fuel. It was a dream of endless possibilities.

This isn't a dream that has died, either. We, almost all of us, are utterly besotted with the life that oil gives us. We can jump on planes or trains or cars to see the world. We can eat basically anything from anywhere because it is wrapped in plastic packaging, shipped by fuel-consuming boats and trains and planes, harvested using oil-powered tools, and only possible in abundance because of petrochemicals used on fields and in greenhouses.

And what happens when you love something so completely and someone comes and tries to take it away? Or, put slightly differently, what happens when you realise you've been sold a nightmare instead of a dream?

You cling with all your might to what you have left.

STRANGE PROPERTY

A striking early example of this was seen during a 1959 event held to mark 100 years of the American oil industry. For this centennial celebration, the Columbia University business school was asked by the American Petroleum Institute to organise a comprehensive symposium for more than 300 government officials, economists, scientists, historians and industry executives. They called the event Energy and Man.[11]

The curated speeches were a veritable orgy of optimism, celebrating oil as the 'prime mover' of humanity, as essential for prosperity and progress, and the greatest liberating force in history. There was just one exception. It was a dissenting speech so direct that it must have felt like someone had brought an axe to the party and cut someone's head off. The man who gave the speech – this axe murderer of mood – was the nuclear physicist Edward Teller.

'Ladies and Gentlemen,' he began, 'I am here to talk to you about energy in the future. I will start by telling you why I believe that the energy resources of the past must be supplemented.' For him to say that other forms of energy were needed was already a bold opening in a room full of oil enthusiasts. But his reasoning was simple: oil is finite. At some point, it will run out and we will need alternatives.

Teller also explained to the symposium attendees that the world needed to move away from oil because of 'the question of contaminating the atmosphere'. And he presented his argument without fuss or grandiosity, basing it entirely on the scientific evidence, which as he said himself, 'anyone can calculate'.

The following quote is what, in 1959, a room full of influential people heard about the risk of burning petroleum:

> Carbon dioxide has a strange property. It transmits visible light but it absorbs the infrared radiation which is emitted from earth. Its presence in the atmosphere causes a greenhouse effect in that it will allow solar rays to enter, but it will, to some extent, impede the radiation from the earth into outer space. The result is that the Earth will continue to heat up until a balance is re-established. Then the Earth will be at a higher temperature and will radiate more. It has been calculated that a temperature rise corresponding to a 10 per cent increase in carbon dioxide will be sufficient to melt the icecap and submerge New York. All the coastal cities would be covered, and since a considerable percentage of the human race lives in coastal regions, I think that this chemical contamination is more serious than most people tend to believe.[12]

The reaction to Teller's speech was muted. Instead of panicking at this apocalyptic prognosis, or discussing it at length, it seems to have been mostly ignored.

Based on the record of the event, apart from one clarifying question from the audience, it wasn't brought up again onstage at all.

Here was a scientist predicting that all coastal cities would be flooded, making climate refugees of most people in the world, and the audience just . . . didn't want to talk about it? Why didn't they immediately want to stop the transfer of hell's fuel to the surface of the Earth, as that man had once warned Colonel Drake?

To understand why, we need to turn to the science of how we form beliefs.

DISCONFIRMATION BIAS

It can be baffling to listen to people who downplay the urgency of the climate crisis, or the role of specific human behaviours in causing it. It is confusing how we, and they, exist in the same society at the same time and have such wildly opposing views of reality. Have they not been paying attention? Are they just idiots?

This question of climate change denialism is also something that baffles scientists. When Edward Teller got on that stage in 1959, he must have assumed that presenting the facts of the greenhouse effect would be enough to convince the audience that they needed to shift away from oil.

But it didn't work. Why?

This is a question that many people today ask themselves too. How audiences can remain unmoved as scientists lay out the facts about the triple planetary crisis – climate change, pollution and biodiversity loss. What does it take to get people to care about, and act on, carefully calculated scientific predictions?

This was what political scientists James Druckman and Mary McGrath wanted to answer when in 2019 they published a review of all the research they could find on when, and why, people change their beliefs related to climate change. They discovered that climate scepticism isn't the result of laziness or low intelligence. It has to do with how people incorporate new information into their way of thinking. Druckman and McGrath found that a model called Bayesian updating was the best way to explain how, and whether, people change their minds.[13] It's a little bit technical, so I am going to walk you through it.

Imagine you are at that symposium in 1959. As you sit down in your chair to listen to Teller give his speech, you already have a set of existing beliefs. These are your best guesses about the true state of the world. These beliefs are your core assumptions about how you think the world works. These assumptions, and the strength of your belief in them, will determine what happens next.

Let's say that one of your existing beliefs is that oil is good for the world. Now, how strongly do you hold that belief? Are you entirely sure that oil is good? Or have you occasionally had doubts?

When Teller gets on that stage, he tells you that, actually, oil is not good for the world. Not only that, but it will have catastrophic consequences. Now it's up to you to decide how to evaluate that new information. One of the big things that will decide what happens next is how credible you find this new information and its source.

You and the 300 other important people in the room know from his introduction that Edward Teller is a renowned nuclear physicist. You might also already know that he is no stranger to communicating bad news. Together with two colleagues, he convinced Einstein to sign a letter that urged the president of the United States to create an atomic weapon during World War II. He then worked on building that weapon, as part of the Manhattan Project, and in the 1950s became the father of the even more powerful hydrogen bomb. He was also born in Austria-Hungary, which would become Soviet-controlled Hungary. This fact would have been an inherent problem for some Americans, given that the Cold War was already underway when the symposium took place.

So, you are listening to this man. But you are also assessing him as a person. If you see him as one of the brightest minds in the world, and a great scientist, then you probably trust his calculations. But if you doubt his scientific integrity because he helped to create the most devastating weapons of mass destruction of all time, then perhaps you don't believe what he says. You think his scientific findings are inherently tainted by his questionable ethics. Or maybe you think that this man born abroad, this foreigner, is trying to undermine the American oil industry by fearmongering and feeding you disinformation.

Now you head into the final step of your Bayesian updating. Depending on the outcome of your credibility calculations, you now need to decide what to do with the information he has presented. Will you change your mind? There are three ways this can go:

The first option is that the new information has no effect on your existing beliefs. You might decide that Teller isn't credible enough, or refuse to believe that New York will be underwater someday because it seems impossible to you.

The second possible outcome is that you are persuaded. You start to believe that oil is not as good for the world as you thought. That there are major downsides, including the greenhouse effect. This can shift your beliefs a little or a lot. It can lead to the early whispers of new questions and doubts, or a full-on crisis in your beliefs.

The third and probably worst outcome for the planet is that Teller's speech causes a backlash in your mind. Your beliefs move further in the opposite direction, and you come to think even more firmly that oil is good. Who does this unethical foreigner think he is, telling you what is good for America? You double down and feel a sense of strength in holding on to your beliefs. That oil is good.

Druckman and McGrath emphasise that effective communication about climate change has to consider who or what the audience thinks is credible. And climate scientists may need to adjust their strategy accordingly.

Rather than statistics about climate change from an academic, an audience may react more strongly to a religious leader talking about the factors that contribute to climate change. Or in a business setting, people may respond better to those who speak their language. People who are emphasising not the biodiversity loss caused by climate change, but the economic losses.

Druckman and McGrath also point to the problem that people want to see big changes in how people think about climate change, and they want change quickly. This means that small shifts can feel underwhelming, go unnoticed, and can be hard to capture in research studies. But in real life, even if the right person is delivering a compelling message, people might only shift their belief about climate change a bit. Fundamental beliefs about how the world works tend to change in incremental steps rather than in a single moment of life-changing epiphany. But this gradual change is still powerful.

There's something else that can get in the way of changing people's minds. Something that to Teller's audience in 1959 probably mattered a whole lot. This was a group of people who were emotionally and financially invested in the oil industry. People who believed it was the fuel of the future. Perhaps they just didn't *want* to believe what Teller was saying?

Disconfirmation bias is when we place a really high bar on what a person needs to say or do to convince us of their view. Anything less, and we are quick to evaluate their objectively sensible statements as outrageous or ridiculous. Rather than wrestling with the fact that we might be wrong, we convince ourselves that they are definitely wrong.

In order for people to change their minds, we need to allow ourselves to accept new information as accurate, and not just undermine everything that contradicts our existing views.

It seems to me that disconfirmation bias is also what led to the Deepwater Horizon disaster.

NONSENSICAL

In May 2010, President Barack Obama announced the creation of the National Commission on the BP Deepwater Horizon Oil Spill and Offshore Drilling, an independent entity set up to figure out exactly what had happened.[14] Their main finding was that 'The explosive loss of the Macondo well could have been prevented.'[15] It seems to have happened because of missed warning signals, a failure to share information, and a lack of appreciation for the risks involved.

This is not at all what you would expect on an oil rig. 'In the oil industry, there is a prevailing safety culture,' oceanographer Ian MacDonald told me. 'Where the work happens, the commitment is intense, fierce even. If you go on a production platform, there are signs everywhere reminding you to *be safe*.' He continued, making sure I understood just how seriously the issue of risk is taken. 'Every shift change starts with a safety briefing, run with the intensity of a prayer meeting. Any employee is supposed to be able to halt production at any time without consequence if they think something unsafe is happening. In this environment, for blatantly unsafe risky things to exist, or choices to be made, is a baffling departure.' Yet in the case of the Deepwater Horizon, precisely that departure was made.

The two managers on the rig, Bob Kaluza and Don Vidrine, would both be charged with negligently and grossly negligently failing to control the well, and for having 'accepted a nonsensical explanation for the abnormal readings'.[16] Negligence means failing to take proper care, resulting in harm. Like a doctor missing a serious diagnosis, or a shop owner failing to put up a 'wet floor' sign after mopping and someone slipping. Gross negligence is far worse, showing extreme carelessness or disregard for safety. Like a surgeon removing the wrong limb, or the same shop owner seeing multiple people almost slip and almost hurt themselves on the wet floor and still not putting up a sign. While both are careless, gross negligence is more extreme.

Negligence is interesting because it is missing one of the key aspects of a crime: intent. Most of the time, it's about someone being careless, rather than trying to cause harm on purpose. No one wanted the Deepwater Horizon rig to explode, or people to die. But much like a doctor removing the wrong leg because they didn't check the patient notes, at some point carelessness becomes a crime.

The rig managers were also initially charged with involuntary manslaughter, for the deaths of eleven of the crew. For each of the men who died, they were also charged with the crime of seaman's manslaughter, which is misconduct or negligence on a ship or boat that leads to the death of a member of the crew.

And, finally, they were charged with the environmental crime of causing the oil spill. Specifically, with violating the Clean Water Act for contaminating the Gulf of Mexico, along with hundreds of miles of coastline in the Gulf states of Louisiana, Mississippi, Alabama and Florida.

The original indictment made it clear that the managers should have consulted their colleagues on land about the alleged 'bladder effect' and stopped preparations to leave the drilling rig. The charges against the two managers were revised several times over the years, and many were dropped. You will learn the outcome of the legal proceedings against the two managers on page 285. But the core question remained: why didn't they believe the facts?

In the aftermath of the disaster, how people dealt with the facts took on an even bigger role.

CLIMATE RISK REALIST

A few days after the blowout at the Macondo oil well, professor of oceanography at Florida State University Ian MacDonald got a call from a friend, John Amos. Amos is the founder of SkyTruth, a conservation organisation whose motto is 'if you can see it, you can change it'. They use various kinds of imaging to hold polluters accountable, including jumping on small planes and taking photos from the air, and using satellite data to track green crimes.[17]

Amos knew that for decades MacDonald had studied how oil released into the Gulf of Mexico impacts biodiversity. So, he pointed MacDonald to a map released to the media by the US Coast Guard. From planes, they had mapped out where they saw oil, and what the oil looked like. This was important, because the colour and shimmer of oil tells you how thick it is. Oil increases in density as it moves from looking like a silver sheen, to rainbow, to metallic, to dark true oil.

The map had lots of little blobs on it, each of which represented an area of oil the pilots had seen. MacDonald sat in his office with a ruler and calculator, and did the maths.

This was a pivotal moment.

MacDonald told me that, after doing the maths, he thought, 'Holy shit. They're just lying. For whatever reason, they're lying about how much oil is coming out.' He immediately sent his results to an academic journal in his field. But the editor called him up with bad news, saying they didn't want to publish his findings, didn't want to get involved. He was asking to withdraw the paper. 'I regret it. But I did,' he told me about choosing not to go ahead with the academic manuscript.

As a scientist with crucial results but no one willing to listen, initially for MacDonald 'it was very lonely'. I'm sure many scientists who do research on climate and environmental issues have felt the same way.

Despite this, he decided to contact the press. 'I went on this radio programme,' he recalled, but the decision to go public wasn't easy, 'I was really conflicted because I felt like I had hung my reputation out. And I could very easily be identified as an alarmist.'

Sociologists Joe Davidson and Luke Kemp have argued that we need to carefully differentiate between 'climate doomists' and 'climate risk realists'. Climate doomists see the climate catastrophe as imminent and unavoidable. Climate risk realists see it as a potential future that we need to work to avoid.

This is an important distinction. In the battle for belief, being seen as a doomist is a sure way for your argument to fall flat, easily dismissed and avoided. In MacDonald's case, even just the fear of being seen as a doomist – or what he called alarmist – almost had the effect of silencing him.

But when we have reality on our side, we are not doomists. We are climate risk realists.

MacDonald pushed through his fears and explained his calculations step-by-step on the radio show. Instead of encountering hostility, he actually found himself faced with a surprisingly receptive audience.

Pressure mounted on BP, and other scientists also began to ring the alarm that the spill was orders of magnitude bigger than the official numbers reported. On 27 April 2010, just a week after the explosion, MacDonald published his findings in a blog. He estimated that the rate of the oil spill was a minimum of 26,500 barrels per day. At this point, the official statistic was still just 1,000. The *New York Times* called this estimate the 'MacDonald Minimum'.[18]

The next day, 28 April 2010, the official estimate only rose to 5,000 barrels per day. And when the scientists kept showing that this was still obviously wrong, they got pushback from BP. 'Essentially, they were just saying shut up and let us worry about how much oil is coming out. It doesn't matter. It's not going to change the trajectory of the response,' MacDonald told me, still in disbelief fifteen years later. 'That's a deeply dishonest and false statement.'

Underestimating the rate by that much also meant they were trying to use the wrong containment methods, because they were treating a flood of oil as a trickle. It was like trying to stop a water hose set to maximum pressure with a paper towel. Futile. This meant more and more oil just kept gushing out. Every day, the underestimations caused harm.

A month later, on 27 May, the estimate was pushed up to 16,000 barrels a day. In June, up to 30,000. Then 48,000. It crept in pathetic slow motion towards the truth.

To get a sense of just how much that is, picture an oil tank truck. Those long shiny tubes on wheels, like sideways aluminium cans, seen on motorways with their many tyres, heading to deliver fuel to petrol stations. The amount of oil that was pouring into the Gulf of Mexico, for eighty-four days, was the equivalent of 305 of those trucks every single day.

'I think they believed their own fantasy. Their own rosy scenario,' MacDonald told me about the underestimate.

Wishful thinking isn't a crime. But it sure makes it easier to commit one. And it's one of the biggest causes of the climate crisis. People don't want to destroy nature. Instead, nature is destroyed by a thousand tiny bad decisions, initiated every time someone whispers 'it can't be that bad'.

Unfortunately, it can.

OIL SHOCK

Ian MacDonald had been doing important ocean research long before he got involved in revealing the truth about the Deepwater Horizon spill. 'Most of my career, I've worked on natural oil seeps in the deep ocean, particularly the Gulf of Mexico,' he told me. 'My work involved going down hundreds of metres with submersibles and submarines and looking at sites where oil and gas were bubbling up to the seafloor and then all the way to the surface of the ocean.'

Oil seeps are small, slow oil leaks from underground reservoirs through cracks in the Earth's crust. For most of the history of oil production, the way that people found oil reservoirs was by looking for leaks, and creeks where oil was floating on the surface persistently, like when Colonel Drake first encountered oil creek.

MacDonald wanted to understand what impact this naturally occurring oil seepage has on ocean health. What he and fellow scientists found changed our understanding of life in the deep sea.

'Long before our society became fuelled by hydrocarbons, there were natural ecosystems that used similar energy,' he explained. Similar to what humans do when they burn oil to create energy, under the sea, in the absence of light, the microorganisms convert the oil into food. 'Instead of finding sick fish, what we found were lush ecosystems in which there were tube worms, mussels, clams, bacteria. Fuelled by hydrocarbons, by oil and gas.'

'One of the really unfortunate tropes that came out of Deepwater Horizon' MacDonald told me, 'was the idea that somehow the Gulf was inoculated against the deleterious effects of oil spills, due to the prevalence of natural seeps.' He called this a 'misstatement of scientific fact'.

But, BP's CEO Tony Hayward used this to publicly downplay the scale of the disaster. 'The Gulf of Mexico is a very big ocean . . . The amount of volume of oil and dispersant we are putting into it is tiny in relation to the total water volume.' A dispersant is something the ocean was sprayed with to break up the oil so it's not just a big flammable sheet on top of the water. After he uttered these words, they hung in the air like a bad joke, earning him the nickname 'Tiny Tony'.[19] But as the oil continued to spew from the wellhead, Hayward doubled down. 'I think the environmental impact of this disaster is likely to be very, very modest.'

The problem MacDonald stressed, is one of scale. Oil seeps release small, steady amounts of oil over decades or centuries, giving ecosystems time to adapt. By contrast, an oil spill is like a shock, flooding a system much faster than it can handle.

There are three primary ways that oil spills harm the environment.

The first is killing off wildlife. Sea turtles, whales, and other marine life that need to breathe at the water's surface have to pass through a toxic layer of oil. These animals develop breathing problems, or even suffocate from the oil entering their lungs.

The second is the impact on marine larvae and plankton. These tiny organisms are the foundation of the marine food web; without them, lots of other animals would starve. Even in low concentrations, crude oil is highly toxic to them when it ends up in places where it doesn't occur naturally. This also has an impact on human food sources because we heavily rely on eating wild fish. During the Deepwater Horizon spill, species like tuna saw devastating losses as their larvae were poisoned before they had the chance to grow.

The third is the huge area that the oil affects, as it can drift for tremendous distances before being sponged up by our shores. This was a particularly big problem in the Deepwater Horizon spill because of the use of dispersant. However, as Ian MacDonald explained, 'You reduce the volume, it's not as unsightly, but it can have just as broad an ecosystem impact.' Instead of making the spill more manageable, the dispersants made it harder to track the affected area as it grew, spreading the toxic effects across the Gulf.

Unfortunately oil spills are not uncommon, though most are drastically smaller in size than the Deepwater Horizon spill. To put this into perspective, between 2011 and 2024, there were more than 2,000 oil spills in the North Sea reported to the UK government. Most of these were small, but they were also often in marine protected areas, where that kind of toxic release is likely to be even more harmful.[20]

Adding to the destruction of the Deepwater Horizon oil spill was the reluctance of BP to share the data that would allow scientists and responders to accurately deal with the consequences.[21] As Ian MacDonald told me, 'Ed Markey was a congressman, he's now a senator. He was a hero in all this.' Markey told BP to release the tapes that showed how much oil was flowing out of the pipes, and threatened to subpoena them if they didn't. 'So they released the tapes . . . They proved that BP had video of oil gushing out of the ruptured pipes on the seafloor from the submersibles they had on scene. They had refused to release them for independent analysis.'

Once people outside of BP had the tapes, the reality turned out to be even worse than MacDonald had anticipated. 'After Markey forced the release, it was immediately clear that the rate of the spill was in the order of 50,000 barrels per day.' Finally, on 2 August, months after the spill began, it was agreed that the well was leaking at the maximum rate. The official estimate ended up being 58,000 barrels a day.

Just a month later, in late September 2010, MacDonald sat before the National Commission on the oil spill.[22] Supported by a presentation of graphs and calculations, he explained how for whatever reason, BP had used their own charts to calculate what the oil on the surface indicated regarding the rate of the spill. They had used their own numbers instead of the official guidelines published by NOAA, the National Oceanic and Atmospheric Administration. The discrepancy was enormous, sometimes a difference of more than 100 times. 'By following this method, the BP technicians who were attempting to analyse the spill magnitude would have gotten a number that was artificially low,' he told Congress.[23]

What were they thinking, making these severe miscalculations? I asked MacDonald, who told me these were 'sloppy engineers who were leaping to conclusions when the conclusions were favourable to their desired outcome'. BP had preferred their own version of the truth.

This is a crushing realisation given that it meant, for months, the clean-up crew that headed out every day was underequipped and underprepared for a spill that was orders of magnitude worse than they were being told.

ECOLOGICAL GRIEF

The horizon was still a dark line between the sky and the sea. As the motley crew drove towards the coast, the familiar salty scent of the Gulf of Mexico hung in the air. It was mixed with something unnatural, a thick, chemical tang that burned with every breath. They hit the decks and as they climbed onto their boats, big and small, they saw that the once-blue water below them was coated with a sheet of crude oil.

On their daily clean-up missions, the crew would occasionally encounter animal graveyards along the coast. Whole pods of dolphins beached after suffocating in the oil. Birds grounded by wings too heavy to lift. Then there were the marshes smothered under layers of sludge. And disgusting blobs of oil washing up on the shore. It looked like the world was dying.

For nearly two months, this was their life. From dawn to

dusk, seven days a week, approximately 11,000 'Vessels of Opportunity' formed an enormous informal fleet that fought to contain the millions of gallons of oil being released into the Gulf. It felt like an impossible battle. Every gallon of oil they managed to clean up was replaced by another, as the well remained uncontained for 87 relentless days. And it would keep leaking at a slower rate for even longer, 152 days in total.

The work was brutal, and the chemical they were spraying, Corexit, seemed to be making people sick. Some would stay sick, and later file lawsuits against BP.[24] But they kept going. The Gulf was choking, and someone needed to save it. When they went home at night they were shattered not just by the work, but by the psychological impact of the environmental horrors they had witnessed. Meanwhile, MacDonald was getting to the truth behind the numbers.

He told me how the sight of oil spreading over an area the size of Scotland created a sense of environmental loss that extended to people around the world. 'They felt this as a sympathetic trauma. People have a sense of tragedy around the demise of the Gulf.'

This relates to the concept of ecological grief. The term was coined in 2018, when two researchers from opposite sides of the world observed the same phenomenon. Ashlee Cunsolo was working in northern Canada, where nature is thick, and weather is extreme by default. Neville Ellis was in the Australian wheatbelt, defined by vast open areas of beige land that have been excessively cleared over the years. They had both been running multi-year research programmes into how people psychologically respond to climate change, and found that many people were experiencing something that didn't yet have a name. They called it 'ecological grief'.[25]

Since then, as more people search for ways to describe their changing relationship with nature, it has become a popular term.

Ecological grief comes in three forms. First, grief linked to physical loss. For example, loss of land, ecosystems or species. The loss can be fast, for example loss caused by a disaster like an oil spill or hurricane. Or it can be slow, gradual and ongoing. Like the dying-off of a forest, the poisoning of an ocean, or the end of predictable weather patterns. These are tangible, measurable realities that are changing.

The second kind of ecological grief is caused by disruptions to environmental knowledge and identity. This particularly affects people who have close connections with the natural world through their daily lives and work. This was captured in a study on the psychological impacts of the Deepwater Horizon oil spill, published in 2024. To explain the far-reaching emotional consequences, the researchers quoted one of their participants, a mother of three children whose husband, a commercial crabber on the Gulf of Mexico, was out of work because of the disaster.

She talked about how her son had 'been on the boat since he could walk', and added: 'My in-laws own a seafood shop. My daddy was in commercial shrimping. We don't know anything else on either side. My husband's family, it's all we've ever known.'[26] Being at sea was part of this family's identity, and for them the grief of losing the ability to fish because of this green crime was catastrophic.

This has also been called 'solastalgia', which describes the feelings of nostalgia, anxiety, stress and worry experienced by individuals living in environments that have deteriorated.[27] It's a sort of homesickness at home.[28]

Third is grief associated with anticipated future ecological losses, mourning a loss you know is coming. We might be sad now that we will one day soon live in a hotter world, not have as many beaches, and be left with few remaining ancient forests to explore as we get older. For people who have already suffered traumatising environmental experiences, this feeling can be even more severe and direct.

The mother interviewed in the 2024 study whose family's seafaring identity was disrupted by the BP oil spill also said 'the fear that it put in my child was, "Is this going to be gone forever?" It was deep thinking, worry. I see just a change in his psychological . . . I mean, everything about his daily routine. He couldn't concentrate in school for worrying about what's going to happen.'[29]

The negative effects of ecological grief are worst in situations where people are powerless about environmental degradation.

With more of nature being eroded every day, ecological grief is almost certainly going to increase. The important thing is to use that feeling to actively do something. Turning ecological grief into action makes it a 'functional' grief. A functional grief is an appropriate response to loss that has a purpose.[30] And it can help to fuel change.

I am sure that the perpetrators of green crime can experience this ecological grief, too. After all, they also need to live in the world they ruin.

We know from other kinds of crime, including when people murder their loved ones, that perpetrators can suffer from tremendous grief, and can even suffer from offence-related post-traumatic stress disorder.[31] And among men who have killed, many mention that in the act of killing another, they also killed a part of themselves.[32] I would expect this is also true for some environmental criminals. But certainly not always.

In May 2010, when the well was still leaking at the maximum rate, Tony Hayward, the CEO of BP, was asked by a reporter whether he could sleep at night given the catastrophic environmental damage the spill had caused. To this he responded, 'Of course I can.' It didn't go down well. Neither did his other myopic comment, 'I would like my life back'. This was taken as a sign of a callous disregard for the eleven men who had died on the rig.

I can't imagine he was unbothered by the environmental impact of the spill. But perhaps he wasn't as traumatised as many of those who had to clean up his company's mess.

There was still the question of recklessness. How did the crew get to a place where they were so willing to accept a nonsensical explanation in such an incredibly high-risk situation?

THE PARADOX OF FEEDBACK

While MacDonald was focused on uncovering bad science, others were investigating corporate failures. Robert Bea, who conducted the forensic engineering investigation of the Deepwater Horizon blowout, sent me his original report from 2010.[33] Together with his colleague William Gale, Bea described shortcuts and repeated risks that were taken in pursuit of faster, cheaper drilling.

One email, from just over a month before the Deepwater Horizon spill, showed just how troubling the mindset had become. In it, a member of BP's Tiger Team, an elite group dedicated to doing pressure predictions and checking at what point rock will start to break, wrote about a totally different incident on the Deepwater Horizon rig in which the crew had received technical readings they 'didn't believe'.

It had been a potentially dangerous situation that was eerily similar to what ended up taking the whole rig down in flames a month later. 'Everyone was aware of the gas, but we decided to drill ahead,' the Tiger Team member wrote. They then experienced a surge of gas. 'I'm not sure it was a lack of communication or awareness as much as a "we can get away with this" attitude,' the team member reflected about his experiences of the culture on board the rig.[34]

In addition to this, as Ian MacDonald told me, 'There was no inspection anymore of the oil wells that were out there, the platforms that are out in the Gulf, because there was no money for the Minerals Management Service, now the Bureau of Safety, Energy and Environment.' The regulators were no longer able to do regular checks, or to fly people offshore and do inspections when they were drilling. 'And so no inspections got done. So nobody said, hey, your blowout preventer hasn't been serviced in three and a half years.'

With no one external coming to inspect, it can be easy for standards to slip. Risks feel more abstract the longer the situation seems fine, and checks that an inspector would do feel unnecessary. On the Deepwater Horizon, this attitude is probably why a number of important backup systems on the rig didn't kick in. Systems which could have stopped the blowout from being such an uncontrollable disaster for months. Which safety checks might have prevented the deaths of eleven men.

Bea and Gale's investigation into the disaster highlighted a failure to learn from previous close calls. As one crew member reflected in the aftermath, 'I don't see us really learning.'

This is not an uncommon issue.

When people experience a near-miss, it can have a counterproductive psychological effect called the paradox of feedback. For example, when a hurricane narrowly misses a town, people breathe a sigh of relief. But that relief can turn into scepticism the next time a warning comes. The fact that the kick of gas the Deepwater Horizon crew experienced the first time – the one which the Tiger Team member wrote about in the email – did not result in a disaster might have felt like proof that certain precautions were unnecessary. This kind of mindset leads to complacency, leaving us vulnerable because we underestimate future risks.

The findings of the presidential commission were even more damning. The final report concluded: 'The immediate causes of the Macondo well blowout can be traced to a series of identifiable mistakes made by BP, Halliburton, and Transocean that reveal such systematic failures in risk management that they place in doubt the safety culture of the entire industry.'[35]

FALLOUT

The Macondo well was finally declared 'dead' on 19 September, 2010. After 152 days, they had finally managed to strategically pump cement into the reservoir and permanently seal it.

The legal fallout that followed was swift. Transocean,

which owned the Deepwater Horizon, was the first to plead guilty to environmental crimes under the Clean Water Act. The company admitted negligence, particularly for ignoring 'clear danger signs',[36] and paid $1.4 billion in penalties.[37] This money funded relief efforts for communities, and ecosystem restoration in the region. Transocean also had to overhaul its risk protocols, in order to address failures.

Halliburton, who made the foamy cement, was the next to pay a penalty, after pleading guilty to destroying evidence related to the spill.[38] The company paid a $200,000 fine and contributed $55 million to the National Fish and Wildlife Foundation.[39]

And then there was BP. The company pleaded guilty to felony manslaughter for the deaths of the eleven workers, as well as environmental crimes under the Clean Water Act and the Migratory Bird Treaty Act. BP also admitted to obstruction of justice for providing false information about the spill's magnitude. In January 2013, the company was sentenced to pay $4 billion in penalties – at that point, the largest criminal resolution in U.S. history.[40] Of this, $2.4 billion was allocated to restoring Gulf ecosystems, and funding crucial research and conservation efforts.

Scientists like Ian MacDonald were instrumental in exposing the truth, and their voices helped to shape the unprecedented focus on environmental harm in the sentencing. This case represented a victory: science had been heard, believed and acted upon. The Gulf of Mexico's battered ecosystems now had a chance to recover.

What about the two managers on the rig? As more details about the disaster emerged during the investigations, most of the charges against the two well site managers were dropped, including the eleven counts of seaman's manslaughter and regular manslaughter.

In December 2015, the day manager, Donald Vidrine, pleaded guilty to a misdemeanour violation of the Clean Water Act.[41] This is a green crime, but it is only a minor one. He was sentenced to ten months' probation.[42] Shortly after this, in 2016, his colleague Robert Kaluza, the night manager, went to trial on the same charges.

During the trial, Vidrine testified. When he was asked in court if he had done something wrong that night, Vidrine said, 'I probably didn't press hard enough,' referring to insufficiently questioning the inconsistent pressure readings on the rig. 'I mean, I thought I had, but I probably didn't press hard enough to get more information or questioned some of the information I got.'[43] By the end of the trial, the jury didn't consider the evidence against Kaluza compelling and he was acquitted.

A couple of years later, Kaluza told a *Forbes* journalist, 'I feel like BP served me up to the government.'[44] He has since spoken out about being falsely accused and having six years of his life stolen by the legal process.[45] Others have echoed that the aggressive use of a highly specialized maritime manslaughter law is an unreasonable legal burden for those at sea.

So, were the managers BP's scapegoats, unjustly tossed to the press and public as the ones to blame? Or should they have been punished more harshly, since they were in fact the two men in charge of the rig?

The answer to that will probably depend on how people frame the event.

A couple of years after the disaster, psychological scientist

Susan Clayton and colleagues set out to learn how people made sense of it, asking hundreds of people how they would characterise the event.[46] Did they think the Deepwater Horizon oil spill was a crime, or a natural disaster?

Most participants felt strongly that it was a crime, and that BP was largely responsible. It was also seen as predominantly an environmental disaster rather than a social one. And, probably surprising the researchers, participants' perceptions weren't influenced by different kinds of media coverage. But one psychological trait emerged as important in people's assessment of the nature of the spill; belief in a just world.

It's the idea that fundamentally people get what they deserve. It is a view of the world as predictable, assuming that good things happen to good people, and bad things to bad people. It is also a worldview that overlaps greatly with political conservatism.

People with high 'belief in a just world' were much more likely to see the event as a natural disaster. As the authors wrote, 'Political conservatives define environmental crises differently than do liberals: as unfortunate events, but not as crimes or acts of injustice.' The participants in Clayton and colleagues' study with high belief in a just world also believed that the spill caused less harm than their more liberal peers.

It's important to recognise our own biases, political or otherwise, and try to overcome them when we are confronted with evidence. I know that science itself isn't inherently unbiased, but it is inherent to science to try to be. And that makes it the most powerful tool we have for understanding and predicting the risks we face in the world.

One of the big questions I get regarding the Deepwater Horizon case is: wasn't it just an accident? The answer is a resounding no. We must take negligence and dangerous risk-taking seriously. They are probably the most common causes of green crime. To downplay or excuse them is to perilously risk our future.

THE SIX PILLARS OF OIL CRIME

The Deepwater Horizon oil spill is another prime example of how the six pillars of green crime can create the conditions for disaster.

Ease led to the use of the foam nitrogen cement, which was faster to apply and easier to remove than heavy cement.

Impunity plagued the rig's culture. Certain safety protocols were ignored, and oversight was lax. Emails revealed a 'we can get away with this' attitude. Although some people were held accountable, it took years of investigation for this to happen.

Greed kept the operation going despite mounting danger. The lure of 'light, sweet crude' outweighed the perceived risks both to the crew and to the planet more generally.

Rationalisation blinded the crew on the rig. Evidence that the cement plug wasn't secure was dismissed. They clung to a flawed explanation, unwilling to confront the reality their own data had revealed.

Conformity stifled dissent. Faulty tests were accepted, and the nonsensical explanation of the group that the high pressure was due to a 'bladder effect' was insufficiently challenged. After the spill, conformity continued as estimates of the oil spill rate that were clearly far too low were repeated.

Desperation emerged as the project fell behind schedule and went over budget. The pressure drove the crew to consider shortcuts.

So, what can we do to avoid catastrophic green crimes like this? In addition to challenging groupthink and bias, I think the answer lies in training our imagination.

DYSTOPIAN DREAMS

I have always loved dystopian climate fiction. Or, cli-fi, as the genre is called.

Each story presents a different future Earth. In *Venomous Lumpsucker* by Ned Beauman, plummeting biodiversity has led to a global system where companies need to buy ever-more elusive credits to eradicate species as they harvest the resources of the world. In *Parable of the Sower* by Octavia Butler, resource scarcity and environmental degradation lead to severe social unrest. In *The Wall* by John Lanchester, much of the world is underwater due to rising sea levels. And *The Ministry for the Future* by Kim Stanley Robinson starts with a gruesome scene of scorching heat caused by climate change.

Each one of these worlds is a lesson in risk, showing the long-term consequences of our modern lives. They are creative manifestations of our climate anxieties, often rooted in science. Cli-fi makes us realise that the Earth and society are inherently entangled. That changing the Earth changes who we are as human beings. And beneath every story lies a single, urgent question. How do we stop this from becoming reality?

The impact of cli-fi on how we think and behave has been

studied by researchers within the broader category of narrative persuasion. This is when someone is trying to convince you of something by embedding the message in a story. Rather than telling you facts about climate change, cli-fi turns it into relatable characters and an exciting plot.

It is an exercise in 'show, don't tell', a strategy that many budding writers will have heard of. This is the difference between writing dialogue for a character to say 'I love her', and describing in vivid detail the feelings which that character experiences every time their love interest enters the room. If you take care to guide people to the relevant feelings and experiences, the understanding comes naturally.

Research on narrative persuasion has found that stories don't just bring issues to life, they also make complicated information easier to understand and more persuasive.[47] And, because of how people immerse themselves in stories, people are more likely to agree with a main character and are less likely to immediately look for counterarguments. This is true for both fiction and non-fiction.

Of course, even if you can persuade someone, it doesn't always result in action. For example, researchers looked at whether watching *An Inconvenient Truth*, a 2006 film about climate change, had an impact on people's behaviour. They found that, yes, there was a small increase in pro-environmental behaviour in the form of voluntary carbon offsets. They called it the 'Al Gore effect' because the movie was presented by former American vice president Al Gore.[48] But the effect was only temporary. A year later, that benefit seemed to have vanished.

Another study looked at whether the beautiful BBC nature documentary series *Blue Planet* changed climate-related beliefs and behaviour. The researchers found that people who watched the show had more knowledge about the environment. But in practice, people did not change their behaviour in line with something fairly basic that the series recommended: that they should buy less plastic.[49]

Then there was yet another study in 2024, a group of behavioural scientists randomly exposed participants to one of five conditions.[50] One group read scientific information about climate change. Three other groups either read, heard or watched a cli-fi story in which a protagonist took intentional pro-environmental actions. And the final group was the control, who read a story unrelated to the environment.

Scientific information presented just as facts was better at fostering policy support and intentions for individual action, while cli-fi videos inspired charitable donations and positive emotions like hope and happiness. As always, it seems that it's important to know who your audience is, and what exactly you are hoping to achieve with any specific communication.

I think the main benefit of cli-fi is that it brings issues that otherwise feel so distant into the here and now. As the saying goes, *he who reads, lives many lives.* When I read, I feel like I am in the world the author has created. By living for a couple of weeks in the climate thought experiment of a fiction book, it feels like those risks aren't so far away. It feels like I have lived them.

This immersion allows us to overcome our tendency towards temporal discounting. We often tend to focus so much on the present that it comes at the cost of our future. Imagining disasters is not about spreading fear; it is about finding the motivation to act before it is too late.

If we cannot imagine the risks, we cannot prepare for them. If we keep telling ourselves comforting stories, we will keep repeating the same mistakes. The future does not just happen to us. We create it. With every decision we make, or choose to avoid.

The tragedy is that we often wait for disaster to snap us out of complacency. Only after the oil rig explodes and the birds begin to fall from the sky do we appreciate the value of the precautions we failed to take.

LIBERATE KNOWLEDGE

When Ian MacDonald sat down in his office to do the calculations on the 'little blobs' on a map, no one was paying him to do it. Yet there he was, doing the math. Trying to figure out just how bad the damage would be to our beloved ocean.

When he put down his pencil, he was faced with the difficult position of knowing the truth. What would he do with it? MacDonald's courage in speaking out is a reminder that having knowledge alone isn't enough. It takes conviction to act on what we know.

Environmental scientists have long been climate risk realists, which has made them the bearers of bad news. And we cannot expect them to carry this burden alone; we need to help them. Ian MacDonald shared with me one way that we can do that. We need to build the infrastructure so that oceanographers and other scientists can really understand the deep seas. Only if we know the baseline of the nature we are extracting from can we know how much we have changed an ecosystem. Then, we need to monitor it.

Some of the money BP had to pay in fines went to the Gulf of Mexico Research Initiative, which has helped us to better understand the ecosystems affected by the spill. This is the kind of long-term research that we need. But we need this before crimes are committed, not after. We cannot retroactively understand what we have lost, or need to restore, if we never understood it in the first place.

Once we have the research, we also need to accept what we find. Even if we don't like it. Scientists are our adventurous explorers. Only if they say it is safe for us to drill, smash and extract should we be going into new areas. Those who spend their lives researching nature tend to be more reliable sources of information about our long-term risks than politicians who look only a few years into the future.

According to MacDonald, oil spills like Deepwater Horizon 'are preventable with better regulation and enforcement'. We have the science, the laws and the risk assessments to prevent these negligent green crimes.

As MacDonald wrote in an impassioned email after President Donald Trump made cuts to the National Oceanic and Atmospheric Administration in 2025, we must resist this 'campaign of wilful ignorance'. In MacDonald's words, 'If we lose the thread of climate research amid the storms and floods and fires, we will wander in darkness toward a precipice. I have legal standing to defend the natural world – we all do – and I will join any lawsuit, testify in any court, or march in any protest to oppose this madness. We all must.'

CONCLUSION: CAPABLE GUARDIANS

YOU HAVE BEEN on a journey with me through the air, forests, oceans, and deep into the ground. Seeing over and over again how the six pillars – ease, impunity, greed, rationalisation, conformity and desperation – are omnipresent in cases of green crime.

Usually, the six pillars prop up different levels within the hierarchies of green crime. The people at the bottom of the pyramid are often most driven by desperation and ease. Those in the middle by rationalisation and conformity. And those at the top are typically driven by impunity and greed. But each factor can sneak its way into any level of power. If we want to stop green crime, we need to address these driving factors.

We also need to stop treating environmental criminals as abstract, unknowable villains. They are, like ourselves, motivated by relatable psychological factors. Influenced by things like poverty and joblessness, social norms and expectations, laws and their enforcement. And by the presence of capable guardians, who catch them breaking rules and hand out adequate penalties.

We also need to stop thinking that we are doomed and alone in the fight for our planet. Because we are not. The protectors of the Earth work tirelessly, and we must keep them in our minds whenever we feel that crushing pull towards the black hole of hopelessness.

To resist doomism and apathy in the face of the triple planetary crisis is a radical act.

Stay strong.

As we have seen, there are many ways to help protect nature from green criminals. The people I have written about can be broadly categorised into three groups, each crucial to safeguarding our Earth: the watchers, the investigators and the enforcers.

Watchers monitor changes in the environment. They are the scientists who track damage to nature and people, cut through stereotypes with real data, and publish findings for all of our benefit. The environmental defenders who see first-hand the land being stripped of the trees, who stand up to bullies and report crimes to the authorities. The journalists who jump on ships to document illegal fishing, or meet anonymous informants in secret locations to expose corporate pollution.

Investigators take a systematic approach to identifying green crimes, and collect evidence. They are the Interpol detectives who help police around the world share information and track down the criminals, to make sure every gillnet or frozen fish is accounted for. The financial investigators who trace money flows, helping banks sever the value chains funding transnational green crimes. The undercover agents, like those from the Environmental Investigation Agency, who infiltrate criminal organisations, heading into warehouses of

CONCLUSION: CAPABLE GUARDIANS

death if they need to. The regulators who run their own tests, painstakingly uncovering deceptions and helping to make the world cleaner and safer for us all. The environmental lawyers who craft and apply treaties or use existing laws creatively to pin down environmental criminals.

Enforcers make sure there are consequences. They are the police officers and customs agents who make arrests, raid apartments, and work to track down the bosses of the organised crime networks. The federal agents who conduct interviews with witnesses, read damning emails, and collaborate with justice departments to press charges. The judges who understand the importance of green crime and hand out appropriate sentences.

There are many others involved in the fight for our future whom I haven't been able to cover in this book. Like the people working for charities who are striving to directly protect our natural resources. The campaigners who take to the streets and push politicians to prioritise green policies. The advertisers who make sustainable options appealing and refuse to engage in greenwashing. Those who help train judges in the unique challenges of convicting and sentencing environmental offenders. And the educators in schools around the world who make sure the next generation are growing up with strong biospheric values, equipping them to protect themselves against those who plan to steal their natural resources.

Every one of us has a place in this fight. Converting our anger and grief about the climate crisis into action is what we need. Right now.

As Chiara Armeni, professor of environmental law at the Université Libre de Bruxelles, told me, 'Participation fosters stewardship.' By getting directly involved with specific environmental issues and groups, 'You get to know about the facts. You get to know about how we shape our environments and what the consequences are . . . you'll be involved in a collective exercise.' Getting involved can be transformative – and not just for the world around us, but for our own minds too. Being part of big decisions helps to create community and psychological ownership, enhancing our desire and motivation to protect rather than harm the Earth.

The fact that you bought and finished this book tells me something very important about you. You will not be the kind of person who does nothing when environmental destruction and injustices are taking place. So, don't allow yourself to put this book down and go back to the way things were before. You are different now. You have a new understanding of environmental harm. You know some of the solutions. And, importantly, you feel things in new ways and have the psychological framework to help mobilise your apathy and fear, your grief and anger.

Now it is time to focus your mind on the big issues that need urgent action. 'One area that I find very interesting at the moment is how foresight comes into play,' Armeni told me about the current research on the psychology of climate change. Like 'imagining London underwater'. What she means by foresight is listening to what scientists predict for our near and distant future, and visualising these plausible futures. Like in cli-fi, this makes it more real, and it allows you to ask yourself: Would I want to live here? If not, how can I prevent this prediction from becoming reality?

She explained how thought experiments can help us anticipate the emotional and cultural shifts. It can give us a sense of belonging that environmental change will bring. Foresight can also activate the mobilising forces of eco-anger and eco-grief to inspire action.

In 2024, a mega-study involving more than 250 researchers and 59,000 participants from sixty-three countries was conducted on how people can be mobilised to engage in pro-environmental behaviour. The researchers found that, by far, one of the most effective ways to get people to act was to ask them to write a letter . . . to themselves.[1]

It's called the 'letter from a future self' exercise. The researchers found that the task forced people to grapple with the consequences of their actions and to articulate their own role in shaping the future. It brought the future into the present, and turned abstract threats into deeply personal ones, closing the psychological distance between now and then.

Here is, almost exactly, what the participants in the study were told to do:

> Picture yourself ten years in the future. You are writing a letter to yourself, as you are today. Take a few moments to imagine your life in that future. Imagine how you will look, where you will be, and who you are with. By then, it will be clear whether keeping climate change under 2°C is still possible. It will be clear whether the necessary change occurred fast enough to match the speed of the changing climate. As the Earth's atmosphere continues to heat up, the effects of climate change will be more apparent: the 'highest observed temperature' records will keep being updated, heatwaves and draughts will become more common, species will continue to become extinct.

Now, please write a letter from this future self.

This should be a letter you are writing to your past self. From the person that you will be in ten years. What role do you think would be appropriate for you in respect to climate change? What do you want to tell yourself in the past? What would you like your past self to do?

Writing to your future self brings into focus how the decisions you make today have a long-term impact. It helps you see yourself not as a passive observer of the world but as an active participant in its future. This kind of reflection is essential. Without it, the enormity of the problem can feel paralysing, leading to inaction and defeatism. With it, we see clearly that change is possible and that our actions matter.

As we close this journey into the psychology of green crime, I invite you to write your own letter to the future. Then to use that letter as a guide.

It is time for you to answer the call.

Become one of Earth's guardians.

ACKNOWLEDGEMENTS

The pages of this book carry the fingerprints of many minds.

More than any other project, there were so many lonely moments where writing this book felt impossible. I was overwhelmed by the scope of the issues, and depth of the stories, that I wanted to tell. But the intelligence, enthusiasm, and support of my contributors and friends carried me through. I feel truly honoured that so many guardians of our future trusted me with their work and their stories.

For the emissions chapter, my thanks go to Alberto Ayala, Executive Director and Air Pollution Control Officer at the Sacramento Metropolitan Air Quality Management District and author of *Three Forks in the Road*. Jack Ewing, journalist and *New York Times* business reporter, and author of *Faster, Higher, Farther*, brought his sharp insights to this chapter. I am also grateful to Harald Frey, a researcher at the Research Centre for Transport Planning and Traffic Engineering at the Vienna University of Technology, and Susan Smith, professor of environmental and natural resources law, former US Department of Justice prosecutor, and author of *Crimes Against the Environment*.

In writing about deforestation, I benefited from the knowledge of Paulo Busse, environmental and human rights lawyer, and David Boyd, associate professor of Law, Policy and Sustainability at the University of British Columbia, former UN Special Rapporteur on Human Rights and the Environment, and author of *The Rights of Nature*. Dolors Armenteras, professor of landscape ecology at the University of Barcelona, provided invaluable perspective, as did Sophie Lemaître, environmental lawyer and anti-corruption researcher.

The poaching chapter owes much to the expertise of Julian Newman, campaigns director at the Environmental Investigation Agency, and Ceres Kam, wildlife campaigner at the same organisation and a psychiatrist. Ted Leggett, research expert for the UN Office on Drugs and Crime, and Oscar Morton, conservation scientist at the University of Cambridge, also contributed their insights. Two rangers who wanted to stay anonymous at a wildlife reserve in South Africa also graciously shared their stories with me.

For the illegal fishing chapter, I am deeply thankful to Peter Hammarstedt, ship captain with the non-profit ocean conservation movement Sea Shepherd, and Ian Urbina, journalist, founder of the Ocean Outlaw Project, and author of *The Outlaw Ocean*. Mario Alcaide, coordinator of control operations with the European Fisheries Control Agency and former chief information officer at Interpol, also provided invaluable expertise.

When exploring illegal mining, I was guided by Vidette Bester, clinical sociologist and author of *The Untold Story of Zama Zama Miners in South Africa*. I also want to thank

Juhani Grossman, head of the environmental corruption division at the Basel Institute.

The oil spill chapter would not have been possible without the help of Ian MacDonald, professor of biological oceanography at Florida State University. Thank you also to Robert Bea, who conducted the forensic engineering investigation of the Deepwater Horizon and sent me his original report.

I would like to extend special thanks to those who reviewed entire chapters: Alberto Ayala and Jack Ewing for emissions; Paulo Busse for deforestation; Ceres Kam for poaching; Peter Hammarstedt and Mario Alcaide for illegal fishing; Vidette Bester for illegal mining; and Ian MacDonald for the BP oil spill chapter.

To my agent, Annette Brüggemann, your steady guidance made this journey possible, and your tireless allyship, conversations, and creative vision really helped me through. Special thanks to my German translator, Ingrid Ickler, who not only carried my words into another language but helped refine the very structure and rhythm of this book. And to my copyeditor, Gemma Wain, who did a huge amount of polishing and checking to make sure the content of this book flows smoothly. To my editor, Simon Thorogood, thank you for believing in this book from the start, and making it possible.

I am also grateful to the many others who helped me understand the underlying issues.

Thank you to Nicholas Pamment, principal lecturer in criminology and criminal justice, and Jac Reed, senior lecturer in criminology and forensic studies, both at the University of Portsmouth. You allowed me to attend your course for an entire semester and spent time every week discussing issues and ideas related to green crime with me. Also thank you to Tanya Wyatt, professor of criminology at Northumbria University, who graciously spent time talking to me about the complexities of green criminology. Thank you to Oulie Keita, executive director of Greenpeace Africa for helping me understand some of the more global issues related to today's environmental movements.

Thank you to the UN for tirelessly pursuing a healthier Earth and hosting the UNICRI winter school on environmental crime which I attended in 2023. As part of the research for this book, I also virtually attended many UN meetings and conferences, including events at the United Nations Climate Change Conference, the meeting and deliberations of the Convention on International Trade in Endangered Species of Wild Fauna, and the conference of the UN Convention against Corruption.

Thank you to Professor David White, director of the Centre for Climate Crime and Climate at Queen Mary University, for inviting me to attend his environmental justice module at Queen Mary University, and to the panel discussion on ecocide he organised.

And thank you to all the scientists whose work I have been able to apply to understanding environmental issues and crimes. I hope that one day soon there will be far more exchange between environmental and social science researchers.

NOTES

INTRODUCTION

1 Stop Ecocide International. (2021). Article 8 ter. Ecocide. https://www.stopecocide.earth/legal-definition.
2 European Parliament News. (2024, February 27). Environmental crimes: MEPs adopt extended list of offences and sanctions. https://www.europarl.europa.eu/news/en/press-room/20240223IPR18075/environmental-crimes-meps-adopt-extended-list-of-offences-and-sanctions.

1 THE CON MEN

1 Disaster at Donora – An epidemiologic study. (1950). *New England Journal of Medicine*, *242*(5), 155–156. https://doi.org//10.1056/NEJM195001262420409.
2 Jacobs, E. T., Burgess, J. L., & Abbott, M. B. (2018). The Donora smog revisited: 70 years after the event that inspired the Clean Air Act. *American Journal of Public Health*, *108*(S2), S85–S88. https://doi.org/10.2105/AJPH.2017.304219.
3 Mills, C. A. (1950). The Donora episode. *Science*, *111*(2873), 67–68. https://doi.org/10.1126/science.112.2899.92.c
4 Disaster at Donora (1950).
5 Disaster at Donora (1950).
6 Disaster at Donora (1950).

7 Mills (1950).
8 Bell, M. L., Davis, D. L., & Fletcher, T. (2004). A retrospective assessment of mortality from the London smog episode of 1952: The role of influenza and pollution. *Environmental Health Perspectives*, *112*(1), 6–8. https://doi.org/10.1289/ehp.6539.
9 Clean Air Act 1956. https://www.legislation.gov.uk/ukpga/Eliz2/4-5/52/enacted.
10 Warren Spring Laboratory. (1959). *Nature*, *184*, 146–149. https://doi.org/10.1038/184146a0.
11 BBC Archive. (1962, December 6). Choking fog spreads across Britain. http://news.bbc.co.uk/onthisday/hi/dates/stories/december/6/newsid_3251000/3251001.stm
12 BBC Archive (1962, December 6).
13 US Environmental Protection Agency. (n.d.). EPA history: The Clean Air Act of 1970. https://www.epa.gov/clean-air-act-overview/clean-air-act-text.
14 US EPA (n.d.). EPA history: The Clean Air Act of 1970.
15 Clean Air Fund. (2024, November 14). The case for action on tropospheric ozone. https://www.cleanairfund.org/resource/action-on-tropospheric-ozone/.
16 US Environmental Protection Agency. (2024, July 16). Nitrogen dioxide (NO_2) pollution. https://www.epa.gov/no2-pollution/basic-information-about-no2.
17 Cruden, J.C., Engel, B., Cooney, N., & Van Eaton, J. (2024). Dieselgate: How the investigation, prosecution, and settlement of Volkswagen's emissions cheating scandal illustrates the need for robust environmental enforcement. *Virginia Environmental Law Journal*, 36(2). https://heinonline.org/HOL/LandingPage?handle=hein.journals/velj36&div=9&id=&page=
18 US Congress. (2015, October 6). Subcommittee on Oversight and Investigations of the House Committee on Energy and Commerce. https://www.congress.gov/114/meeting/house/104046/documents/HHRG-114-IF02-Transcript-20151008.pdf.
19 Gewin, V. (2015). Turning point: Daniel Carder. *Nature*, *527*(7578), 401. https://doi.org/10.1038/nj7578-401a

20 Morgan, D. (2015, September 24). West Virginia engineer proves to be a David to Volkswagen's Goliath. *Reuters Business.* https://www.reuters.com/article/us-usa-volkswagen-researchers-idUSKCN0RM2D720150924/.
21 US Environmental Protection Agency. (n.d.). Cummins Engine Company diesel engine Clean Air Act settlement. https://www.epa.gov/enforcement/cummins-engine-company-diesel-engine-clean-air-act-settlement.
22 U.S. EPA (n.d.). 2024 Cummins Inc. Vehicle Emission Control Violations Settlement.
23 US EPA (n.d.). Cummins Settlement.
24 US Environmental Protection Agency Office of Inspector General (2018). VW Notice of Violation. https://www.epa.gov/enforcement/learn-about-volkswagen-violations
25 US Environmental Protection Agency Office of Inspector General (2018, May 15). The EPA did not identify Volkswagen emissions cheating; Enhancing controls now provide reasonable assurance of fraud detection (Report No. 18-P-0181). https://www.oversight.gov/reports/audit/epa-did-not-identify-volkswagen-emissions-cheating-enhanced-controls-now-provide.
26 United Nations Development Programme. (2024). Peoples' Climate Vote results. https://peoplesclimate.vote/download.
27 Stanley, S. K., Hogg, T. L., Leviston, Z., & Walker, I. (2021). From anger to action: Differential impacts of eco-anxiety, eco-depression, and eco-anger on climate action and wellbeing. *Journal of Climate Change and Health, 1,* 100003. https://doi.org/10.1016/j.joclim.2021.100003.
28 Stanley et al. (2024).
29 UNDP. (2024). Peoples' Climate Vote.
30 Cruden et al (2024)
31 The Detroit News (n.d.). VW engineer's 40-month sentence 'sends . . . message'. https://eu.detroitnews.com/story/business/autos/foreign/2017/08/25/vw-engineer-laing-sentencing-diesel-emissions-scandal/104935982/.
32 Automotive News Europe (2017, December 7). Schmidt's

statement showed a broken man with misplaced faith in VW. https://europe.autonews.com/article/20171207/BLOG15/312079926/schmidt-s-statement-showed-a-broken-man-with-misplaced-faith-in-vw.

33 Luan, Y., Zhao, K., Wang, Z., & Hu, F. (2023). Exploring the antecedents of unethical pro-organizational behavior (UPB): A meta-analysis. *Journal of Business Ethics, 187,* 119–136. https://psycnet.apa.org/doi/10.1007/s10551-022-05269-w.

34 Federal Trade Commission. (2016, March 29). FTC charges Volkswagen deceived consumers with its 'Clean Diesel' campaign. https://www.ftc.gov/news-events/news/press-releases/2016/03/ftc-charges-volkswagen-deceived-consumers-its-clean-diesel-campaign.

35 FTC (2016, March 29).

36 Meyer, M., & Choo, C. W. (2024). Harming by deceit: Epistemic malevolence and organizational wrongdoing. *Journal of Business Ethics, 189*(3), 439–452. https://doi.org/10.1007/s10551-023-05370-8.

37 Choo, C. W., & Meyer, M. (2023). Information misbehavior: How organizations use information to deceive. *Journal of the Association for Information Science and Technology, 74*(9), 1081–1085. https://doi.org/10.1002/asi.24804.

38 Shaw, J., Porter, S., & ten Brinke, L. (2013). Catching liars: Training mental health and legal professionals to detect high-stakes lies. *Journal of Forensic Psychiatry and Psychology, 24*(2), 145–159. https://doi.org/10.1080/14789949.2012.752025.

39 Shaw, J. (2024). How to actually catch a liar, according to the new science of lie detection. *Science Focus.* https://www.sciencefocus.com/the-human-body/how-to-catch-a-liar.

40 European Commission. (2023, March 22). Questions and answers on European green claims. https://ec.europa.eu/commission/presscorner/detail/en/qanda_23_1693.

41 European Parliament. (2023). EU to ban greenwashing and improve consumer information on product durability. https://www.europarl.europa.eu/news/en/press-room/20230918IPR05412/

eu-to-ban-greenwashing-and-improve-consumer-information-on-product-durability.

42 Bisschop, L., Hendlin, Y., & Jaspers, J. (2022). Designed to break: Planned obsolescence as corporate environmental crime. *Crime, Law and Social Change, 78*, 271–293. https://doi.org/10.1007/s10611-022-10023-4.

43 Kuhn, S., Thøgersen, J., & Kutzner, F. (2023). No trust in the choice architect? No problem! On the minor role of trust for the effectiveness of default interventions promoting the choice of energy-efficient appliances. *Journal of Environmental Psychology, 91*, 102115. https://doi.org/10.1016/j.jenvp.2023.102115.

44 Robertson, J. L., Montgomery, A. W., & Ozbilir, T. (2023). Employees' response to corporate greenwashing. *Business Strategy and the Environment, 32*(7), 4015–4027. https://doi.org/10.1002/bse.3351.

45 Bae, S., Liu, X., & Ng, S. (2022). We are more tolerant than I: Self-construal and consumer responses toward deceptive advertising. *Marketing Letters, 33*, 277–291. https://doi.org/10.1007/s11002-021-09593-5

46 Golec de Zavala, A., & Lantos, D. (2020). Collective narcissism and its social consequences: The bad and the ugly. *Current Directions in Psychological Science, 29*(3), 273–278. https://doi.org/10.1177/0963721420917703.

47 Cislak, A., Cichocka, A., Wojcik, A. D., & Milfont, T. L. (2021). Words not deeds: National narcissism, national identification, and support for greenwashing versus genuine pro-environmental campaigns. *Journal of Environmental Psychology, 74*, 101576. https://doi.org/10.1016/j.jenvp.2021.101576.

48 US Department of Justice Archives. (2017, January 11). Volkswagen AG agrees to plead guilty and pay $4.3 billion in criminal and civil penalties; Six Volkswagen executives and employees are indicted in connection with conspiracy to cheat U.S. emissions tests. https://www.justice.gov/opa/pr/volkswagen-ag-agrees-plead-guilty-and-pay-43-billion-criminal-and-civil-penalties-six.

49 US DOJ Archives (2017, January 11).
50 Federal Trade Commission. (2020, July 28). In the final court summary, FTC reports Volkswagen repaid more than $9.5 billion to car buyers who were deceived by 'Clean Diesel' ad campaign. https://www.ftc.gov/news-events/news/press-releases/2020/07/final-court-summary-ftc-reports-volkswagen-repaid-more-95-billion-car-buyers-who-were-deceived-clean.
51 US Department of Justice Archives. (2017, January 11). Attorney General Loretta E. Lynch delivers remarks at a press conference announcing criminal and civil actions against Volkswagen. https://www.justice.gov/opa/speech/attorney-general-loretta-e-lynch-delivers-remarks-press-conference-announcing-criminal.
52 US Department of Justice Archives. (2018, May 3). Former CEO of Volkswagen AG charged with conspiracy and wire fraud in Diesel Emissions Scandal. https://www.justice.gov/opa/pr/former-ceo-volkswagen-ag-charged-conspiracy-and-wire-fraud-diesel-emissions-scandal.
53 US Environmental Protection Agency. (n.d.). Current EPA fugitives. https://www.epa.gov/enforcement/epa-fugitives#neusser.
54 Leggett, T. (2024, September 3). Trial of former VW boss begins over 'Dieselgate' scandal. BBC News. https://www.bbc.co.uk/news/articles/cn5r9rgg6yno.
55 Nixon, R. (2013). *Slow Violence and the Environmentalism of the Poor*. Harvard University Press.
56 EU EUR-Lex. (2021, December 15). Explanatory memorandum to COM(2021)851 – Protection of the environment through criminal law. https://www.eumonitor.eu/9353000/1/j4nvhdfdk3hydzq_j9vvik7m1c3gyxp/vloreuvgdhxc.
57 US Attorney's Office. (2017, August 25). Volkswagen engineer sentenced for his role in conspiracy to cheat U.S. emissions tests. https://www.justice.gov/usao-edmi/pr/volkswagen-engineer-sentenced-his-role-conspiracy-cheat-us-emissions-tests.
58 US Department of Justice Archives. (2017, December 6). Volkswagen senior manager sentenced to 84 months in prison

for role in conspiracy to cheat U.S. emissions tests. https://www.justice.gov/opa/pr/volkswagen-senior-manager-sentenced-84-months-prison-role-conspiracy-cheat-us-emissions-tests.
59. Bloomberg (2023, May). Ex-Audi Boss Rupert Stadler Admits He Turned Blind Eye to Diesel-Rigged Cars.
60. Deutsche Welle. (2023, June 27). Ex-Audi boss given suspended sentence in 'dieselgate' case. https://www.dw.com/en/ex-audi-boss-given-suspended-sentence-in-dieselgate-emissions-scandal/a-66040769.
61. Deutsche Welle (2023, June 27).
62. McGuinness, D. (2023, June 27). Ex-Audi boss Stadler avoids jail in VW emissions scandal. BBC News. https://www.bbc.co.uk/news/world-europe-66029634.
63. Tagesschau. (2023, July 3). Stadler legt Revision gegen Diesel-Urteil ein. https://www.tagesschau.de/wirtschaft/unternehmen/stadler-urteil-revision-100.html?utm_source=chatgpt.com
64. NY Times (2025). Four Former VW Managers Found Guilty in Emissions Trial. https://www.nytimes.com/2025/05/26/business/volkswagen-emissions-trial.html
65. European Parliament News. (2024, February 23). Environmental crimes: MEPs adopt extended list of offences and sanctions. https://www.europarl.europa.eu/news/en/press-room/20240223IPR18075/environmental-crimes-meps-adopt-extended-list-of-offences-and-sanctions.
66. Capital. (2024, February 15). Der Selbstgerechte: Winterkorn hat die Justiz lächerlich gemacht. https://www.capital.de/wirtschaft-politik/der-selbstgerechte--martin-winterkorn-macht-die-justiz-laecherlich-34462112.html.
67. Meyer, M., Bernard, Y., German, J., & Dallmann, T. (2023). Reassessment of excess NOx from diesel cars in Europe following the Court Justice of the European Union rulings. International Council on Clean Transportation. https://theicct.org/publication/dieselgate-emissions-diesel-cars-europe-mar23/

2 THE MURDERERS

1 Climate Counsel Online Evidence Platform. (2022). Crimes in the State of Pará. brazil-crimes.org.
2 Globo. (2011, May 25). Ambientalistas do Pará foram mortos em tocaia, diz delegado. G1. https://g1.globo.com/brasil/noticia/2011/05/ambientalistas-do-para-foram-mortos-em-tocaia-diz-delegado.html
3 Globo (2011, May 25).
4 Climate Counsel Online Evidence Platform (2022).
5 Climate Counsel Online Evidence Platform (2022).
6 Ribeiro, Z. C. (2011, February 2011) Killing trees is murder: Zé Cláudio Ribeiro at TEDxAmazonia. https://www.youtube.com/watch?v=XO2pwnrji8I
7 Globo. (2013, April 4). Ministra quer punição para acusados de assassinar casal de extrativistas. G1. https://g1.globo.com/pa/para/noticia/2013/04/ministra-quer-punicao-para-acusados-de-assassinar-casal-de-extrativistas.html.
8 Globo. (2013, April 1). Acusados de assassinar casal de extrativistas vão ao banco dos réus. G1. https://g1.globo.com/pa/para/noticia/2013/04/acusados-de-assassinar-casal-de-extrativistas-vao-ao-banco-dos-reus.html.
9 Sutter, J. D. (2014, August 13). Why do environmentalists keep getting killed around the world? *Smithsonian Magazine*. https://www.smithsonianmag.com/science-nature/why-do-environmentalists-keep-getting-killed-around-world-180949446/
10 Capriles, J. M., Lombardo, U., Maley, B., Zuna, C., Veit, H., & Kennett, D. J. (2019). Persistent Early to Middle Holocene tropical foraging in southwestern Amazonia. *Science Advances*, 5(4), eaav5449. https://doi.org/10.1126/sciadv.aav5449.
11 Motta, M. M. M. (2005). The Sesmarias in Brazil: Colonial land policies in the late eighteenth century. *e-Journal of Portuguese History*, 3(2), 1–12. https://www.brown.edu/Departments/Portuguese_Brazilian_Studies/ejph/html/issue12/html/mmotta.html
12 Cobo, M. J. R. (1986). Study of the problem of discrimination

against indigenous populations: Conclusions, proposals, and recommendations (Vol. V). United Nations. https://digitallibrary.un.org/record/133666?ln=en&v=pdf.
13. Climate Counsel Online Evidence Platform (2022)
14. UN Department of Economic and Social Affairs (n.d.). UNPFII Mandated Areas – Environment. https://www.un.org/development/desa/indigenouspeoples/mandated-areas1/environment.html.
15. Greenpeace UK. (n.d.). Amazon rainforest. https://www.greenpeace.org.uk/challenges/forests/amazon-rainforest/.
16. U.S. Department of Agriculture, Foreign Agricultural Service. (2023). Brazil: Livestock and products annual. https://fas.usda.gov/data/brazil-livestock-and-products-annual-10.
17. Poelhekke, F. G. M. N. (1982). The Struggle for Land in Brazilian Amazonia, Consequent on the Expansion of Cattle-Raising. *Boletín de Estudios Latinoamericanos y del Caribe*, *33*, 11–33. https://www.jstor.org/stable/25675151.
18. Le Tourneau, F. M., & Beaufort, B. (2017). Exploring the boundaries of individual and collective land use management: institutional arrangements in the PAE Chico Mendes (Acre, Brazil). *International Journal of the Commons*, *11*(1). https://doi.org/10.18352/ijc.589.
19. Beattie, M., Fa, J. E., Leiper, I., Fernández-Llamazares, Á., Zander, K. K., & Garnett, S. T. (2023). Even after armed conflict, the environmental quality of Indigenous Peoples' lands in biodiversity hotspots surpasses that of non-Indigenous lands. *Biological Conservation*, *286*, 110288. https://doi.org/10.1016/j.biocon.2023.110288.
20. Intergovernmental Panel on Climate Change. (2022). Cross-Chapter Paper 1: Biodiversity Hotspots. In: *Climate Change 2022: Impacts, Adaptation and Vulnerability*. Contribution of Working Group II to the Sixth Assessment Report of the Intergovernmental Panel on Climate Change. https://www.ipcc.ch/report/ar6/wg2/.
21. Burton-Chellew, M. N., & West, S. A. (2021). Payoff-based

learning best explains the rate of decline in cooperation across 237 public-goods games. *Nature Human Behaviour*, 5(10), 1330–1338. https://doi.org/10.1038/s41562-021-01107-7.

22 Eichenseer, M. (2023). Leading-by-example in public goods experiments: What do we know?. *The Leadership Quarterly*, 101695. https://doi.org/10.1016/j.leaqua.2023.101695.

23 Barron, K., & Nurminen, T. (2020). Nudging cooperation in public goods provision. *Journal of Behavioral and Experimental Economics*, 88, 101542. https://doi.org/10.1016/j.socec.2020.101542.

24 Araujo, C., Bonjean, C. A., Combes, J. L., Motel, P. C., & Reis, E. J. (2009). Property rights and deforestation in the Brazilian Amazon. *Ecological economics*, 68(8–9), 2461–2468. https://doi.org/10.1016/j.ecolecon.2008.12.015.

25 Preston, S. D., & Gelman, S. A. (2020). This land is my land: Psychological ownership increases willingness to protect the natural world more than legal ownership. *Journal of Environmental Psychology*, 70, 101443. https://doi.org/10.1016/j.jenvp.2020.101443.

26 Baragwanath, K., & Bayi, E. (2020). Collective property rights reduce deforestation in the Brazilian Amazon. *Proceedings of the National Academy of Sciences*, 117(34), 20495–20502. https://doi.org/10.1073/pnas.1917874117.

27 United Nations Environment Programme. (2023). Environmental rule of law: Tracking progress and charting future directions. https://doi.org/0.59117/20.500.11822/43943.

28 Climate Counsel Online Evidence Platform (2022).

29 Ribeiro (2011).

30 United Nations (2012, September 10). Forest heroes – Jose Claudio Ribeiro and Maria do Espirito Santo, special award. YouTube. https://www.youtube.com/watch?v=iJ5NH3-sFkY.

31 Ribeiro (2011).

32 SOS Amazônia (2020, September 4). Carta deixada por Chico Mendes inspira a criação para o festival 'Jovens do Futuro'. https://sosamazonia.org.br/tpost/olhbcmhzuo-carta-deixada-por-chico-mendes-inspira-a.

33 United Nations (2012, September 10).
34 United Nations Environment Programme (n.d.). Who are environmental defenders? https://www.unep.org/explore-topics/environmental-rights-and-governance/what-we-do/advancing-environmental-rights/who.
35 EJAtlas (n.d.). Global Atlas of Environmental Justice. https://ejatlas.org.
36 Buil-Gil, D., Medina, J., & Shlomo, N. (2021). Measuring the dark figure of crime in geographic areas: Small area estimation from the Crime Survey for England and Wales. *The British Journal of Criminology*, *61*(2), 364–388. https://doi.org/10.1093/bjc/azaa067.
37 United Kingdom. (2023). Public Order Act 2023: Part 1 – Offences relating to locking on. UK Government. https://www.legislation.gov.uk/ukpga/2023/15/part/1/crossheading/offences-relating-to-locking-on.
38 Associated Press (2022, October 27). 'Girl with a Pearl Earring' targeted by climate activists in latest art protest. *Los Angeles Times*. https://www.latimes.com/world-nation/story/2022-10-27/girl-with-a-pearl-earring-targeted-by-climate-activists.
39 Global Witness (2023, September 13). Almost 2,000 land and environmental defenders killed between 2012 and 2022 for protecting the planet. https://globalwitness.org/en/press-releases/almost-2000-land-and-environmental-defenders-killed-between-2012-and-2022-protecting-planet/.
40 Global Witness (2024, September 10). The violent erasure of land and environmental defenders. https://globalwitness.org/en/campaigns/land-and-environmental-defenders/missing-voices/.
41 Le Billon, P., & Lujala, P. (2021). Environmental defenders: Killings, perpetrators, and drivers of violence. In *Environmental Defenders* (pp. 64–75). Routledge.
42 Globo (2013, April 3). Acusados de assassinar casal de extrativistas são julgados no Pará. https://oglobo.globo.com/politica/acusados-de-assassinar-casal-de-extrativistas-sao-julgados-no-para-8013153.

43 Globo. (2016, December 1). Acusado de envolvimento na morte de casal de extrativistas é condenado. https://g1.globo.com/pa/para/noticia/2016/12/acusado-de-envolvimento-na-morte-de-casal-de-extrativistas-e-condenado.html.
44 Climate Counsel Online Evidence Platform (2022).
45 Buil-Gil, Medina & Shlomo (2021).
46 Kaiser, F., Huss, B., & Reinecke, J. (2022). Revisiting the experiential effect: How criminal offending affects juveniles' perceptions of detection risk. *Journal of Developmental and Life-Course Criminology, 8*(1), 47–74. https://doi.org/10.1007/s40865-021-00186-4.
47 Nagin, D. S. (2013). Deterrence in the twenty-first century. *Crime and justice, 42*(1), 199–263. https://doi.org/10.1086/670398.
48 Nagin (2013).
49 Nery, F. S., & Nadanovsky, P. (2020). Homicide impunity in Brazil between 2006 and 2016. *Revista de saude publica, 54*, 144. https://doi.org/10.11606/s1518-8787.2020054002284.
50 GI PA (2013, April 3) Começa julgamento de acusados de assassinar casal de extrativistas no PA. https://g1.globo.com/pa/para/noticia/2013/04/acusados-de-assassinar-casal-de-extrativistas-vao-ao-banco-dos-reus.html.
51 G1 Globo (2013, April 3). Acusados de assassinar casal de extrativistas vão ao banco dos réus. https://g1.globo.com/pa/para/noticia/2013/04/acusados-de-assassinar-casal-de-extrativistas-vao-ao-banco-dos-reus.html.
52 UOL. (2013, April 3). Testemunha afirma ter visto acusado no local do crime e gera bate-boca em julgamento no Pará. Notícias. https://noticias.uol.com.br/cotidiano/ultimas-noticias/2013/04/03/testemunha-afirma-ter-visto-acusado-no-local-do-crime-e-gera-bate-boca-em-julgamento-no-para.htm.
53 Carta Capital (2012, April 4).). Familiares do casal de extrativistas assassinado recebem intimidações no Pará. https://www.cartacapital.com.br/sociedade/familiares-do-casal-de-extrativistas-assassinado-recebem-intimidacoes-no-para/.

54 Direct communication with Paulo Busse.
55 Pública. (2013, July 8). Marcadas para morrer: Laisa luta pela terra, pela memória da irmã. https://apublica.org/2013/07/marcadas-para-morrer-laisa-luta-pela-terra-pela-memoria-da-irma/
56 UOL (2012, March 6). Três acusados do homicídio de casal de extrativistas no Pará vão a júri popular https://noticias.uol.com.br/cotidiano/ultimas-noticias/2012/03/06/tres-acusados-do-homicidio-de-casal-de-extrativistas-no-para-vao-a-juri-popular.htm.
57 CNN Brasil. (2023, May 4). Foragido desde 2015, condenado por matar extrativistas é recapturado no Pará. https://www.cnnbrasil.com.br/nacional/foragido-desde-2015-condenado-por-matar-extrativistas-e-recapturado-no-para/.
58 US Department of Agriculture. (2022, January 25). Brazilian economic and agricultural overview. USDA Foreign Agricultural Service. https://apps.fas.usda.gov/newgainapi/api/Report/DownloadReportByFileName?fileName=Brazilian%20Economic%20and%20Agricultural%20Overview%20_Sao%20Paulo%20ATO_Brazil_01-25-2022.pdf
59 Secretaria de Comunicação Social. (2024, July 16). Brazilian agribusiness exports reach USD 15.20 bi in June, total USD 82.39 bi in first half of 2024. https://www.gov.br/secom/en/latest-news/2024/07/brazilian-agribusiness-exports-reach-usd-15-20-bi-in-june-total-usd-82-39-bi-in-first-half-of-2024.
60 New Zealand Legislation. Te Urewera Act 2014. https://www.legislation.govt.nz/act/public/2014/0051/latest/whole.html,
61 Georgetown University Political Database of the Americas. (2008). Constitution of the Republic of Ecuador (English version). https://pdba.georgetown.edu/Constitutions/Ecuador/english08.html.
62 Stop Ecocide International. (n.d.). Ecocide: Legal definition. Stop Ecocide. Retrieved September 5, 2024, from https://www.stopecocide.earth/legal-definition.
63 Falk, R.A. (1973). Environmental Warfare and Ecocide – facts,

appraisal, and proposals. *Bulletin of Peace Proposals*, 4(1), 80–96. https://www.jstor.org/stable/44480206.
64 Reuters (2025, February 17). Brazil targets illegal logging in major Amazon raids. https://www.reuters.com/world/americas/brazil-targets-illegal-logging-major-amazon-raids-2025-02-17/.

3 THE TRAFFICKERS

1 Cowie, H. L. (2021). *Victims of Fashion*. Cambridge University Press.
2 Cowie (2021).
3 Cowie (2021).
4 Bentham, J. (1879). *The Principles of Morals and Legislation*. Clarendon Press.
5 Camilleri, L., Gill, P. R., & Jago, A. (2020). The role of moral disengagement and animal empathy in the meat paradox. *Personality and Individual Differences*, *164*, 110103. https://doi.org/10.1016/j.paid.2020.110103.
6 Eating Better (2022, June 17). Cost and choice are key to sustainable eating finds 2022 public poll from Eating Better. https://www.eating-better.org/news-and-reports/news/eating-better-2022-public-attitudes-survey-results/.
7 CITES (n.d.) What is CITES? https://cites.org/eng/disc/what.php.
8 United Nations Office on Drugs and Crime (2016). *World Wildlife Crime Report 2016*. https://doi.org/10.18356/e70581eb-en.
9 Interpol (2019). Global Wildlife Enforcement: Strengthening Law Enforcement Cooperation Against Wildlife Crime. https://www.interpol.int/en/Crimes/Environmental-crime/Wildlife-crime.
10 United Nations Office on Drugs and Crime (2024).
11 Shivanand, P., Arbie, N. F., Krishnamoorthy, S., & Ahmad, N. (2022). Agarwood – the fragrant molecules of a wounded tree. *Molecules*, *27*(11), 3386. https://doi.org/10.3390/molecules27113386.

12 Interpol (2023, November 6). Illegal wildlife trade has become one of the 'world's largest criminal activities'. https://www.interpol.int/en/News-and-Events/News/2023/Illegal-wildlife-trade-has-become-one-of-the-world-s-largest-criminal-activities.
13 World Bank Group (n.d.). Urban Development. https://www.worldbank.org/en/topic/urbandevelopment/overview.
14 Soga, M., & Gaston, K. J. (2018). Shifting baseline syndrome: causes, consequences, and implications. *Frontiers in Ecology and the Environment*, *16*(4), 222–230. https://doi.org/10.1002/fee.1794.
15 Ripple, W. J., Newsome, T. M., Wolf, C., Dirzo, R., Everatt, K. T., Galetti, M., . . . & Van Valkenburgh, B. (2015). Collapse of the world's largest herbivores. *Science Advances*, *1*(4), e1400103. https://doi.org/10.1126/sciadv.1400103.
16 Ceballos, G., Ehrlich, P. R., & Dirzo, R. (2017). Biological annihilation via the ongoing sixth mass extinction signaled by vertebrate population losses and declines. *Proceedings of the National Academy of Sciences*, *114*(30), E6089–E6096. https://doi.org/10.1073/pnas.1704949114.
17 Morton, O., Scheffers, B. R., Haugaasen, T., & Edwards, D. P. (2021). Impacts of wildlife trade on terrestrial biodiversity. *Nature Ecology & Evolution*, *5*(4), 540–548. https://doi.org/10.1038/s41559-021-01399-y.
18 Janzen, D. H. (1970). Herbivores and the number of tree species in tropical forests. *The American Naturalist*, *104*(940), 501–528. https://www.jstor.org/stable/2459010.
19 Schweinfurth, G. A. (1874). The Heart of Africa: Three Years' Travels and Adventures in the Unexplored Regions of Central Africa, From 1868 To 1871 (Vol. 2). S. Low, Marston, Low, and Searle. https://archive.org/details/heartofafricathr02schw.
20 WWF. (2024). World Elephant Day. https://www.wwf.org.uk/learn/world-days/world-elephant-day.
21 Global Conservation (n.d.). *African Savanna Elephant*. https://globalconservation.org/endangered-species/african-savanna-elephant?rq=million%20elephants.

22 Belecky, M., Singh, R. and Moreto, W. (2019). *Life on the Frontline 2019: A Global Survey of the Working Conditions of Rangers*. WWF. https://www.worldwildlife.org/publications/life-on-the-frontline-2019-a-global-survey-of-the-working-conditions-of-rangers.

23 Galliers, C., Cole, R., Singh, R., Ohlfs, J., Aisha, H., Koutoua, A. B., . . . & Malvido, M. Á. (2022). Conservation casualties: an analysis of on-duty ranger fatalities (2006–2021). *Parks*, *28*(1), 39–50. https://www.npshistory.com/publications/ranger/p-v18n1-2022.pdf.

24 Titeca, K. (2018). Understanding the illegal ivory trade and traders: evidence from Uganda. *International Affairs*, *94*(5), 1077–1099. https://doi.org/10.1093/ia/iiy115.

25 Hariohay, K. M., Ranke, P. S., Fyumagwa, R. D., Kideghesho, J. R., & Røskaft, E. (2019). Drivers of conservation crimes in the Rungwa-Kizigo-Muhesi game reserves, Central Tanzania. *Global Ecology and Conservation*, *17*, e00522. https://doi.org/10.1016/j.gecco.2019.e00522.

26 Kuiper, T., Altwegg, R., Beale, C., Carroll, T., Dublin, H. T., Hauenstein, S., . . . & Milner-Gulland, E. J. (2023). Drivers and facilitators of the illegal killing of elephants across 64 African sites. *Proceedings of the Royal Society B*, *290*(1990), 20222270. https://doi.org/10.1098/rspb.2022.2270/

27 Appeal Verdict, Kanwen Wan.

28 TRAFFIC. (2020). The people beyond the poaching. https://www.traffic.org/beyond-the-poaching/.

4 THE OUTLAWS

1 Interpol. (2013, May 27). Countries unite to identify illegal fishing vessel via INTERPOL. https://www.interpol.int/en/News-and-Events/News/2013/Countries-unite-to-identify-illegal-fishing-vessel-via-INTERPOL.

2 Kroon, D. (2019). The End of Freedom of the Seas?. *The International Lawyer*, *52*(2), 299–326. https://www.jstor.org/stable/27009665.

3 Grotius, H. (1901). *The Rights of War and Peace*. New York: M. Walter Dunne.
4 Berlin, I. (1969). *Two Concepts of Liberty*. Oxford University Press.
5 The Pew Charitable Trusts. (2023). Despite progress, illegal catch continues to reach the market. https://www.pewtrusts.org/en/research-and-analysis/issue-briefs/2023/08/despite-progress-illegal-catch-continues-to-reach-the-market.
6 WWF (2003, January 9). Cyanide: An easy but deadly way to catch fish. https://wwf.panda.org/wwf_news/?5563/Cyanide-an-easy-but-deadly-way-to-catch-fish.
7 Mondal, S., Samanta, G., & De la Sen, M. (2022). Dynamics of oxygen-plankton model with variable zooplankton search rate in deterministic and fluctuating environments. *Mathematics*, *10*(10), 1641. https://doi.org/10.3390/math10101641.
8 Gruber, N., Bakker, D. C., DeVries, T., Gregor, L., Hauck, J., Landschützer, P., . . . & Müller, J. D. (2023). Trends and variability in the ocean carbon sink. *Nature Reviews Earth & Environment*, *4*(2), 119–134. https://doi.org/10.1038/s43017-022-00381-x.
9 Cheng, L., von Schuckmann, K., Abraham, J. P., Trenberth, K. E., Mann, M. E., Zanna, L., . . . & Lin, X. (2022). Past and future ocean warming. *Nature Reviews Earth & Environment*, *3*(11), 776–794. https://doi.org/10.1038/s43017-022-00345-1.
10 Food and Agriculture Organisation of the United Nations (2022). The state of world fisheries and aquaculture 2022. https://www.fao.org/3/cc0461en/online/sofia/2022/world-fisheries-aquaculture-production.html.
11 The Ocean Outlaw Project (n.d.). About. https://www.theoutlawocean.com/about/.
12 Urbina, I (2023, October 9). *Crimes at Sea: A Fleet Prone to Captive Labor and Plunder*. Ocean Outlaw Project Report: https://www.theoutlawocean.com/investigations/china-the-superpower-of-seafood/a-fleet-prone-to-captive-labor-and-plunder/.
13 Global Initiative (2023). The Illegal, Unreported, and

Unrefulated Fishing Risk Index. https://globalinitiative.net/analysis/iuu-fishing-risk-index-2023/.
14. Stop Illegal Fishing (2015, October 20). Guilty verdicts in the Thunder case. https://stopillegalfishing.com/news-articles/guilty-verdicts-in-the-thunder-case-4/.
15. Butler, N. M. (1923). Law and Lawlessness. *American Bar Association Journal*, *9*(2), 98–102. http://www.jstor.org/stable/25711152.
16. Dau, P. M., Vandeviver, C., Dewinter, M., Witlox, F., & Vander Beken, T. (2023). Policing directions: A systematic review on the effectiveness of police presence. *European Journal on Criminal Policy and Research*, *29*(2), 191–225. https://doi.org/10.21428/cb6ab371.47e2db59.
17. Belhabib, D., & Le Billon, P. (2022). Fish crimes in the global oceans. *Science Advances*, *8*(12). https://doi.org/10.1126/sciadv.abj1927.
18. Sea Shepherd Global. (2018, April 17). Pirate Fishing Tycoon Hit with €8.2 Million Fine in Spain. https://www.seashepherdglobal.org/latest-news/thunder-owner-fined/.
19. United Nations Office on Drugs and Crime. (n.d.). *Crimes in the Fisheries Sector.* https://www.unodc.org/unodc/en/environment-climate/fisheries.html.
20. United Nations Office on Drugs and Crime. (2020). Maritime Domain Awareness (MDA) courses catalogue. UNODC Global Maritime Crime Programme. https://www.unodc.org/unodc/en/piracy/index.html.
21. Blue Justice (2023, September 7). Blue Justice Ocean Surveillance Programme launch.https://www.youtube.com/watch?v=msEE7EFgkew&t=2s.

5 THE THIEVES

1. South African Government Opinion Pieces (2024). The stand-off at Stilfontein must be resolved peacefully and safely. https://www.gov.za/blog/stand-stilfontein-must-be-resolved-peacefully-and-safely.

2 *The Guardian* (2024, November 19). South African officials weigh up rescue mission for illegal miners underground. https://www.theguardian.com/world/2024/nov/19/south-african-officials-weigh-up-rescue-mission-for-miners-underground.
3 South African Government Media Statements (2023, November 9). Presidency on authorisation of SANDF members employment in cooperation with SAPS in operation against illegal mining. https://www.gov.za/news/media-statements/presidency-authorisation-sandf-members-employment-cooperation-saps-operation.
4 Burgess, A. (2018). *Heist!: South Africa's Cash-In-Transit Epidemic Uncovered*. Penguin Random House South Africa.
5 Polity (2023, October 13). Deploying 'badly overstretched' army not the solution to cash-in-transit heists, defence experts say. https://www.polity.org.za/article/deploying-badly-overstretched-army-not-the-solution-to-cash-in-transit-heists-defence-experts-say-2023-10-13.
6 Magistrate Barberton. Inquest Number 26/2021. Judgment. Inquest into the circumstances attending to the presumed death of Solomon Emmanual Nyirenda, Yvonne Mnisi, Pretty Winnie Nkambule.
7 United Nations Environment Programme (2020). Mineral resource governance in the 21st Century: Artisanal and Small Scale Mining, 79–104. https://doi.org/10.18356/89a57af1-en.
8 World Bank (2020). 2020 State of the Artisanal and Small-Scale Mining Sector. https://documents1.worldbank.org/curated/en/884541630559615834/txt/Delve-2020-State-of-the-Artisanal-and-Small-Scale-Mining-Sector.txt.
9 McCurry, J. (2006). Japan remembers Minamata. *The Lancet*. https://doi.org/10.1016/s0140-6736(06)67944-0.
10 Eto, K., Yasutake, A., Nakano, A., Akagi, H., Tokunaga, H., & Kojima, T. (2001). Reappraisal of the historic 1959 cat experiment in Minamata by the Chisso factory. *Tohoku Journal of Experimental Medicine*, *194*(4), 197–203. https://doi.org/10.1620/tjem.194.197.

11 United Nations News (2021, October 30). First Person: Telling the tragic story of mercury poisoning in Japan. https://news.un.org/en/story/2021/10/1103842?123=.
12 McCurry (2006).
13 United Nations Environment Programme (2023). Minamata Convention on Mercury – Text and Annexes. https://minamataconvention.org/en/resources/minamata-convention-mercury-text-and-annexes
14 UNEP (2024, November 24). Minamata Convention on Mercury.
15 Fashola, M. O., Ngole-Jeme, V. M., & Babalola, O. O. (2016). Heavy metal pollution from gold mines: environmental effects and bacterial strategies for resistance. *International Journal of Environmental Research and Public Health*, *13*(11), 1047. https://doi.org/10.3390/ijerph13111047.
16 UNEP (2023). Decisions adopted by the Conference of the Parties to the Minamata Convention on Mercury at its fifth meeting. MC-5/7: Artisanal and small-scale gold mining. https://minamataconvention.org/en/documents/artisanal-and-small-scale-gold-mining-0.
17 Laker, M. C. (2023). Environmental Impacts of Gold Mining – With Special Reference to South Africa. *Mining*, *3*(2), 205–220. https://doi.org/10.3390/mining3020012.
18 Harvard Law School (2016). The Cost of Gold: Environmental, Health, and Human Rights Consequences of Gold Mining In South Africa's West and Central Rand. https://cer.org.za/wp-content/uploads/2016/10/Cost-of-Gold-South-Africa-Report-Exec-Summary-Oct-2016.pdf.
19 Marais, L., Kemp, D., van der Watt, P., Matebesi, S., Cloete, J., Harris, J., Li Ern, M. A., & Owen, J. R. (2024). The catastrophic failure of the Jagersfontein tailings dam: an industrial disaster 150 years in the making. *International Journal of Disaster Risk Reduction*, *109*, 104585. https://doi.org/10.1016/j.ijdrr.2024.104585.
20 Lydia, O., Godwin, A., & Isaac, L. (2022). 'We have done

nothing wrong':Youth miners' perceptions of the environmental consequences of artisanal and small-scale mining (ASM) in Ghana. *The Extractive Industries and Society*, *12*, 101179. http://dx.doi.org/10.1016/j.exis.2022.101179.
21. Veiga, M. M., & Fadina, O. (2020). A review of the failed attempts to curb mercury use at artisanal gold mines and a proposed solution. *The Extractive Industries and Society*, *7*(3), 1135–1146. http://dx.doi.org/10.1016/j.exis.2020.06.023.
22. United Nations Environment Programme (2016, May 27). The rise of environmental crime: a growing threat to natural resources, peace, development and security. https://www.unep.org/resources/report/rise-environmental-crime-growing-threat-natural-resources-peace-development-and.
23. News24 (2021, November 9). Lily Mine inquest: Witness says zama zamas could have become trapped along with 3 employees. https://www.news24.com/News24/lily-mine-inquest-witness-says-zama-zamas-could-have-become-trapped-along-with-3-employees-20211109.
24. ActionAid (2019). Regularising informal artisanal mining in South Africa: An evidence-based report 2019.
25. Magistrate Barberton. Inquest Number 26/2021.
26. Said by Tanya Wyatt at the annual UN convention against corruption (CoSP) session on combating corruption to protect the environment, on 13 December 2023.
27. Transparency International (n.d.). What is corruption? https://www.transparency.org/en/what-is-corruption.
28. United States Institute of Peace. (n.d.). *Section 10: Corruption-related offenses and other offenses involving a public official.* https://www.usip.org/sites/default/files/MC1/MC1-Part2Section10.pdf
29. Weißmüller, K. S., & Zuber, A. (2023). Understanding the micro-foundations of administrative corruption in the public sector: Findings from a systematic literature review. *Public Administration Review*, *83*(6). https://doi.org/10.1111/puar.13699
30. Sundström, A. (2019). Exploring performance-related pay as an anticorruption tool. *Studies in Comparative International*

Development, 54, 1–18. https://doi.org/10.1007/s12116-017-9251-0.

31 Siegel, S., & Veiga, M. M. (2009). Artisanal and small-scale mining as an extralegal economy: De Soto and the redefinition of 'formalization'. *Resources Policy, 34*(1–2), 51–56. https://doi.org/10.1016/j.resourpol.2008.02.001.

32 Sundström, A. (2016). Violence and the costs of honesty: Rethinking bureaucrat's choices to take bribes. *Public Administration, 94*(3), 593-608. https://doi.org/10.1111/padm.12242.

33 United States Institute of Peace. (n.d.). Section 10: Corruption-related offenses and other offenses involving a public official. https://www.usip.org/sites/default/files/MC1/MC1-Part2Section 10.pdf.

34 News24 (2021, November 4). Lily Mine inquest: Families refuse to believe that loved ones trapped underground since 2016 are dead. https://www.news24.com/news24/lily-mine-inquest-families-refuse-to-believe-that-loved-ones-trapped-underground-since-2016-are-dead-20211104.

35 Magistrate Barberton. Inquest Number 26/2021.

36 South African Government Media Statements (2023, November 9). Presidency on authorisation of SANDF members employment in cooperation with SAPS in operation against illegal mining. https://www.gov.za/news/media-statements/presidency-authorisation-sandf-members-employment-cooperation-saps-operation.

37 Altay, S., & Acerbi, A. (2024). People believe misinformation is a threat because they assume others are gullible. *New Media & Society, 26*(11), 6440–6461. https://doi.org/10.1177/14614448231153379.

38 Ulucanlar, S., Fooks, G. J., & Gilmore, A. B. (2016). The policy dystopia model: An interpretive analysis of tobacco industry political activity. *PLoS medicine, 13*(9), e1002125. https://doi.org/10.1371/journal.pmed.1002125.

39 Root, T. (2019, May 16). Inside the long war to protect plastic. The Centre for Public Integrity. https://publicintegrity.org/

environment/pollution/pushing-plastic/inside-the-long-war-to-protect-plastic/.
40 NPR Investigations (2020, September 11). How Big Oil Misled the Public into believing plastic would be recycled. https://www.npr.org/2020/09/11/897692090/how-big-oil-misled-the-public-into-believing-plastic-would-be-recycled.
41 NPR Investigations (2020, September 11).
42 *The Guardian* (2024, October 1). Most soft plastic collected for recycling is burned, campaigners say. https://www.theguardian.com/environment/2024/oct/01/soft-plastic-collected-for-recycling-burned-tesco-sainsburys-campaigners.
43 Lancaster University News (2024, November 14). Research into UK's use of plastic packaging finds households 'wishcycle' rather than recycle – risking vast contamination. https://www.lancaster.ac.uk/news/research-into-uks-use-of-plastic-packaging-finds-households-wishcycle-rather-than-recycle-risking-vast-contamination.
44 Smith, O., & Brisman, A. (2021). Plastic waste and the environmental crisis industry. *Critical Criminology*, *29*, 289309. https://doi.org/10.1007/s10612-021-09562-4.
45 European Commission News (2024, December 2). EU regrets lack of conclusion on global plastics treaty. https://environment.ec.europa.eu/news/eu-regrets-inconclusive-global-plastics-treaty-2024-12-02_en.
46 NPR Investigations (2020, September 11).
47 Ecker, U. K., Lewandowsky, S., Cook, J., Schmid, P., Fazio, L. K., Brashier, N., . . . & Amazeen, M. A. (2022). The psychological drivers of misinformation belief and its resistance to correction. *Nature Reviews Psychology*, *1*(1), 13–29. https://doi.org/10.1038/s44159-021-00006-y.
48 Ecker et al. (2022).
49 Ecker et al. (2022).
50 BBC News (2024, November 16). Police vow to arrest South African miners as standoff continues. https://www.bbc.co.uk/news/articles/czj71kj1jlmo,

51 Times Live (2024, December 18). Six more illegal miners arrested in Stilfontein after resurfacing. https://www.timeslive.co.za/news/south-africa/2024-12-18-six-more-illegal-miners-arrested-in-stilfontein-after-resurfacing/.

52 TimesLive (2024, December 1). Pretoria high court grants emergency aid to illegal miners amid police crackdown. https://www.timeslive.co.za/news/south-africa/2024-12-01-pretoria-high-court-grants-emergency-aid-to-illegal-miners-amid-police-crackdown/.

53 Lawyers for Human rights press statement (2024, December 1). Pretoria High Court grants urgent interim relief for humanitarian aid for artisanal miners trapped at Buffelsfontein Gold Mine. https://www.lhr.org.za/lhr-news/press-statement-pretoria-high-court-grants-urgent-interim-relief-for-humanitarian-aid-for-artisanal-miners-trapped-at-buffelsfontein-gold-mine/.

54 South African Police Service Media Statements (2025, February 19). Process underway to identify suspected illegal miners bodies. saps.gov.za/newsroom/msspeechdetail.php?nid=59054.

55 New Zimbabwe News (2015, February 21). Bodies of 90 illegal Stilfontein miners remain unclaimed. https://www.newzimbabwe.com/bodies-of-90-illegal-stilfontein-miners-remain-unclaimed/.

56 BBC News (2025, January 13). Dead bodies seen in videos from South African mine. https://www.bbc.co.uk/news/articles/c70k4ke4r49o.

6 THE NEGLIGENT

1 U.S. Government Printing Office (2011). *Deep Water: The Gulf Oil Disaster and the Future of Offshore Drilling. Report to the President.* The National Commission on the BP Deepwater Horizon Oil Spill and Offshore Drilling.

2 GPO (2011). *Deep Water*.

3 Beckman, E. (2012). An Oil Well Named Macondo: Latin American Literature in the Time of Global Capital. *PMLA*, *127*(1), 145–151. https://doi.org/10.1632/pmla.2012.127.1.145.

4 GPO (2011). *Deep Water.*
5 GPO (2011). *Deep Water.*
6 *United States of America v. Kaluza and Vidrine*, Criminal No. 12-265 (E.D. La. 2012). Superseding indictment for involuntary manslaughter, seaman's manslaughter, and Clean Water Act violations.
7 Nevins, A, & Dunlop, R. G. (2019). *Energy and Man: A Symposium.* Pickle Partners Publishing.
8 Nevins & Dunlop (2019).
9 GPO (2011). *Deep Water.*
10 Belt, B. C. (1956). Louisiana and Texas Offshore Prospects, Drilling, 119. As cited in GPO (2011). *Deep Water.*
11 Nevins & Dunlop (2019).
12 Nevins & Dunlop (2019).
13 Druckman, J. N., & McGrath, M. C. (2019). The evidence for motivated reasoning in climate change preference formation. *Nature Climate Change, 9*(2), 111–119. https://doi.org/10.1038/s41558-018-0360-1.
14 GPO (2011). *Deep Water.*
15 GPO (2011). *Deep Water.*
16 *United States of America v. Kaluza and Vidrine.*
17 https://skytruth.org/.
18 Joye, S. B. (2015, April 29). *Written testimony of Samantha B. Joye, Ph.D., Athletic Association Distinguished Professor of Arts & Sciences, Professor of Marine Sciences, University of Georgia.* Testimony presented before the U.S. Senate Committee on Commerce, Science, and Transportation. Hearing: Five years after Deepwater Horizon: Improvements and challenges in prevention and response.
19 Fitz-Henry, E. (2020). Conjuring the past: Slow violence and the temporalities of environmental rights tribunals. *Geoforum, 108,* 259–266. https://doi.org/10.1016/j.geoforum.2019.09.001.
20 McCulloch, M. (2023, October 13). North Sea oil spills threat to marine protected areas. *The Ferret.* https://theferret.scot/north-sea-oil-spills-threat-marine-protected-areas/.

21 MacDonald (2010).
22 C-SPAN (2010, September 27). Gulf of Mexico Oil Spill Commission, Scientists Panel. https://www.c-span.org/video/?295668-3/gulf-mexico-oil-spill-commission-scientists-panel.
23 C-SPAN (2010, September 27).
24 *The Guardian* (2023, April 20). They cleaned up BP's massive oil spill. Now they're sick – and want justice. https://www.theguardian.com/environment/2023/apr/20/bp-oil-spill-deepwater-horizon-health-lawsuits
25 Cunsolo, A., Ellis, N. R. Ecological grief as a mental health response to climate change-related loss. *Nature Clim Change* 8, 275–281 (2018). https://doi.org/10.1038/s41558-018-0092-2.
26 Meltzer, G. Y., Merdjanoff, A. A., Gershon, R. R., Fothergill, A., Peek, L., & Abramson, D. M. (2024). Adverse Effects of the Deepwater Horizon oil spill Amid Cumulative Disasters: A Qualitative Analysis of the Experiences of Children and Families. *Journal of Child and Family Studies*, *33*(6), 1995–2011. https://doi.org/10.1007/s10826-024-02815-0.
27 Cáceres, C., Leiva-Bianchi, M., Serrano, C., Ormazábal, Y., Mena, C., & Cantillana, J. C. (2022). What is Solastalgia and how is it measured? SOS, a validated scale in population exposed to drought and forest fires. *International Journal of Environmental Research and Public Health*, *19*(20), 13682. https://doi.org/10.3390/ijerph192013682.
28 Albrecht, G. (2006). Solastalgia: Environmental damage has made it possible to be homesick without leaving home. *Alternatives Journal*, 32 (4–5), 34–36. https://link.gale.com/apps/doc/A161545303/AONE?u=anon~664c6410&sid=googleScholar&xid=8758c4b4.
29 Meltzer et al. (2024).
30 Cunsolo et al (2020).
31 Crisford, H., Dare, H., & Evangeli, M. (2008). Offence-related posttraumatic stress disorder (PTSD) symptomatology and guilt in mentally disordered violent and sexual offenders. *The

Journal of Forensic Psychiatry & Psychology, 19(1), 86–107. https://doi.org/10.1080/14789940701596673

32 Ferrito, M., Needs, A., Jingree, T., & Pearson, D. (2020). Making sense of the dark: a study on the identity of men who committed homicide. *Journal of Forensic Psychology Research and Practice, 20*(2), 163–184. https://doi.org/10.1080/2473285 0.2020.1714399.

33 Bea, R. G., & Gale, W. E. (2011). Rule 26 report on BP's Deepwater Horizon Macondo Blowout. Report prepared for the Plaintiff Steer Committee (PSC) for MDL No. 2179 by order of the Judicial Panel on Multi District Litigation.

34 Bea & Gale (2011).

35 GPO (2011). *Deep Water.*

36 US Department of Justice Press Release (2013, January 3). Transocean Agrees to Plead Guilty to Environmental Crime and Enter Civil Settlement to Resolve U.S. Clean Water Act Penalty Claims from Deepwater Horizon Incident. https://www.justice.gov/archives/opa/pr/transocean-agrees-plead-guilty-environmental-crime-and-enter-civil-settlement-resolve-us.

37 US DOJ (2013, January 3).

38 US Department of Justice Press Release (2013, July 25). Halliburton pleads guilty to destruction of evidence in connection with Deepwater Horizon disaster and agrees to pay maximum statutory fine. https://www.justice.gov/opa/pr/halliburton-pleads-guilty-destruction-evidence-connection-deepwater-horizon-disaster-and.

39 US DOJ (2013, July 25).

40 Department of Justice (2013). BP Exploration and Production Inc. Pleads Guilty, Is Sentenced to Pay Record $4 Billion for Crimes Surrounding Deepwater Horizon Incident. https://www.justice.gov/archives/opa/pr/bp-exploration-and-production-inc-pleads-guilty-sentencedto-pay-record-4-billion-crimes

41 Reuters. (2015, December 3). BP spill manslaughter charges dropped, one guilty of environmental crime. https://www.reuters.

com/article/business/environment/bp-spill-manslaughter-charges-dropped-one-guilty-of-environmental-crime-idUSK BN0TL26J

42 Reuters (2015, December 3).
43 Associated Press News (2017). BP supervisor on ill-fated Deepwater Horizon rig dies at 69. https://apnews.com/general-news-739a808148da4a1e93661ff115d4c89e.
44 Forbes (2018, June 5). Two Years After Ruling, BP Engineer Still Carries Burden of Prosecution. https://www.forbes.com/sites/walterpavlo/2018/01/08/two-years-after-ruling-bp-engineer-still-carries-burden-of-prosecution/.
45 Forbes (2018, June 5).
46 Clayton, S., Koehn, A., & Grover, E. (2013). Making sense of the senseless: Identity, justice, and the framing of environmental crises. *Social Justice Research*, *26*, 301–319. https://psycnet.apa.org/doi/10.1007/s11211-013-0185-z
47 Bullock, O. M., Shulman, H. C., & Huskey, R. (2021). Narratives are persuasive because they are easier to understand: examining processing fluency as a mechanism of narrative persuasion. *Frontiers in Communication*, *6*, 719615. https://doi.org/10.3389/fcomm.2021.719615.
48 Jacobsen, G. D. (2011). The Al Gore effect: an inconvenient truth and voluntary carbon offsets. *Journal of Environmental Economics and Management*, *61*(1), 67–78. https://doi.org/10.1016/j.jeem.2010.08.002.
49 Dunn, M. E., Mills, M., & Veríssimo, D. (2020). Evaluating the impact of the documentary series *Blue Planet II* on viewers' plastic consumption behaviors. *Conservation Science and Practice*, *2*(10), e280. https://doi.org/10.1111/csp2.280.
50 Shreedhar, G., Sabherwal, A., & Malconado, R. (2024). Cli-fi videos can increase charitable donations: Experimental evidence from the United Kingdom. *Frontiers in Psychology*, *14*. https://doi.org/10.3389/fpsyg.2023.1176077.

CONCLUSION: CAPABLE GUARDIANS

1 Vlasceanu, M., Doell, K. C., Bak-Coleman, J. B., Todorova, B., Berkebile-Weinberg, M. M., Grayson, S. J., . . . & Lutz, A. E. (2024). Addressing climate change with behavioral science: A global intervention tournament in 63 countries. *Science Advances*, *10*(6), eadj5778. https://doi.org/10.1126/sciadv.adj5778.

INDEX

abuse of functions 222, 229
acid mine drainage 213
acid rain 19
activism 75, 79, 81–3, 91
advertising 31–2, 33, 34, 37, 39, 140, 295
agar-wood 120
Agostinho, Rodrigo 102, 103
agribusiness 92
air pollution 9, 13–17, 18, 19, 51, 52
Alcaide, Mario 156, 177–81, 186, 187, 188, 196, 197
algae 168
'Al Gore effect' 289
Amazon region 59, 62–3, 66–7, 69, 71, 73–5, 77–9, 83, 91–5, 102–4
American Petroleum Institute 261
Amos, John 270
anger 24, 25–7
animal feed 67, 73, 92
animal poaching *see* poaching
Antarctica 154, 157–9, 161, 167–9, 173, 176, 181, 186, 191, 195, 196, 198
aquaculture 170
Armeni, Chiara 295–6
Armenteras, Dolors 68, 69, 70, 94–5
artisanal and small-scale mining (ASM) 207–9, 211–12, 214–18, 227, 241

asthma 19, 24, 213
Audi 24, 46
Audobon Society 112
Ayala, Alberto 7–13, 17, 20–4, 27–8, 30–1, 44, 47, 50, 53–5
Three Forks in the Road 10

Bandit Six 158, 159, 194, 197, 198
Barker, Bob 158
Basel Institute 229, 230
Bayesian updating 264, 265
Bea, Robert 281, 283
Beauman, Ned, *Venomous Lumpsucker* 288
beef production 67, 79, 92
behaviour
  change 138–41
  labelling 72, 97
belief formation 263, 264, 266–7
belief in a just world 286
Bentham, Jeremy 113–14
Bertone, Steve 249–50, 251, 252, 258
Bester, Vidette 202, 207, 208–9, 212, 214, 216, 220, 235–6, 240–1
'Big Oil' 238, 258
biodiversity
  crisis 123, 124
  hotspots 69–70, 71
  loss 264, 266
  oil spills 270

INDEX

biospheric values 4, 183, 184, 295
bird conservation 111–13, 115, 153
blue crimes 170
Blue Justice Ocean Surveillance Programme 199
Blue Planet (TV series) 289–90
Bob Barker (ship) 157–60, 166, 173, 174, 179, 188, 190, 196
Bolsonaro, Jair 73
Boyd, David 97–8, 99
BP 251, 253, 254, 256, 272, 274, 276–8, 280–6, 292
Brazil 57, 63, 66–7, 74–5, 83, 87, 89, 91–3, 102–3, 162
bribery 220, 222, 227–8, 229, 230
British Wild Birds Act 112, 115
Bureau of Safety, Energy and Environment 282
bushmeat 124
Busse, Paolo 57, 58, 76, 90–3, 94, 103
Butler, Nicholas 189
Butler, Octavia, *Parable of the Sower* 288

cacti 120–1
CAFEE *see* Center for Alternative Fuels, Engines, and Emissions
California 12, 17–18, 22, 99
California Air Resources Board (CARB) 10, 12, 17, 22, 24
capable guardians 190, 198, 293
CARB *see* California Air Resources Board
carbon 10, 69–70, 80, 103, 169, 289
carbon dioxide (CO2) 70, 262
Carder, Daniel 23
carmakers 10–12, 17, 20, 30, 38, 49–51, 55 *see also* Volkswagen
cars
  air pollution 18, 19–22
  electric cars 181, 183–4
  emissions fraud 7–13, 23
  emotional attachment 37
  Model T 260
Carson, Rachel, *Silent Spring* 16–17
cash-in-transit (CIT) heists 204–5

Cataldo, Captain Luis Alfonso Rubio 185–6, 188
cattle farming 67, 79, 84, 124
Center for Alternative Fuels, Engines, and Emissions (CAFEE) 22, 23
CEOs 5, 40, 47, 48, 49
charismatic megafauna bias 111
China
  illegal fishing 171–2, 191
  ivory trade 108–9, 119, 122, 127, 129–31, 136, 139–40, 143–6, 148
Chisso petrochemical factory 210–11
choice architecture 35–6
Choo, Chun Wei 33
Chrysler 23
CIT (cash-in-transit) heists 204–5
CITES (UN Convention on International Trade in Endangered Species of Wild Fauna and Flora) 115, 116, 127, 141, 143, 144
cities, wildlife in 122–3
civil disobedience 82
Clayton, Susan 286
clean air 10, 13, 15–16, 17
Clean Air Acts
  UK 15–16
  US 17, 18, 23, 39
'clean diesel' 10, 12, 21, 22, 32, 35, 36, 53
Clean Water Act 269, 284, 285
cli-fi (climate fiction) 288–9, 290
climate action 10, 25, 26, 295, 296, 297
climate change
  bad decisions 273
  belief formation and credibility 266–7
  deforestation 69, 70, 71
  denialism 27, 27, 237, 263, 264
  doomists and risk realists 271, 291, 294
  eco-anger 25, 26–7
  ecological grief 278
  emissions fraud 29, 55
  and environmental crime 1–2

forest crime 103
An Inconvenient Truth (2006 film) 289
'letter from a future self' exercise 297–8
plastic waste 240
psychology of 182–184
regulators 54
scepticism 264
climate fiction (cli-fi) 288–9, 290
climate velocity 70–1
clothing 183
CO2 *see* carbon dioxide
coal 15, 260
Cobo report 64, 65, 68
Cod Wars 165
colonisation 63–4, 67, 235
combustion 18
comingling 152
conceptual normativity 222
conceptual tribunal 164, 166, 181
conformity 5, 53, 96, 149, 196, 242, 287, 293
conscience 164
conservation 110–13, 115–16, 121–2, 126, 140–1, 143, 149, 153
COP28 summit 102
core international crimes 100
Corexit 278
corporate fraud 8–9, 28, 39
Corral, Florindo González 194, 195
corruptibility 4, 223, 225
corruption 45, 119, 202, 220–6, 227–31
Cowie, Helen 111, 113
credibility 264–6
crime
    'dark figure' of unreported crimes 85
    environmental offences as 2–3
    psychology of impunity 85–7
criminal psychology 1, 34, 42
crocodile parts 120
crown pillar 205–6, 218, 221, 232, 233
crude oil 251, 253, 275, 277
culling animals 124
Cummins Engine Company 23

Cunsulo, Ashlee 278
cyanide fishing 167

'dancing cat fever' (Minamata disease) 209–11
'dark figure' of unreported crimes 85
'dark ships' 171
Davidson, Joe 271
DDT 17
debunking 240, 243
deception detection 34
deep sea life 273–4, 291
Deepwater Horizon oil spill 251–2, 254–8, 267–76, 279, 281–4, 286–8, 291–2
default choices 35–6
defeat devices 13, 20–4, 30, 33, 36, 50, 53–5
defenders *see* environmental defenders
deforestation 60, 67, 68–70, 74, 85–6, 91, 102, 103, 170
Democratic Republic of Congo (DRC) 207
denialism 27, 237, 263, 264
descriptive norms 181–2, 184
desperation 5, 53, 96, 149, 196, 216–17, 242, 288, 293
detection, fear of 189–90
deterrence theory 86, 190
diamond mining 208
diesel 9, 10, 12, 18–24, 27, 44, 49–51, 253, 260
    'clean diesel' 10, 12, 21, 22, 32, 35, 36, 53
Diesel, Rudolf 260
Dieselgate 9, 10, 16, 32, 49, 54
dinosaurs 123, 126
disconfirmation bias 3, 267
disinformation 236, 237, 239, 243, 244
disruption 149, 152–3
DOJ *see* US Department of Justice
Donora disaster 13–15, 19
doomists 271, 291, 294
Douglas, William O. 99
downlisting species 141, 142, 143
Drake, Colonel Edwin 258–9, 263, 273

INDEX

Druckman, James 264, 266
drug smuggling 122
dumping 152–3, 163, 168

ease 4, 52–3, 95, 148, 196, 241, 287, 293
Ecker, Ullrich 242, 243
eco-anger 4, 9, 25–7, 297
eco-anxiety 25, 26
ecocide 2, 58, 100–2
eco-depression 25, 26
eco-feminist exchanges 75
ecological grief (eco-grief) 4, 278–80, 297
economic growth 17
Ecuador 98
educators 295
EIA *see* Environmental Investigation Agency
Einstein, Albert 265
electric cars 182, 183–4
electronics waste 152
elephants 106, 109–10, 117–19, 125–8, 131–2, 134–8, 140–1, 143–5, 153
Ellis, Neville 278
embezzlement 222
emissions 9–10, 12–13, 15, 18–24, 27, 29, 32, 36–7, 39, 45, 50–4
emotional attachment 37, 114
endangered species 108, 115–16, 120–1, 128, 131, 138, 142–4, 146, 167
Energy and Man event 260
energy resources 261–2
enforcers 43–4, 294, 295
environmental activism 75, 79, 81–3, 91
environmental crime
    and climate crisis 1–2
    'dark figure' of unreported crimes 85
    definition 3
Environmental Crime Directive 3
environmental defenders 2, 57, 62, 65, 76, 78, 80–1, 83, 87, 90–1, 93, 95–6, 103, 294

Environmental Investigation Agency (EIA) 107, 118, 122, 126, 128–31, 138, 141–3, 145–6, 148, 294
Environmental Justice Atlas 80, 83
Environmental Protection Agency (EPA) 23, 24, 39
environmental sustainability, social responsibility and transparent governance (ESG) 195
epistemic malevolence 32–3, 34, 50
ethics 156, 164, 222
ethnocentrism 64–5
European Fisheries Control Agency (EFCA) 178
European Parliament 3, 34, 44, 47–8
European Union (EU) 48, 49, 50, 51, 191
e-waste 152
Ewing, Jack 20, 28–9, 31, 36, 50, 53
Faster, Higher, Farther 28
exotic birds 111
exotic pets 120
experiential effect 85
extinction 71, 98, 108, 111–13, 115, 120, 123, 125, 127, 153
Extractivism Settlement Projects 68, 77

factories 14, 15, 16, 18, 19
factory farming 113
Falk, Richard 101
false flags 193
false narratives 236–7, 242–4
farming 113, 170
fashion trade 111, 113, 115
FBI (Federal Bureau of Investigation) 27, 45
feathers trade 111, 113
Federal Trade Commission (FTC) 32, 33, 39
felonies 39, 284
Fernandez, Luis Miguel Perez 186
fiction 288–9, 290
Fidelity Group 204
financial flows 150
financial investigators 294

fines   23, 43, 46, 48, 50, 103, 138, 195, 284, 292
fish consumption   211, 213, 275
fishing   5, 115, 156–61, 165–73, 176–81, 184–8, 190—9, 227, 279
flagging ships   171, 192–3
flagship species   126
food security   170, 187
Ford, Henry   260
foresight   296–7
forestry industry   229, 230
forests   60, 63, 67–73, 75–8, 84, 91–7, 99, 102–3, 125
fossil fuels   237, 253
fraud   8–9, 28, 39, 45, 46, 49, 103, 119
freedom of the seas   161, 164, 166
Frey, Dr Harald   18–20, 51
FTC *see* Federal Trade Commission

Gabon   198
Galamsey   215
Gale, William   281, 283
Galicia   177, 181, 184, 194, 196
game hunting   124
game reserves   131
gas   12, 253–4, 255, 258, 274, 282, 283
gender division of labour   217
General Motors   23
Geneva Convention on the Law of the Sea   164
Germany   12, 37, 40, 44–6, 48, 49, 82, 156, 179
Ghana   215
ghost nets   168, 176
gillnets   167–8, 175, 195
globalisation   172
Global Maritime Crime Programme   198
global warming   19, 262
Global Witness   83
gold mining   200–1, 203–8, 211–16, 218–19, 230–6, 245–7
Gore, Al   289
Great Smog   15, 16
greed   5, 30, 53, 95, 148–9, 176, 196, 242, 287, 293
green corruption   229, 230, 231

green crime
  overview   1–6
  capable guardians   293–8
  deaths in the Amazon   56–104
  definition   3
  emissions fraud in US   7–55
  illegal fishing in Antarctica   154–99
  oil spill in Gulf of Mexico   249–92
  poaching syndicates from China   105–53
  zama zama miners in South Africa   200–48
greenhouse effect   12, 262, 263, 266
Greenpeace   67, 91
green psychology   4
greenwashing   5, 9, 28, 34–5, 36–8, 39, 54
grief, ecological   4, 278–80, 297
Grossmann, Juhani   229–31
gross negligence   269
Grotius, Hugo   161, 162, 164, 181
  Mare Liberum   161–3
Guerreiras da Floresta (Warriors of the Forest)   75
Gulf of Mexico   251, 253, 260, 269, 270, 273–5, 277–9, 282, 284, 292
Guterres, António   211

Halliburton   256, 257, 283, 284
Hammarstedt, Peter   156–61, 168, 173–7, 184, 185, 188, 190, 194, 197–9
Harris, Kamala   27
hat making   111, 153, 210
Hayward, Tony   252, 274, 281
health   14, 15, 17, 19–20, 55
heists   204–5
herbivores   123, 125
high seas   165, 166, 171, 191
hitmen   59, 62, 84, 87, 89, 93, 96
honesty   227, 228
Hong Kong   139, 143
houseplants   120–1
human rights   2, 57, 65–6, 91, 99, 172–3, 247
hunting   107, 124–5, 133–8

INDEX

ICCT (International Council on Clean Transportation) 22
Iceland 165
illegal mining *see* mining
illegal, unreported and unregulated (IUU) fishing 167, 171 *see also* fishing
illicit enrichment 222
illicit financial flows 150
illness 14, 15, 209–11
illusion of truth effect 239–40
illusion of unique invulnerability 43
imprisonment 2, 40–5, 47, 48–9, 86, 138
impunity
  overview 4–5, 293
  deaths in the Amazon 93, 94, 95
  emissions fraud 44, 52, 53
  fish crime 177, 180, 196
  illegal mining 241
  oil crime 287
  psychology of 85–7
  wildlife crime 148
An Inconvenient Truth (2006 film) 289
INCRA 84
Indigenous peoples 58, 63–70, 74–5, 80, 91–2, 94, 96, 98–9, 102–3, 259
Indonesia 198
influence peddling 222–3
information, false 236–7, 242–4
injunctive norms 181, 184
innocent passage 164
Instituto Zé Cláudio e Maria 75
insurance 194–5
International Convention for the Prevention of Pollution from Ships (MARPOL) 187
International Council on Clean Transportation (ICCT) 22
International Court of Justice 157
International Criminal Court 57, 76, 91, 101, 103
International Maritime Organization 171
International Union for the Conservation of Nature 132

Interpol 121, 156, 177–9, 193–5, 198, 229, 294
  Purple Notices 158–9, 193, 194–5
  Red Notices 40
  investigators 294–5
IUU *see* illegal, unreported and unregulated (IUU) fishing
ivory trade 106–10, 117–19, 121, 122, 126–32, 135–40, 143–9, 153

Jagersfontein mine dam 213
Johannesburg 212
journalism 170, 294

Kaluza, Robert 268, 285
Kam, Ceres 107, 138–9, 140–1, 143, 144, 145
Kemp, Luke 271
kerosene 259

labelling behaviours 72, 97
labour
  gender division 217
  trafficking 172
Lacey Act (1900) 112
Lanchester, John, *The Wall* 288
landfills 152
land ownership 63, 72–5, 84, 88, 89, 93
land rights 58, 66, 68
law enforcement 43–4, 47–8, 49–50, 87
lawlessness 156, 177, 189, 196
lawsuits 51, 81, 278
lawyers 295
Lawyers for Human Rights 247
Leggett, Ted 119, 121–2, 124, 126, 136, 137, 138
legislation 43, 47–8, 49–50
Lemaître, Sophie 101, 149–50, 151, 244
Lemon, Margaretta 112
'letter from a future self' exercise 297–8
liability 48, 49
licences 226, 227, 230
lie acceptability 37

lie detection 34
light bulbs 35
Lily gold mine 204–8, 211, 212, 218–21, 224, 231–4, 241–2, 245–7
lions 124
litigation 51, 81, 278
Llanos de Moxos 62
lobbying 223, 237, 238
'locking on' 82
logging 60, 61, 62, 67, 71, 78, 79, 103
London 15, 16, 111
Los Angeles 18, 20
Lula da Silva, Luiz Inácio 102
Lynch, Loretta 38–40, 46

Māori peoples 97
MacDonald, Ian 251, 253, 268, 270–8, 281, 282, 284, 291, 292
Macondo oil well 249–51, 253, 254, 256, 268, 270, 283
mammoth tusks 109, 127
Manders, Antonius 47, 48, 49, 50
Mandiberg, Susan 41
Manhattan Project 265
Marianas oil rig 254
marine resources 165
Maritime Domain Awareness courses 198
Markey, Ed 276
MARPOL (International Convention for the Prevention of Pollution from Ships) 187
maximum sustainable yield 116
McGrath, Mary 264, 266
meat consumption 35–6, 114, 213
meat production 67, 73, 92, 136–7
Mendes, Chico 78–9
mercury 201, 207, 209–12, 214, 215–16
methane 253
Meyer, Marco 33
Migratory Bird Treaty Act 112, 284
Mills, Clarence 15
Milton, Charlotte 152–3

Minamata Convention 211, 215–16
Minamata disease 209–11
Mineral King Valley 99
Minerals Management Service 282
minimisation 180, 214
mining 200–9, 211–21, 223, 224, 227, 230–7, 240–2, 244–7
misinformation 236–7, 240, 242, 243, 244
Mnisi, Yvonne 234
Model T 260
money laundering 195, 222
moral disengagement 114–15
moral hazards 195
moral locus of accountability 224
Moreira, José Rodrigues 84, 87, 88, 89–90, 95–6
Morton, Oscar 123, 124, 125, 126
Mother Earth 65, 78, 80, 98
Mozambique 110, 117–18, 119, 128, 129, 136
Mr Charlie oil rig 260
Mr K 136, 137
Mr X 203–4, 205, 206, 207, 211, 218–19, 234

Nambule, Pretty 234
narrative persuasion 289
Nascimento, Alberto Lopes do 61, 89
National Commission on the BP Deepwater Horizon Oil Spill 252, 256, 268, 276, 283
National Fish and Wildlife Foundation 284
national narcissism 37–8
National Oceanic and Atmospheric Administration (NOAA) 276, 292
natural disasters 286
natural gas 253
nature, rights of 2, 58, 74–5, 76, 95, 96–100, 103
negative freedom 162, 164, 165, 196
negligence 268–9, 284, 287
nets, fishing 167–8, 176, 178, 195
Newman, Julian 107, 128–9, 137, 142–3, 145–6, 148, 153

INDEX

New Zealand 97
Nigeria 193
nitrogen dioxide (NO2) 19–20
nitrogen oxides (NOx) 16, 18–24, 27, 32, 38, 50, 51
NOAA *see* National Oceanic and Atmospheric Administration
Noda, Kaneyoshi 209
norms 181–2
North Sea oil spills 276
NOx *see* nitrogen oxides
Ntshavheni, Khumbudzo 201
Nyirenda, Solomon 234

Obama, Barack 268
observer effect 163–4
obsolescence, planned 35
oceans 156, 161–6, 169, 199
oil 165, 249–51, 252–61, 262–9, 270–6, 277–83, 284–8, 291–2
Oil Creek, Pennsylvania 259, 273
Operation Amazonia 67
Operation Maravalha 103
Operation Vala Umgodi ('Close the Hole') 202, 246, 247
organised crime 5, 107, 128, 133, 149–53
Osei, Lydia 215
oud 120
Ou Haiqiang 105, 106, 108–10, 117–18, 128, 130, 136, 147, 148
Outlaw Ocean Project 170, 171, 172
overfishing 2, 5, 158, 165, 172
ownership 4, 72–5
oxygen 169
ozone 19, 27

Pacha Mama 98
palm oil 81
Panama 192, 193
pangolin scales 109, 119–20, 146, 147, 151
Pará 77, 78, 96
paradox of feedback 4, 283
participation 295–6, 298
Patagonian toothfish 157, 158, 167, 175, 179, 180, 191
pay levels 225, 226

Pemba, Mozambique 110, 118, 128, 129, 136
penalties 23, 39, 41, 43, 47, 48, 284
performance-related pay 226
perfumes 120
permits 226, 229, 230
'perp walks' 45
pesticides 17
petrol 12, 18, 23, 238, 253, 258–62
pets, exotic 120
Phillips, Eliza 112
photochemical smog 18
plankton 169, 275
planned obsolescence 35
plant trade 120–1
plastics 168, 237–9, 260, 261, 290
poaching
    anti-poaching 107, 116, 131–3, 138, 141
    illegal fishing 158, 180, 191
    ivory trade 110, 117, 124–6, 128, 129, 143, 153
    plants 120–1
    the poachers 133–8
    wildlife crime 119–20
poisoning 209–11, 215
policing 86, 87, 190–1, 197, 199, 229
policy dystopia model 237
'polluter pays' laws 48
pollution
    air pollution 13–17, 18, 19, 51
    denialism 264
    dirty technology 5
    eco-anger 27
    mercury poisoning 209–11
    plastic waste 239
    ships and seas 187, 188
portable emissions testing 23
Portugal 63, 67, 162
positive freedom 166
post-traumatic stress disorder 280
Potas, Mr 219
poverty 5, 96, 136, 138, 149, 216, 217, 241
prebunking 242–3
prevention, and punishment 47
preventive mobilisation 81
prison 2, 38, 40–5, 47–9, 86, 138, 189

Project LEAF 229
Projetos de Assentamento (PAEs) (Extractivism Settlement Projects) 68, 77
property rights 74, 98
protected species 229
protests 78, 81, 82
psychological ownership 4, 74–5
public goods 72
public health 55
public opinion 164, 181, 182
public order laws 82
public sector corruption 221, 223
public service motivation 225
punishment 43, 44, 47, 86, 189

racism 65, 124
radioactive waste 213
rainforests 59, 60, 63, 67–71, 77–8, 83
Ramaphosa, Cyril 200, 202, 234, 247
rangers 107, 131–3, 136
rationalisation 5, 29, 53, 95–6, 149, 196, 214, 223, 242, 287, 293
recycling 26, 238–9, 240
red tape argument 224
regulators 10–12, 22, 27, 29, 33, 35, 44, 54, 94, 282, 295
relative deprivation 225
religion 41
respiratory diseases 19
Rey, Agustín Dosil 186
rhino horn 109, 119–20, 121
rhinos 132, 142, 143
Ribeiro, José Cláudio see Zé Cláudio
rights
    animal rights 113
    human rights 2, 57, 65–6, 91, 99, 172, 247
    Indigenous peoples 65–6
    land rights 58, 66, 68
    property rights 74, 98
    rights of nature 2, 58, 76, 95, 96–100
risk 50, 85–6, 195, 268, 271, 282–4, 287, 288, 291, 292
risk realists 271, 291
Robinson, Kim Stanley, *The Ministry for the Future* 288

Rocha, Lindonjonson Silva 61, 84, 89, 90, 95
Royal Society 135
Royal Society for the Protection of Birds (RSPB) 112
rubbish disposal 152, 237–9
ruralist caucus 92

safety 268, 282, 283
salary satisfaction 225, 226
Salgueiro, João 136
salvage laws 175
Sam Simon (ship) 157, 158, 159, 174, 175, 188
Santo, Laísa do Espírito 56–7, 59, 60, 88–9
Santo, Maria do Espírito 56–60, 62, 71, 77–8, 80, 83–4, 87–8, 90–1, 93, 95–6, 104
Santos, Claudelice Silva dos 75–6, 104
Santos, Raimunda 60
São Tomé and Príncipe 173, 179, 184, 186, 187, 188, 193
sapphire mining 208
satellite monitoring 198
Schmidt, Oliver 40, 45
Schweinfurth, Georg 127
scuttling 187
sea cucumbers 109, 148
sea levels 262, 263
seas 161–5, 169, 171, 187, 188
Sea Shepherd 156–60, 168, 173, 177, 191, 197–9
selfishness 71–2, 223, 224
shipwrecks 186, 188
Shuidong syndicate 107–8, 116–17, 122, 126, 128–31, 136, 138, 144–9, 153
Simon, Sam 157
Sithole, Aaron 232–3
situational crime prevention theory 52
'six pillars' model
    overview 4–5, 293
    conformity 5, 53, 96, 149, 196, 242, 287
    desperation 5, 53, 96, 149, 196, 242, 288

ease 4, 52–3, 95, 148, 196, 241, 287
greed 5, 53, 95, 148–9, 196, 242, 287
impunity 4–5, 53, 95, 148, 196, 241, 287
rationalisation 5, 53, 95–6, 149, 196, 242, 287
crimes against environmental defenders 95–6
illegal fishing 196–7
illegal mining 241–2
oil crime 287–8
Volkswagen emissions fraud 52–4
wildlife crime 148–9
SkyTruth 270
slavery 98
Smith, Susan 41–2
smog 14–17, 18, 19
smuggling 120, 122, 147
social desirability bias 163
social norms 181–2
social responsibility 195
soda ash 81
solastalgia 279
South Africa
  anti-poaching 107, 131, 133, 142
  corruption and pay 226
  gangs research 122
  illegal fishing 227
  illegal mining 200–5, 209, 212–14, 216–18, 230, 234–5, 240–2, 244–7
South America 57, 58, 71, 83
Soweto 213
soybeans 67, 92
space race 260
Spain 177, 189
speciesism 113
species loss 113, 124–6
Stadler, Rupert 46
Stanley, Samantha 25, 26
Steg, Linda 182, 183
Stilfontein gold mine 200–1, 234, 245–7
Stop Ecocide Now 100
stories 288–9, 290, 291

stratospheric ozone 19
Sundström, Aksel 226, 227
sustainability 80, 116, 166, 169, 181–4, 195, 241
syndicates 128, 132, 133 *see also* Shuidong syndicate

tailings 212–14
Tanzania 110, 128
targeted policing 190, 191
tax havens 191
Teller, Edward 261–3, 264, 265, 266, 267
temporal discounting 3–4, 42–3, 290
Tesla 183, 184
Te Urewera 97
Thailand 127, 140, 198
third-person effect 236
thought experiments 290, 296
Thunder (ship) 154, 156–61, 167, 168, 173–80, 184–8, 190, 192–8
Tiger Team (BP) 281–2, 283
toothfish 157, 167, 168, 169, 175, 179, 180, 188, 191, 194
toxic waste 2, 209–14, 229
Toyota 23
trade bans 141–2
trading in influence 222–3
traditional Chinese medicine 108, 119–20
trafficking
  illicit financial flows 150
  ivory trafficking 105–7, 117–19, 122, 126–31, 136, 144, 148
  labour trafficking 171
  wildlife crime 108
tragedy of the commons 71, 73, 94
Transocean 254, 283–4
Transparency International 221
transparent governance 195
Travel Ivory Free 139
trees 67–71, 77–8, 91, 93, 120, 231
trophic cascade 168
tropospheric ozone 19
Trump, Donald 292
tuna 165, 275
tusks trade 106, 109, 117–18, 125, 127–30, 135–7, 139, 145–7

UNCLOS *see* United Nations Convention on the Law of the Sea
unethical pro-organisational behaviour 31
unethical prosocial behaviour 3
United Nations (UN) 66, 75, 102, 126, 171, 222, 239
United Nations Convention against Corruption 228
United Nations Convention on International Trade in Endangered Species of Wild Fauna and Flora (CITES) 115, 116, 127, 141, 143, 144
United Nations Convention on the Law of the Sea (UNCLOS) 165, 166, 187, 192
United Nations Forest Heroes (Heróis de Floresta) Award 77
United Nations Office on Drugs and Crime 119, 198
United Nations Peoples' Climate Vote 25, 26, 27
United Nations Permanent Forum on Indigenous Issues 66
Urbina, Ian 170–1, 172–3
US Department of Justice (DOJ) 23, 27, 39, 41, 45

value chains 150–1, 153
van den Berg, Dirk 204, 207, 218, 231
van der Merwe, Annamarie 234
vegans 182
Vidrine, Donald 268, 285
vigilantes 197
violence 42, 75, 83, 96, 201, 204, 235–6
volatile organic compounds (VOCs) 18
Volkswagen 7–10, 12–13, 20–4, 27–33, 36–40, 43–7, 49–55

Wang Kangwen 106, 109, 117–18, 128, 130, 136, 147
Warren Spring Laboratory 16
waste crime 152–3, 163, 209–14, 237–9, 240
watchers 294
water quality 10, 213, 215, 269
weather 70–1
Weißmüller, Kristina 223, 224, 228Whyte, David 100
wildlife crime 107, 119–22, 148–9, 230
wildlife loss 122–4
wildlife rangers 131–3
William, Prince 140
Williams, Mike 250, 251
Winterkorn, Martin 40, 49
'wishcycling' 238–9
women
  bird conservation 112
  gender division of labour 217
  illegal mining 217, 220, 235
  land ownership 75
wood 120
World Bank 208
World Wildlife Crime Report 119, 126, 136
World Wildlife Federation (WWF) 131, 139

xenophobia 235
Xie Xingbang 108, 109, 110, 117–18, 128, 130, 136, 147, 148

Yster 219

zama zamas (illegal miners) 200–6, 212, 216, 217–20, 231–2, 234–6, 240–2, 244–6
Zé Cláudio (José Cláudio Ribeiro) 56–62, 65–8, 71, 76–80, 83, 84, 87–91, 93, 95–6, 103–4
Zuber, Anna 223, 224, 228